The Structure of Romans

The Structure of Romans

The Argument of Paul's Letter

Paul B. Fowler

Fortress Press
Minneapolis

THE STRUCTURE OF ROMANS

The Argument of Paul's Letter

Cover image: Yellow grunge paper background ©iStock/Thinkstock

Oxyrhynchus 209, manuscript of the New Testament, designated by P10 on the list Gregory-Aland, page with text of Epistle to the Romans 1:1-7. 4th century. PD-old-100. 26 February 2016 / Wikimedia Commons.

The Apostle Paul (detail), 1000 A.D. PD-old-100. 26 February 2016 / Wikimedia Commons.

Cover design: Ivy Palmer Skrade

Library of Congress Cataloging-in-Publication Data

Print ISBN: 978-1-5064-1618-2

eBook ISBN: 978-1-5064-1619-9

The paper used in this publication meets the minimum requirements of American National Standard for Information Sciences — Permanence of Paper for Printed Library Materials, ANSI Z329.48-1984.

Manufactured in the U.S.A.

This book was produced using Pressbooks.com, and PDF rendering was done by PrinceXML.

Contents

Preface

The question may be raised: Why another book on Romans? "Of making many books there is no end" (Eccles. 12:12, RSV), especially books on Romans. Nevertheless, I propose that we add this book to that number for these reasons. First, its purpose is to help those studying Romans to understand the nature of what it is they are studying. It provides a fresh look at Romans and issues related to its interpretation. It challenges the idea that doctrinal themes are guiding the narrative. For too long we have regarded Romans as a book of doctrine merely to be analyzed. We have failed to realize that both the doctrinal and exhortation passages were written to address pressing issues in Rome. Those issues were driving the narrative. The interactive rhetoric was guiding the narrative.

Second, it pulls together arguments for the view that Romans is a letter addressing major circumstances in Rome. The surface structure of the letter points to the issues being addressed. The issues concern circumstances in Rome of major consequence. They are primarily twofold: (1) the precarious nature of living as Christians in Rome and (2) the strained relationships between Jews and gentiles.

Third, it challenges the consensus that Romans is a letter-"essay," that the bookends (1:1-17 and 15:14–16:27) have the markings of a letter while the body should be viewed as an essay. This follows a long line of tradition that the body reflects Paul's own concerns, his desire to introduce himself to the church in Rome in line with his coming visit, to preserve his theology and gospel, and so on. Hence, what we see in the body is theology and a progression of themes unrelated to circumstances in Rome. Proponents argue that the body of Romans lacks interactive discourse with the recipients; thus it is an essay. Contrary to this majority view, I find that the body of the letter is quite interactive with its readers. Its rhetoric, grammar, and extensive use of questions and groups of questions with embedded epistolary formulas combine to make the body of Romans an interactive letter. When Romans is treated as an essay and structured on the level of ideas, the flow of Paul's dialogue is obscured. Such outlines fail to account for Paul's "bold" (15:14) and disruptive rhetoric. But when Romans is treated as a letter, Paul's dialogue becomes engaging as we witness how his gospel addresses the issues facing Roman believers.

Fourth, commentators have overlooked and/or misinterpreted Paul's use of questions and answers in Romans. They have viewed the question-and-answer passages primarily as a means of answering critics or entering into a discussion with an imaginary person. They hold that Paul, while writing Romans, was heavily influenced by a literary convention (genre) known as Hellenistic diatribe. Such diatribe was used by philosophers and teachers with their students. The consensus is that Paul used diatribe as a literary device to aid his internal argument. The entire body of the letter (chaps. 1–11) is structured around the objections and false conclusions from such interlocutors. This understanding of the rhetoric is not only wrong, but also contributes to Romans being viewed more as theological argument than as interactive discourse relating faith to life. Rather, I hold that Paul's extensive use of questions and answers in chapters 2–11 serves to guide the narrative and to point to the underlying circumstances that were driving the narrative. The question-and-answer format helps us realize how the parts of the letter fit together as a whole.

Fifth, this book also takes issue with the premise that Paul, though writing primarily to a gentile constituency, is actually engaged in a debate with Jews. This premise supports the view that Paul is involved in defending himself, his doctrine, or his gospel. Romans is not involved in such a debate.

Sixth, as stated above, this author agrees with the minority position that Paul is primarily addressing circumstances in Rome. Paul is using bold language to exhort gentile believers in Rome to be at one with their Jewish brothers and sisters in Christ. He is also addressing their precarious life existence in Rome. The circumstances in Rome are striking. The church is young, has already gone through persecution, and is about to go through severe persecution. Jewish believers are in the process of returning to Rome following their expulsion in 49 CE, and there are internal relationship issues that need to be resolved. That is precisely what Paul is addressing, and he does so by lifting up the Jews before their fellow believers. He also takes pains to show how the gentiles are now joined to the Jews as the people of God.

Finally, understanding the relational and acoustical effect of the letter's rhetoric and grammar is essential for interpretation. Paul was writing a letter that would be heard orally by the believers in Rome. That interactive rhetoric would be guiding them through the letter. That interactive rhetoric is the key to the organization of the letter. Any outline or structure we impose should conform to that interaction. In addition, Paul was very careful as to how he wrote the letter. It took time to dictate such a long letter and to do so with an amanuensis. He had plenty of time to think of how he would state each sentence as well as frame the entire letter. He was trained to think carefully in order to communicate orally. By this time in his life, approximately sixty years of age, he had an extensive repertoire from which he could draw. The words he used and thoughts he had came from a lifetime of communicating the gospel. For this reason, I believe Paul was very careful even in the placement of words orally for his audience. This is why I have sought to provide a more literal translation of passages in Romans, especially the questions in chapters 2–11. I would add that while the translations are my own, I always compared my translations with other translations that (1) were done by committees of scholars and (2) were primarily word-for-word translations. Paul also had to frame his letter (which was quite long by standards of that day) in a way that would guide his readers through its content. The letter would be read to the believers in Rome. How would Paul keep their attention and lead them through the content of such a long letter? He did so in an interesting way, a way that provided an oral map for the believers as they listened to the letter being read. I would also suggest that that same oral map served as a mental outline for the apostle to follow as he dictated the letter.

Why did Paul begin the body of the letter with a description of the ungodliness of humanity? Why did Paul focus on the Jews and their advantage? Why did Paul spend a whole chapter on all believers being part of the lineage of Abraham? Why did Paul focus on the importance of being "in Christ" and living "in the Spirit" and the Spirit dwelling in believers? Why did Paul plea passionately for the Jews in chapters 9–11? Are any of the exhortations in chapters 12–15 aimed at addressing specific circumstances in Rome? All these questions can be answered once we understand the rhetoric of the letter and the circumstances in Rome toward which the rhetoric is directed. This is why I focus on the structure of the letter. Its structure is found in the rhetoric used by Paul, and the rhetoric is driven by the circumstances of the recipients.

I wish to thank Fortress Press and its editors for publishing this book. Their encouragement and support through the editing process has been very much appreciated. I especially want to thank Dr. Neil Elliott, the acquiring editor in biblical studies, for his encouragement and support. The gracious support I received from the staff of Bridwell Library at Perkins School of Theology has been much appreciated. I am also sincerely grateful to several friends who have sacrificed their time to review and critique this book. Dr. David Lowery met with me after each chapter was initially written and helped with the editing. Dr. Dan McCartney made invaluable comments, as did Dr. Guy Waters. The Rev. Steve Baker and the Rev. Mark Belonga, as well as my son John, helped edit the work. More than anyone else, the time and energy given for the study and writing of this book were a gift from my wife, Camma, whose constant love and encouragement made this book possible.

Abbreviations

BR	*Biblical Research*
ExpTim	*Expository Times*
IBC	Interpretation: A Bible Commentary for Teaching and Preaching
ICC	International Critical Commentary
Int	*Interpretation*
JSNTSup	Journal for the Study of the New Testament Supplement Series
NAC	New American Commentary
NCB	New Century Bible
NICNT	New International Commentary on the New Testament
NTS	*New Testament Studies*
PiNTC	Pillar New Testament Commentary
SBLDS	Society of Biblical Literature Dissertation Series
SBT	Studies in Biblical Theology
ScrB	*Scripture Bulletin*
SD	Studies and Documents
SP	Sacra Pagina
ST	*Studia Theologica*
Str-B	Strack, Hermann Leberecht, and Paul Billerbeck. *Kommentar zum Neuen Testament aus Talmud und Midrasch.* 6 vols. Munich: Beck, 1922–1961.
TNTC	Tyndale New Testament Commentary
WBC	Word Biblical Commentary

WUNT   Wissenschaftliche Untersuchungen zum Neuen Testament

ZNW   *Zeitschrift für die neutestamentliche Wissenschaft und die Kunde der älteren Kirche*

1

Assumptions of This Study

One might think there is nothing more to be written about Paul's Letter to the Romans. In fact, basic issues of an introductory nature are yet to be resolved. These issues do not have to do with authorship, date, or place of origin. Paul is the author, the date is around 57–58 CE, and the place of origin is presumably Corinth. There is general consensus that the text we have is the text of the letter Paul sent to Rome, with a possible exception being the doxology in 16:25-27. The unresolved issues have to do with the purpose of the letter, the audience being addressed, and the structure of the letter. This latter issue is the primary focus of my study. There is a "surface structure" that guides the discourse of the letter. To understand that structure is to understand the flow of thought of the letter and the coherence of its parts. Contrary to prevailing opinion, Romans is not a letter-essay or a diatribe meant to serve Paul's own self-interests such as preserving his gospel or answering his critics. Rather, Romans is a carefully constructed letter from Paul to the church in Rome, written to address a specific set of circumstances in Rome. This is the thesis of this study. Underlying this thesis is the conviction that the questions and answers in chapters 3–11 are guiding the flow of ideas and pointing to issues of concern. The exhortations in chapters 12–15 are not general exhortations but paraenesis directed to specific circumstances in Rome. If acknowledged, this would represent a major shift for many in their approach to Romans. My purpose is to show what I consider to be the surface structure of the letter. It is rhetoric that interacts with the recipients, which it should if Romans is a letter written to address their circumstances. The surface structure guides the discourse of the letter and enables the listening audience to follow Paul's line of thought.

To arrive at the surface structure of the letter, some preliminary steps are needed. My first step will be to review outlines of Romans to probe whether they adequately convey the progression of Paul's thought. As a second step, I will seek to resolve the issue of whether the body of Romans is an essay or an actual letter interacting with its recipients. Having demonstrated the epistolary hallmarks of the letter, I will then show how the rhetoric provides the key for unlocking the progression of thought. From that point on, I will determine the surface structure of the letter, seek to resolve entrenched issues that remain, and attempt to explain the underlying circumstances in Rome that demanded Paul's attention. But let me begin by addressing the issues of purpose and audience and indicate where my preferences lie, for they influence my approach to the structure and interpretation of the letter.

The Purpose of Romans

There are multiple reasons given as to why Paul wrote Romans.[1] Some focus on circumstances surrounding Paul,[2] while others focus on

---

1. For an extended overview of views regarding the purpose of Romans, see Richard Longenecker, *Introducing Romans: Critical Issues in Paul's Most Famous Letter* (Grand Rapids: Eerdmans, 2011), 92–166; see also Robert Jewett, *Romans*, Hermeneia (Minneapolis: Fortress Press, 2007), 80–91; see also the monograph by A. J. M. Wedderburn, *The Reasons for Romans* (Edinburgh: T&T Clark, 1988).

2. Reasons for circumstances surrounding Paul include the following: to introduce himself to the church at Rome; to prepare for his coming visit; to establish a base for further missionary outreach to the west as far as Spain; to establish his authority over the Roman church as the apostle to the gentiles; to indoctrinate the Romans in the essential nature of the gospel; to write a coherent theological essay on major doctrines of theology, anthropology, Christology, and soteriology; to write his last will and testament; to write a brief prepared for Paul's defense when

circumstances surrounding the Christians in Rome.[3] Scholars have referred to the pursuit of Paul's purpose as an "enigma"[4] and "in a state of confusion."[5] C. E. B. Cranfield reserves discussion of the purpose until the end of his commentary, seeking to arrive at his conclusion inductively. He refers to the letter as "a complex of purposes and hopes."[6] It is safe to say that we need to be speaking not of Paul's purpose, but purposes (plural). Instead of choosing between Paul's "personal" self-interests and his "pastoral" interests in Rome, we need to consider multiple purposes combining both. The letter was written not only from a person but also to persons in Rome. If it was written only due to Paul's self-interests, that would be very unlike Paul. If it was written only due to circumstances in Rome, how do we account for the occasion of the letter and what Paul says about his desire to visit Rome and to proceed on to Spain? It is fair to assume that a primary purpose of Paul was to enlist support for his mission to bring about the obedience of faith among gentiles along the northern shore of the Mediterranean Sea.

However, we should avoid the assumption that Paul's purpose for writing is to be found only in the bookends of the letter (1:1-17 and 15:14–16:27). Overemphasis on the bookend passages causes interpreters to divorce the body of the letter from the circumstances of believers in Rome. Do we really want to assume that the body of the letter was written solely to preserve Paul's theology or gospel from criticism (or some similar aim) without any concern for pressing issues

he arrives in Jerusalem; to write an encyclical letter to preserve his doctrine and gospel; and to defend himself from criticism and misunderstandings of his gospel.

3. Reasons proposed for addressing circumstances in Rome include the following: to oppose Jewish particularism, potential or actual; to counter a possible Judaizing threat in Rome; to bring about the obedience of faith of the gentiles in Rome; to effect reconciliation between "the strong" and "the weak"; to resolve conflict and bring unity to the factions in Rome; to counsel Christians regarding their relation to the Roman government and paying taxes; to impart some spiritual gift by applying the gospel to those in Rome (1:11-15).

4. Wedderburn, *Reasons for Romans*, 1. On p. 2 he writes, "The very plethora of suggestions and alternative perspectives offered may leave even the experienced students of Paul with a feeling of frustrated bewilderment."

5. Karl P. Donfried, "False Presuppositions in the Study of Romans," in *The Romans Debate*, ed. Karl P. Donfried (Peabody, MA: Hendrickson, 1991), 102–24 (here 102).

6. C. E. B. Cranfield, *A Critical and Exegetical Commentary on the Epistle to the Romans*, ICC (Edinburgh: T&T Clark, 1975), essay 1, "Paul's Purpose or Purposes in Writing Romans," 2:814–23.

in Rome? I think not and would propose that the letter as a whole is designed to address the real-life issues in Rome.

Second, some have assumed that since Paul had never been to Rome, he could not have been addressing circumstances there. Franz Leenhardt writes, "Paul is not here concerned to remonstrate with Christians at Rome, whom he does not know any more than he knows their special problems."[7] Others have expressed similar sentiments that Paul had little or no knowledge of his audience. However, was Paul really that ignorant of the circumstances in Rome? Was communication between parts of the Roman Empire all that limited? Communication between Corinth and Ephesus was not limited, as evidenced in the Corinthian correspondence. Nor was travel limited between those cities. Consider how many were traveling with Paul from Corinth to Jerusalem.[8] Think of all those who were with Paul at some point during his imprisonment in Rome (Luke, Tychicus, Timothy, Epaphroditus, Onesimus, Aristarchus, Mark, Justus, Epaphras, and Demas).[9] Could not the same level of correspondence and travel have taken place between Corinth and Rome? Paul was in or near Corinth when he wrote to Rome, and Rome was not that far away. He stayed with Prisca and Aquila when they were together in Corinth and had kept up with them (Acts 18:2-3, 18, 26; 1 Cor. 16:19; cf. 2 Tim. 4:19). Now they are in Rome. Paul had numerous friends in Rome, as evidenced in chapter 16.[10] Was there no interaction between them? That would have been quite unlikely. Phoebe, who was from the nearby port city of Cenchreae, was about to travel to Rome. According to William Sanday and Arthur Headlam, "Never in the course of previous history had there been anything like the freedom of circulation and movement which now existed in the Roman Empire . . . and its general

---

7. Franz J. Leenhardt, *The Epistle to the Romans: A Commentary* (London: Lutterworth, 1961), 345–46. William Barclay, Martin Dibelius, Günther Bornkamm, Everett F. Harrison, and a host of other scholars have held this same view.

8. Acts 20:4-5; there were at least eight, representing churches from Achaia, Macedonia, and Asia.

9. Acts 28; Phil. 2:19, 25; Col. 4:7-14; Philem. 23-24.

10. Notice the terms of endearment Paul uses to refer to so many in chapter 16: "beloved," "helper," kinsmen," my "mother," "fellow prisoners," "first convert in Asia." Paul was clearly acquainted with those believers.

trend was to and from Rome."[11] We can be quite assured that Paul was aware of what was happening in Rome.

A third assumption to be avoided is that the body of the letter is a theological essay or summary of the gospel addressing issues involving the gospel and justification and the law of God. For example, J. B. Lightfoot held that Romans was written at leisure, expanding his teaching in Galatians in a systematic way.[12] Günther Bornkamm calls it Paul's "last will and testament," in which he "summarizes and develops the most important themes and thoughts of his message and theology."[13] Werner Kümmel calls it a "theological confession" that sets forth Paul's gospel, "the basic truths of Christianity as he sees and teaches it."[14] Some have held that since it was in essay form, it could and perhaps was sent to other churches as well, that it was a circular letter,[15] or that its destination in addition to Rome was Ephesus.[16] For support, they point to textual variants in Romans. One set of variants omits the words "in Rome."[17] The other set of variants relates to the placement or omission of benedictions and the doxology at the end of the letter, as well as a shortened form of the letter.[18] There is also the

---

11. William Sanday, and Arthur C. Headlam, *The Epistle to the Romans* (New York: Charles Scribner's Sons, 1897), xxvi.
12. J. B. Lightfoot, *Saint Paul's Epistle to the Galatians* (London: Macmillan, 1865), 49.
13. Günther Bornkamm, "The Letter to the Romans as Paul's Last Will and Testament," in *The Romans Debate*, ed. Karl P. Donfried, rev. and expanded ed. (Peabody, MA: Hendrickson, 1991), 16–28 (here 27–28).
14. Werner Georg Kümmel, *Introduction to the New Testament*, trans. Howard Clark Kee (Nashville: Abingdon, 1975), 312–14. It should be noted that while Kümmel agrees with Bornkamm that the letter may be called a testament, he does allow that it is at the same time a concrete message to Christians in Rome. Cranfield (*Romans*, 23) contends that while the occasion of the letter is evident from its epistolary frame, it is less evident why Paul included 1:16b–15:13 in his letter. Then in an appendix of his commentary (ibid., 814–23), he concludes that the body of the letter is an orderly summary of his gospel as he had come to understand it. T. W. Manson ("St. Paul's Letter to the Romans—and Others," in Donfried, *Romans Debate*, 3–15 [here 15]) describes Romans as "a manifesto setting forth his deepest convictions on central issues."
15. Ernst Renan and Kirsopp Lake (as referenced by Longenecker, *Introducing Romans*, 99) held that the letter was a circular letter with distinct and appropriate endings sent to several churches. J. B. Lightfoot (*Biblical Essays* [London: Macmillan, 1893], 352, 374) suggested the letter was first written to Rome, but then later shortened to send to other churches.
16. Manson ("St. Paul's Letter," 13) contends that the original version of Romans was 1:1–15:33, and that chapter 16 was added and sent to Ephesus with the references to Rome in 1:7 and 15 omitted.
17. The phrase *en Rhōmē* is missing from 1:7, and *tois en Rhōmē* from 1:15 in the following ninth-to-eleventh-century manuscripts: G, 1739mg, 1908mg, itg. The omissions were probably made to make the letter appear to be addressed to a more general audience. See Bruce M. Metzger, *A Textual Commentary on the Greek New Testament* (New York: United Bible Societies, 1971), 505–6.
18. Regarding the variants at the end of the letter, see ibid., 533–36. Metzger suggests that the

view that while the letter was sent to Rome, the intended audience was really Jerusalem.[19] Neil Elliott notes that for a majority of interpreters, the letter serves Paul's own self-interests (as he masterfully enumerates in this extended sentence; italics his):

> to "show [the Romans] *in advance* what his gospel *will* be," to offer "an *example* of the kind of preaching or teaching he *will* practice when among them," "to present his gospel" to them so that they might "know more about its character and his mode of argumentation," to introduce to them "the teaching activity Paul *hopes to do* at Rome" or "the gospel *to be . . . proclaimed* [in Spain]," . . . to "[provide] a sustained account of his understanding of the gospel" to "justify his message and mission" by "clarifying and defending his beliefs," to "inform the church [in Rome] about his missionary theology" so that they would "know his thinking."[20]

Elliott then responds, "Paul says nothing in the letter to indicate that he is presenting his own ideas to garner his readers' approval of himself or his mission."[21]

All the above views find Paul's purpose for writing not in the Roman situation but only in Paul himself at the time of writing.[22] While we can hardly doubt that the circumstances of Paul account partly for his purpose of writing, I will show below that the letter was written not only from a specific situation but also to a specific situation. Karl Donfried's "Methodological Principle I" is this: "Any study of Romans

shortened form (omitting chapters 15–16 in certain Latin manuscripts) was probably due to Marcion or his followers. For a thorough discussion of the authenticity and integrity of the letter as we have it, see Cranfield, *Romans*, 1:1–11. Harry Gamble has shown that the textual variants are the result of a later process of "catholicizing" the Pauline corpus (*The Textual History of the Letter to the Romans*, SD 42 [Grand Rapids: Eerdmans, 1977]; also Gamble, "The Redaction of the Pauline Letters and the Formation of the Pauline Corpus," *JBL* 94 (1975): 403–18 [here 414–18]). Some also find discrepancies between the opening and closing of the letter—the opening focusing on Paul's eagerness to evangelize and spend time in Rome, and the closing on his policy not to evangelize where others have done so and his plans to go to Spain.

19. Jacob Jervell ("The Letter to Jerusalem," in Donfried, *Romans Debate*, 53–64) advocates that Romans was written in anticipation of the debates Paul would have when he arrived in Jerusalem with the collection. It is the defense he would make before the church in Jerusalem. The letter is addressed to Rome for the purpose of seeking their support and intercession on his behalf.

20. Neil Elliott, *The Arrogance of Nations: Reading Romans in the Shadow of Empire* (Minneapolis: Fortress Press, 2008), 17 (emphasis original).

21. Ibid.

22. Anders Nygren (*Commentary on Romans*, trans. Carl C. Rasmussen [Philadelphia: Fortress, 1949], 4) writes, "The characteristic and peculiar thing about Romans, differentiating it from the rest of Paul's epistles, is just the fact that it was not, or was only in slight degree, aimed at circumstances within a certain congregation. Its purpose is not to correct maladjustments."

should proceed on the initial assumption that this letter was written by Paul to deal with a concrete situation in Rome."[23] His rationale? All of Paul's authentic letters, without exception, are addressed to specific situations in churches; and the burden of proof is on those who would argue that Romans is an exception to that pattern. J. Christiaan Beker distinguishes between the coherent content of Paul's gospel and its situational contingency. All of Paul's letters are "words on target," meaning they are addressed to particular, concrete situations.[24] Hence, his choice of theological content is governed by and is relevant to the historical situation he is addressing. It would be out of character for Paul to be writing simply for his own self-interests, as it were, to preserve his own gospel for posterity or to send an indirect message to believers in Jerusalem. Paul has a dual purpose for writing: to secure a new mission base and to deal with issues within the Roman church revolving around the Jew/gentile question. The former presents a natural reason for him to be writing. The latter is the more necessary goal of the letter, for the gospel cannot be separated from the circumstances it seeks to address. The letter is not abstract thinking. If the assumptions of Donfried and Beker are correct, and I think they are, then we need to ask what those pressing circumstances were that needed to be addressed by Paul. The answer will be found in the text itself, in both the bookends and the body of the letter. This I will demonstrate once I have resolved the surface structure of the letter.

The Audience of Romans

The issue regarding the audience of the letter has to do not only with the composition of the audience but also with the parties being addressed. Regarding its composition, was it predominantly Jewish or gentile? Clearly it was mixed; it was neither purely Jewish nor purely gentile. Appeals to both would be meaningless if both were not part of the community. Many hold that since the church in Rome was probably

---

23. Donfried, "False Presuppositions," 103–4.
24. J. Christiaan Beker, *Paul the Apostle: The Triumph of God in Life and Thought* (Philadelphia: Fortress Press, 1984), chaps. 2, 3 and 5, esp. 12, 24, 62–63.

established by Jewish Christians, the church must still be predominantly Jewish. Jewish missionaries would have converted more Jews to the church.[25] Nevertheless, the consensus is that when Paul wrote Romans, the majority were gentile.[26] Cranfield says that it is impossible to prove the ratio of Jew or gentile Christians in Rome, that while there must have been a good number of Jewish Christians, they did not form the majority.[27] If we include chapter 16 in the original letter to Rome, which I do,[28] we find that only a handful of the twenty-six listed names are of Jewish origin. According to Peter Lampe (who has carefully analyzed the twenty-six names, not counting Aristobulus or Narcissus, who were non-Christians and possibly deceased at the time Paul wrote),[29] only three are positively identified as Jews with the attribute *syngenēs*—Andronicus, Junia, and Herodion.[30] Aquila can be positively added to that list, and probably Prisca as well (Acts 18:2).[31]

25. William Hendriksen lists multiple arguments for this view (*Romans* [Grand Rapids: Baker, 1981], 20–21). He also lists defenders of this view, including F. C. Baur, T. Zahn, W. Manson, N. Krieger, J. A. C. Van Leeuwen and D. Jacobs. Others include Fahy, Krieger, Leenhardt, Lietzmann, O'Neill, Renan, and Ropes. We do not know when or by whom Christianity first came to Rome. Various answers have been proposed—converts from Pentecost, converts of Paul, Andronicus and Junia being sent as apostolic missionaries from Jerusalem (16:7). Neither Peter nor Paul founded the church. Most assume Jewish missionaries brought Christianity to Rome, and that the Christian community began within the Jewish synagogues. In support of this view is the apparent conflict between Jews and Christians in the 40s leading up to Claudius's edict expelling the Jews in 49. This is strong evidence that Christianity in Rome began with Jewish missionaries in Jewish synagogues. Sanday and Headlam (*Romans*, xxvi–xxviii) argue that the likely origin came from the missionary activities of Paul, that it was more probable that converts of Paul would have had the vision of taking the gospel message to Rome than for converts or evangelists from Jerusalem to do so.
26. Hendriksen (*Romans*, 21) lists multiple arguments for this view. He lists adherents including Sanday and Headlam, Lagrange, Ridderbos, and Murray.
27. Cranfield, *Romans*, 1:18–21. Cranfield comments that the expression "among whom you are also" (1:6) may mean no more than that the whole Roman church was situated in a gentile world, and that the expression in 1:13, "as among the rest of the gentiles," may be viewed as "inexact." This seems quite unlikely in light of the entire text of 1:13-15.
28. See Karl P. Donfried, "A Short Note on Romans 16," in Donfried, *Romans Debate*, 44–52; Peter Lampe, "The Roman Christians of Romans 16," in Donfried, *Romans Debate*, 216–30 (here 217–21).
29. Lampe, "Roman Christians," 216–30. This study is based on his book *Die stadtrömischen Christen in den ersten beiden Jahrhunderten*, WUNT 2/18 (Tübingen: Mohr, 1987).
30. Lampe, "Roman Christians," 224. Lampe observes that the term *syngenēs* does not occur in other Pauline letters (only in Rom. 9:3; 16:7, 11, 21), and that Paul obviously had a "special interest" in using that term in Romans, especially in light of chaps. 9–11. He concludes, "Having this kind of special theological interest in emphasizing the Jewish kinship of Christians in Romans—and only in Romans—Paul probably applies the term 'kins(wo)man' rather consistently to all Jewish Christians he can identify in the group of Romans 16" (ibid., 224–25). Aquila is an exception due to the many things Paul attributes to him.
31. Most of us assume Prisca is Jewish, being married to Aquila. However, this is not specifically stated anywhere in Scripture.

Maria is doubtful.[32] Others may have been Jewish as well, for Jews often bore Greek or Latin names, and their names do not necessarily reflect their race.[33] However, Lampe argues that Paul had a special interest in emphasizing the Jewish origin of Christians and only a minority (15 percent) of those greeted were thus identified, thereby supporting the view that the vast majority of Christians in Rome were gentile. Another interesting finding of Lampe is that he believes "more than two-thirds of the people . . . have an affinity to slave origins."[34] He claims that four names are definitely not those of slaves or freed(wo)men—Urbanus, Prisca, Aquila, and Rufus. Ten definitely are, and twelve cannot be determined. This pattern, if it mirrored the church as a whole, would correspond proportionately to Roman society as a whole. In this light, perhaps the same could be said for the proportion of Jewish names to that of gentile, which is estimated at that time to be around 10 percent of the population.[35] Another not insignificant fact regarding the ratio of Jew and gentile believers has to do with Claudius' edict eliminating many Jewish believers from the Roman church for an extended period of time, from 49 to 54 CE. By the time Paul wrote in 57, some had returned to Rome, as did Prisca and Aquila, but not all.

I assume, then, that the gentiles were in the majority, the Jews in the minority. But the ratio and numbers of each are not that important. Paul was addressing the entire church. There are those who posit multiple groups of recipients and try to pinpoint just what groups are being addressed in particular sections of the letter. An admirable example of this would be Paul Minear, who unabashedly posits at least five distinct factions in 14:1–15:13, and then proposes that Paul shifts his attention from one group to another throughout the rest of the letter.[36] Though his conclusions may be questioned,[37] Minear has made

32. Maria was a fairly common Latin name in Rome (Lampe, "Roman Christians," 225). Theodor Zahn disagrees and views the name as the Hebrew Miriam (*Introduction to the New Testament* [Edinburgh: T&T Clark, 1909], 1:429).

33. Aquila and Prisca are Latin names; Andronicus and Junia and Herodion are Greek names; however, all five are Jewish Christians.

34. Lampe, "Roman Christians," 228.

35. Harry Joshua Leon (*The Jews of Ancient Rome* [Peabody, MA: Hendrickson, 1995], 135–36) estimates the size of the Jewish community in Rome during the first century CE as around 40,000–50,000 Jews. This may be compared to a total population of Rome of 400,000–500,000.

a good-faith effort to identify the various parties. Many scholars view 1:18-32 (or 1:18–2:16) as addressed to gentiles, and 2:1–3:20 (or 2:17–3:20) as addressed to Jews. Some view chapters 1–4 as addressed primarily to Jews, and 6–8 to gentiles. Richard Longenecker and Ben Witherington hold that Paul is addressing Jews in 1–4 and 9–11, and gentiles in 5–8 and 12–15.[38] Kümmel holds that while Romans is addressed to gentiles, Paul is really carrying on a debate with Jews.[39] According to Stanley Stowers, 2:1-5 is an apostrophe of a pretentious gentile, chapter 2 begins with "warning a Greek" and ends with "debating a fellow Jew," and 3:1-9 is dialogue with a fictitious Jew.[40]

There is no need to divide the letter in these ways. We should distinguish between the composition of the audience and the parties to which Paul refers. We need to ask for what reason Paul referred to parties for the benefit of the whole church whom he was addressing. Yes, there were Jewish and gentile Christians in Rome. He says on the one hand, "I am speaking to you who are gentiles"; on the other, "But if you bear the name Jew...." But Paul wrote this from the perspective that the entire church, both Jew and gentile, both the weak and the strong in faith, would be listening as the letter was being read. It is one thing to demonstrate that there were different elements within

36. Paul S. Minear (*The Obedience of Faith: The Purposes of Paul in the Epistle to the Romans*, SBT 2/19 [London SCM, 1971], 8–14, 45n8) divides the Roman Christians into what he perceives to be five groups: group 1: the "weak in faith" who condemned the "strong in faith"; group 2: the "strong in faith" who scorned and despised the "weak in faith"; group 3: the doubters; group 4: the "weak in faith" who did not condemn the "strong in faith"; group 5: the "strong in faith" who did not despise the "weak in faith." Minear then identifies the specific groups he believes Paul is addressing in the various sections of Romans: All readers in the introduction, 1:1-17, but with distinctions recognized; the "weak in faith," group 1, in 1:18–4:15; and then 4:16–5:21 is addressed to all the church; the "strong in faith," group 2, is addressed in chapter 6; while the "weak in faith" is addressed in 7:1–8:8; the "doubters," group 3, are addressed in 8:9–11:12; and the "weak in faith," group 2, in 11:13–13:14. Paul's desire, according to Minear, was for groups 1–3 to move toward groups 4–5 (ibid., 14).

37. See responses by Robert J. Karris, "Romans 14:1–15:13 and the Occasion of Romans," in Donfried, *Romans Debate*, 77–79; and Donfried, "False Presuppositions," 125–27.

38. Ben Witherington III, *Paul's Letter to the Romans: A Socio-rhetorical Commentary*. Grand Rapids: Eerdmans, 2004, 20; Richard Longenecker, "The Focus of Romans: The Central Role of 5.1–8.39 in the Argument of the Letter," in *Romans and the People of God*, ed. Sven K. Soderlund and N. T. Wright (Grand Rapids: Eerdmans, 1999), 49–69 (here 61, 67–68). Longenecker holds that Romans 5–8 is a distinctive message to the gentiles.

39. Kümmel, *Introduction*, 309.

40. Stanley K. Stowers, *A Rereading of Romans: Justice, Jews, and Gentiles* (New Haven: Yale University Press, 1994), 100, 126, 159.

the Roman audience who would be receiving the letter. It is another to divide the letter up by saying that this section was written to this element, and that section to that element. I doubt that the various groups in Rome recognized that this or that section was or was not written specifically to them. Every part of the letter was written with the whole church in mind and for a singular purpose, to unify the body of Christ in Rome. Therefore, when we have an exhortation that appears to be addressed directly to one or the other of these groups, we must view it in the context of how it would be heard within a mixed Jewish-gentile Christian community. Paul was assuming that the entire church, at one time or the other, in house congregations or in larger gatherings, would be listening to the contents of the letter together. His references to the various sectors of the church should be so understood.

Parenthetically, we must remind ourselves that there was no central worship facility where everyone would be gathered to hear the letter. Christians in Rome gathered in house churches.[41] Their homes were no doubt scattered throughout Rome, though perhaps some purposely lived close to each other, as did many Jews. They worshiped in multiple congregations, and one may assume that some were composed primarily of Jewish Christians, while others would attract gentile Christians. Minear finds at least five house churches in Rome (16:5, 10, 11, 14, 15).[42] Lampe projects that there were at least seven or perhaps eight house churches represented by the twenty-six names in chapter 16.[43] Multiple house churches do not in themselves indicate a divided Christian community, but they do leave open that possibility. It is instructive that nowhere in the letter does Paul address the Roman church as a whole as an *ekklēsia*, not even in his opening remarks in 1:1-7. The only reference to an *ekklēsia* in Rome is in 16:5, where Paul

---

41. It seems evident that in the initial stages of mission activity, believers met in homes (Acts 2:46; 12:12; 16:15, 40; 1 Cor. 16:19; Col. 4:15; and Rom. 16:23). There were obviously more than a few house churches in Rome (Rom. 16:3-5, 14-15), being such a large city.

42. Minear, *Obedience*, 7.

43. Lampe, "Roman Christians," 229-30. This stands contrary to Zahn's suggestion that all those mentioned in vv. 5-13 were members of the house church of Prisca and Aquila (Zahn, *Introduction*, 1:429–30).

11

refers to the "church" that is in the house of Prisca and Aquila.[44] The "divided" or "diverse" nature of the Roman Christian community helps bring our perception of them into better balance. The point is this. The letter was meant to be read to all the believers in Rome in whatever circumstances they found themselves. Paul was not jumping to one or the other constituent in his remarks. Nor were the gentiles sitting there listening to Paul debate with Jews for several chapters, or even with an imaginary Jewish interlocutor.

Nevertheless, while Christian Jews were among the audience of Paul's letter, they were not the primary focus of his remarks. Paul's mission as the apostle to the gentiles was to bring about the gentiles' obedience of faith. Thus, while addressing his remarks to the entire body of believers in Rome, and while making reference to specific parties in Rome, Paul is primarily concerned that the gentiles respond to his message. Yes, the letter as a whole is addressed specifically "to all the saints in Rome" (1:7). Paul uses the second-person plural "you" constantly from 1:8-15—"I give thanks for you all" (1:8), "I unceasingly make mention of you always in my prayers" (1:9-10), "I long to see you in order to impart some spiritual gift to you" (1:11). From this use of the plural "you," one could conclude that Paul was being inclusive, referring to both Jew and gentile Christians in Rome, and in part he was.[45] But in 1:13-15 Paul clearly restricts his use of the second-person plural to gentiles in a carefully constructed statement (literally translated):[46]

---

44. The other four references to *ekklēsia* in Romans 16 (vv. 1, 4, 16, 23) refer respectively to the church at Cenchrea, all the churches of the gentiles, all the churches of Christ, and the church of which Gaius is host in Corinth.
45. One would think Prisca and Aquila would be included in the salutation as well as Paul's prayers and thanksgivings for them.
46. This literal translation also reflects the literal order of words in the original text.

¹³But I want you [pl.] to know, brothers and sisters,

that many times I planned to come to you [pl.],   A

and I was hindered until now,

in order that some fruit I might have even among you [pl.]

    as also among the rest of the gentiles [pl.].   B

    ¹⁴Both to the Greeks and to the barbarians,   B

    both to the wise and to the foolish [pl.]

    I am a debtor.

¹⁵Thus I am eager also to you [pl.] who are in Rome   A

    to proclaim the gospel.

Whether or not we want to see a chiasm here is not the issue, though the asyndeton as well as the word order introducing verse 14 do seem to suggest it.[47] The order of the clauses and of the words within clauses is revealing. It is quite clear that Paul is narrowing his focus to the gentiles. He is writing with them in mind. This narrowing of focus on gentiles occurs just prior to the body of the letter.

Immediately following the body of the letter, in 15:14-18, Paul again restricts his use of the second-person plural to gentile believers. He uses sacral terminology for his role in bringing about the "obedience of the gentiles."

¹⁴And I have been persuaded, my brothers, even I myself, concerning you [pl.], that you [pl.] yourselves [pl.] are full of goodness, having been filled with all knowledge and able also to admonish one another.
    ¹⁵But I have written more boldly to you [pl.] on some points, so as to remind you [pl.] again because of the grace given to me by God, ¹⁶to be a minister [*leitourgon*] of Christ Jesus unto the gentiles, serving as a priest

---

47. Cranfield (*Romans*, 1:83) acknowledges the presence of the asyndeton and thinks it adds "solemnity" to the statement. Commentators debate whether these pairings refer to the whole of humanity (including Jews) or the whole of the gentile world. *Hellēsin* probably refers to those of Greco-Roman culture, and *barbarois* to those of foreign culture. *Hellēn* can certainly be restricted to the pagan gentile, or non-Jew. According to James D. G. Dunn (*Romans 1-8*, WBC 38A [Waco: Word, 1988], 32–33), these terms came to be used generally of all races and classes within the gentile world. Wise and foolish is another way of classifying humankind as a whole, synonymous with the preceding contrast. So the function of these designations is to include all of gentile humanity. This leads naturally into v. 15, and the necessary inference that this restriction to gentiles applies to "all" who are in Rome as well. Romans 1:13-15 is clearly restricted to the gentiles.

[*hierourgounta*] the gospel of God, so that the sacrifice [*hē prosphora*] of the gentiles may be acceptable, sanctified [*hēgiasmenē*] by the Holy Spirit.....

[18]For I will not presume to speak of anything except that which Christ has accomplished through me unto the obedience of the gentiles in word and deed.

Paul presents himself as a priest presiding over offerings to God. The gentiles are that offering,[48] and the result is "acceptable," namely, sanctified by the Holy Spirit—a distinctly Jewish way of referring to his calling as the apostle to the gentiles. It is quite unmistakable that Paul is concerned to direct his remarks to the gentiles in Rome, whether or not they constituted a majority. He refers to the grace given him as the apostle to the gentiles (1:5-6; 11:13; 12:3; 15:15-16). He identifies his readers as gentiles (1:13-15; 11:13; 15:14-18). He addresses his concerns about his "kinsmen according to the flesh" to gentiles (chaps. 9–11). He recalls their former sinful lives as heathen (6:17-22) and states that he wants to bear some fruit among them as among the rest of the gentiles (1:11-15). Perhaps his purpose is best stated in 1:5: "to bring about the obedience of faith among all the gentiles for his name's sake."[49]

We come, then, to note these important realities as we read Romans. Paul is addressing the entire letter to the entire body of believers in Rome. While addressing the entire body of believers, Paul makes reference to specific parties within the church as well as to sectors of society at large. That is only natural to do, and the entire body understands that he is referring to this or that sector of believers (or nonbelievers). However, as one given grace as the apostle to the gentiles to bring about their obedience of faith, Paul is primarily addressing his remarks to gentile believers in Rome. This is how we approach Paul's entire dialogue in the letter. Whether we are

---

48. Dunn (*Romans 9–16*, WBC 38B [Waco: Word, 1989], 860–61) notes that *hē prosphora tōn ethnōn* can be either (1) the act of presenting an offering (e.g., Acts 24:17; Heb. 10:14, 18) or (2) the offering itself (Acts 21:26; Eph. 5:2; Heb. 10:5, 8). If *tōn ethnōn* is a genitive of apposition, then Paul would be viewing the gentiles as the offering itself, acceptable as sanctified by the Holy Spirit.

49. Stowers (*A Rereading of Romans*, 29–30) speaks of the letter's "explicitly encoded audience," the gentiles; and he remarks that "it was once fashionable for scholars to say that Romans was addressed to Jewish Christians, but owing to the objections raised by Johannes Munck and others this position is no longer plausible." See Johannes Munck, *Paul and the Salvation of Mankind* (Richmond, VA: John Knox, 1959), 196–209. Elliott (*Arrogance of Nations*, 177n67) says that "Romans must be interpreted as an argument directed to the explicit addressees."

interpreting his exposition of the wrath of God in 1:18-32, or the litany of questions in 3:1-9, or the appeal for Israel in chapters 9–11, or the exhortations to the strong and weak in 14:1–15:6, the hermeneutic is the same. Paul is writing to the whole church in Rome. He may refer directly to this or that party within the church, but he never forgets that the whole church is listening. Moreover, he is writing with his primary audience in mind, the gentile believers in Rome. How will his letter influence their obedience of faith?

The occasion for his writing was his anticipated trip to Rome. He wanted to encourage their spiritual growth in Christ and to enlist their involvement in his mission to go beyond Rome as far as Spain. He explains all of this in the bookends of the letter. My thesis is that the body of the letter serves to address circumstances in Rome. I make a distinction in this study between the "surface structure" that "guides" the audience through the letter, and the "underlying issues" that "govern" or "drive" the content of the letter. As is the case in other letters of Paul, the surface structure of Romans guides the narrative and in the process points to the underlying issues that are driving the narrative. The more clearly we understand the surface structure of Romans, the more credible will become our understanding of why Paul wrote Romans. In the end, the coherence of the entire letter should become evident.

2

The Structure of Romans

We turn now to the unresolved issue of the structure of Romans. The most obvious place to start is with the "bookends" of Romans. There is general agreement that the opening of the letter is 1:1-17, the closing is 15:14–16:27, and the body is 1:18–15:13.[1] There does appear to be an *inclusio* of sorts, in two ways. First, Paul's expressed desire to proclaim the gospel to the gentiles in Rome concludes the opening (1:13-15) and commences the closing (15:14-19). Second, Paul's thematic statement that the gospel is the power of God for salvation to the Jews first and also to the Greeks (1:16-17) has its counterpart in his concluding statement that God's mercy extends first to the "circumcision" and then to the gentiles who are to glorify God together with "his people" (15:8-13).[2] These structural features affirm that one cannot divorce Paul's repeated statements about the gospel from the body of material they bracket.

---

1. For an analysis of Hellenistic epistography and its relation to the letters of Paul, see John Lee White, *The Form and Function of the Body of the Greek Letter*, SBLDS 2 (Missoula, MT: Scholars Press, 1972); see also David E. Aune, "Epistolography," in *The Westminster Dictionary of New Testament and Early Christian Literature and Rhetoric* (Louisville: Westminster John Knox, 2003), 162–68.
2. Other corresponding phrases include his being hindered thus far in coming to them (1:13; 15:22), and his coming being a means of imparting some spiritual gift or blessing (1:11; 15:29).

There is also a consensus regarding major breaks within the letter. Chapter 8 concludes the prior section with expressions of praise that are of almost hymnic proportion, while chapter 9 begins a new subject without any connective (asyndeton) to the prior section. Chapter 11 ends with an ecstatic doxology to God, while chapter 12 begins with the words, "Therefore I exhort you, brothers" (parakalō oun hymas adelphoi), followed by a series of exhortations. Thus there are three major blocks of discourse—1:18–8:39, 9:1–11:36, and 12:1–15:13. This is not to say that these three sections are detached or isolated from each other, for they are closely related. I am simply pointing to clear breaks within the body of the letter.

There are two issues about which there is no consensus. The first has to do with the placement of chapter 5. Many interpreters view chapter 5 as concluding chapters 1–4, whereas it is becoming popular to view chapter 5 as introducing chapters 6–8.[3] The second issue has to do with perceived digressions of thought, more precisely, the entirety of chapters 9–11 and the rhetorical questions in 3:1–9a. In the past, many have viewed chapters 9–11 as a parenthetical digression due to Paul's great desire for his Jewish kins(wo)men and not particularly related to the subject matter in Romans. More recent commentators are taking the opposite view, that chapters 9–11 are central to Paul's line of thought. The rhetorical questions in 3:1–9a are generally viewed as Paul's defensive response to a Jewish interlocutor who is objecting to what Paul said in 2:17-25. Commentators are prone to mention these verses in passing, not realizing their significance for the progression of thought in Romans. These issues will be dealt with below, where I will maintain that both chapters 9–11 and 3:1–9a are anything but digressions.[4]

Thematic Approaches

Some commentators have offered an outline similar to this.

---

3. This issue will be considered below in chap. 5.
4. See chap. 4.

I. The Doctrine of Sin and Salvation, 1–8

II. The Problem of Israel, 9–11

III. The Practical Application of Doctrine, 12–16

Behind this is the assumption that in chapters 1–8 we have a clear statement of Paul's doctrine of justification by faith; in chapters 9–11 we have a statement regarding the future of Israel; and in chapters 12–16 we have practical exhortations for the church at large.[5] The earlier chapters, including 1–11, develop a theological grid on which the final exhortations are based. For some, Paul was dealing with justification in chapters 1–5 and sanctification in chapters 6–8.[6] For others, he was developing the theme of justification throughout chapters 1–11.[7] Of course, the themes of justification and sanctification are present in these chapters, but is the progression of thought governed by these themes? The concern many have with these and similar outlines is that theological loci appear to be governing one's approach to the text.

More favored, exegetically, is to follow the themes laid out in the letter. Anders Nygren suggests that the organizing theme is the quotation of Hab. 2:4 in Rom. 1:17, and what follows is an exposition of that text:

5. According to Charles Hodge (*A Commentary on the Epistle to the Romans* [1886; repr., Grand Rapids: Eerdmans, 1950], 13), "The epistle consists of three parts. The first, which includes the first eight chapters, is occupied in the discussion of the doctrine of justification and its consequences. The second, embracing chs. ix.–xi., treats of the calling of the Gentiles, the rejection and future conversion of the Jews. The third consists of practical exhortations and salutations to the Christians at Rome." Heinrich August Wilhelm Meyer (*The Epistle to the Romans* [New York: Funk & Wagnalls, 1884], 25) notes that after the salutation and introduction of Romans (1:1-15), Romans "falls into two main portions, a theoretical and a hortatory, after which follows the conclusion (xv.14–xvi.27)." The theoretical portion includes chaps. 1–11 and bears the theme of righteousness by faith for both Jew and gentile. The hortatory section includes chaps. 12–15.

6. For example, William Sanday and Arthur Headlam, *The Epistle to the Romans* (New York: Charles Scribner's Sons, 1897), xlvii–l. A. E. Garvey's outline (*Romans*, NCB [New York: Oxford University Press, n.d.], 41) includes: "The Doctrine of Justification, i.18–v.21," "The Doctrine of Sanctification, vi–viii," and "The Doctrine of Election, ix–xi." Garvey's outline is similar to the one this author was initially taught, that chaps. 1–8 proceeded from the doctrine of sin (1–2), to justification (3–5), to sanctification (6:1–8:17), to glorification (8:18-39), and that 9–11 was a parenthesis.

7. For example, William Hendriksen, *Romans* (Grand Rapids: Baker, 1981), 30, 308.

The Theme: "He who through faith is righteous . . . shall live" (1:17).

 I. **He Who through Faith Is Righteous,** 1:18–4:25

  A. Under the Wrath of God, 1:18–3:20
  B. The Righteousness of God, 3:21–4:25

 II. He Who through Faith is Righteous **Shall Live,** 5:1–8:39

  A. Free from Wrath, 5:1-21
  B. Free from Sin, 6:1-23
  C. Free from the Law, 7:1-25
  D. Free from Death, 8:1-39

Nygren's view is that the letter had nothing to do with circumstances in Rome. It was simply a doctrinal letter, a "theological treatise," written to deal with a major purpose in life—the new relation we have by faith in Christ apart from works of the law.[8] C. E. B. Cranfield expands the theme to include 1:16b-17, but he essentially follows Nygren's outline.[9] Paul Achtemeier insists that viewing 1:17 and "righteousness by faith" as the central theme of the letter is problematic. Grammatically, 1:17 is merely one member of a series of causal clauses, and to find "the" theme of the letter in just one of the clauses is "to overload the grammar to the point of ignoring it."[10] Clearly, the "righteousness of God" is a major theme, but it is not alone the central organizing theme of the letter.

Most commentators view the entirety of 1:16-17 as the theme of the letter. Here are a few examples.

C. H. Dodd's outline:[11]

The Prologue, 1:1-15
 The Theme, 1:16-17

 I. The Universal Sway of Sin and Retribution, 1:18-3:20

8. Anders Nygren, *Commentary on Romans*, trans. Carl C. Rasmussen (Philadelphia: Fortress Press, 1949), 26–41, with outline for chaps. 1-8 on p. 38. Numerous commentators have been influenced by Nygren's approach, especially his captions for chapters 5-8.
9. C. E. B. Cranfield, *A Critical and Exegetical Commentary on the Epistle to the Romans*, ICC (Edinburgh: T&T Clark, 1975), 1:28–29, 87–102.
10. Paul Achtemeier, *Romans*, IBC (Atlanta: John Knox, 1985), 21.
11. C. H. Dodd, *The Epistle of Paul to the Romans* (London: Fontana, 1970), vii–viii (outline in abbreviated form).

  II.   The Righteousness of God in Justification, 3:21–4:25
  III. The Righteousness of God in Salvation, 5:1–8:39
  IV. The Divine Purpose in History, 9–11
  V.   The Righteousness of God in Christian living, 12:1–15:13

The Epilogue, 15:14–16:27

Douglas J. Moo's outline:[12]

  I.   The Letter Opening, 1:1-17
      The Theme of the Letter, 1:16-17
  II.   The Heart of the Gospel: Justification by Faith, 1:18–4:25
  III. The Assurance Provided by the Gospel: The Hope of Salvation, 5:1–8:39
  IV. The Defense of the Gospel: The Problem of Israel, 9:1–11:36
  V.   The Transforming Power of the Gospel: Christian Conduct, 12:1–15:13
  VI. The Letter Closing, 15:14–16:27

James Dunn's outline is a bit more involved:[13]

I. Introduction, 1:1-17
Summary Statement of the Letter's Theme (1:16-17)
II–V. The Righteousness of God—From God's Faithfulness to Man's Faith (1:18–11:36)
    II–III. The Righteousness of God—To Man's Faith (1:18–5:21)
        II. The Wrath of God on Man's Unrighteousness, 1:18–3:20
        III. God's Saving Righteousness to Faith, 3:21–5:21

    IV–V. The Outworking of This Gospel in Relation to the Individual and to the Election of Grace (6:1–11:36)
        IV. The Outworking of the Gospel in Relation to the Individual, 6:1–8:39
        V. The Righteousness of God—From God's Faithfulness: The Outworking of the Gospel in Relation to Israel, 9:1–11:36

VI. The Outworking of the Gospel for the Redefined People of God in Everyday Terms, 12:1–15:13

VII. Conclusion, 15:14–16:27

Dunn speaks for many when he states that "vv. 16-17 is clearly the

---

12. Douglas Moo, *The Epistle to the Romans*, NICNT (Grand Rapids: Eerdmans, 1996), 33–35 (outline in abbreviated form).
13. James D. G. Dunn, *Romans 1–8* WBC 38A (Waco: Word, 1988), vii–xi (outline in abbreviated form).

thematic statement for the entire letter." Attention should not be focused exclusively on verse 17, and especially not limited to the quote from Hab. 2:4, which is there simply to provide scriptural support for the text of the letter. Dunn views 1:16b as tying the whole letter together (chapters 1–15), and 1:17 as providing the text for the main didactic portion of the letter (chapters 1–11).[14]

However, there are those who have taken exception to this thematic approach to the letter. J. Christiaan Beker is concerned that when the body of Romans is separated from its frame, and the exhortations of chapters 12–15 are detached from the main body, what is left becomes increasingly viewed as an "abstract core." This is especially true if you treat chapters 9–11 as an appendix or afterthought, leaving only chapters 1–8, which become the dogmatic core of the letter. Rather, Beker says, we must realize that Romans is only a letter and that "letters are words on target because of their contingency." Paul wrote "a variety of contingent letters. Thus we must acknowledge their epistolary integrity and avoid treating them as merely the accidental pretext for a systematic statement of a 'timeless' Pauline thought."[15] Beker laments that commentators such as Nygren have focused on chapters 1–8 and viewed them as timeless theological truth apart from the rest of the letter. Beker then points out the inconsistencies in Nygren's outline—that 5:1-11 focuses more on joy and hope than wrath, that 6:1-23 is concerned as much with life and death as with sin,

---

14. Ibid., 37–38. However, we should not leave unnoticed commentators such as Joseph A. Fitzmyer (*Romans: A New Translation with Introduction and Commentary*, AB 33 [New York: Doubleday, 1992], viii–xi, or 98–99, Arabic numbers 4–30) who view 1:16-17 as the theme statement for 1:18–4:25, and 5:1-11 as the theme statement for 5:12–8:39. While we may find major theme statements initially in any discourse, in a prolonged discourse it would seem evident that there would be repeated or added statements of the theme.

15. J. Christiaan Beker, *Paul the Apostle: The Triumph of God in Life and Thought* (Philadelphia: Fortress Press, 1984), 62; see 61–74. For his reference to Nygren, see p. 65. Beker also points out that Karl Barth in his commentary pays no attention to 1:1-15 and 15:14–16:25, and bypasses the historical issues (Beker, *Paul the Apostle*, 65). He writes: "The presupposition that Romans is a 'theological confession' or a 'dogmatics in outline' is the real reason for the immense interest in the letter's architectonic structure and the neglect of its 'frame'" (ibid., 62). "The attractiveness of these structural schemes should not tempt us. . . . The diligent search for the architectonic structure of Romans—whether in its totality or in 'craters'—suffers from an unexamined presupposition, for it imposes a dogmatic premise on the exegetical task. Dogmatic language requires systematic coherence and architectonic logic (cf. *loci*-dogmatics), and far too often New Testament scholarship has not resisted this dogmatic prejudice in its investigation of Romans" (ibid., 68–69).

that 7:1-25 has more to do with trying to do the law than freedom from the law, and that freedom from death is only one theme among many in chapter 8. He concludes that "the aesthetic beauty and clarity of this outline should not deceive us, for it attributes to Paul an architectonic rigor that cannot stand close scrutiny."[16]

To the extent that scholars have imposed on Romans theological classifications not warranted from the text, Beker's objections are surely warranted. I agree with Beker that Romans is a contingent letter, written to circumstances in Rome, and should not be labeled a "theological treatise," as Nygren has done. Of course, this should not keep us from pursuing exegetically theological themes throughout the letter. Paul argues theologically, and logically. For example, 3:21 follows quite logically from 3:19-20, and 5:1 is based on what is clearly stated in 3:21-26 (and 3:27–4:25); and these passages expand on the theme of righteousness by faith introduced in 1:16-17. So theological themes do play an important role in the structure and content of the letter. However, it is wrong to assume that themes alone guide the dialogue of the letter.

A similar sentiment has been expressed by Thomas Tobin, SJ, who cautions against understanding the structure of Romans based on theological themes. He argues that when one structures Romans thematically, the themes take on a life of their own and thereby tend to hide the historical setting. In fact, it inhibits attempts to understand Paul's arguments in terms of his own situation, that of the Christians in Rome, and the relationship between the two. Furthermore, a thematic protocol inhibits attempts to deal adequately with the literary structure of the letter itself. He asks, "Are there literary rather than theological cues in Romans that reveal how Paul structured his arguments in the letter?"[17] He then finds that there are differences of style between sections of the text. Some sections are calm and expositional in tone; others are quite argumentative or polemic in style. "In terms of ancient rhetoric, the expository sections roughly

16. Ibid., 65–66.
17. Thomas H. Tobin, SJ, *Paul's Rhetoric in Its Contexts: The Argument of Romans* (Peabody, MA: Hendrickson, 2008), 82–84, esp. 84.

correspond to the positive argumentation of a speech; the more polemical sections correspond to the part of the speech devoted to the refutation of objections."[18] After analyzing the differences, he proposes this overall structure of the letter:

1:16-17 (proposition)

1. 1:18–3:20

   a. 1:18-32 (expository)
   b. 2:1–3:20 (argumentative)

2. 3:21–4:25

   a. 3:21-26 (expository)
   b. 3:27–4:25 (argumentative)

3. 5:1–7:25

   a. 5:1-21 (expository)
   b. 6:1–7:25 (argumentative)

4. 8:1–11:36

   a. 8:1-30 (expository)
   b. 8:31–11:36 (argumentative)

5. 12:1–15:7 (exhortatory)
   15:8-13 (conclusion)

In the expositional sections, Paul is highlighting shared beliefs with the Roman believers, while in the argumentative sections that follow and are significantly longer he is defending his positions on various issues. He does so by using a common literary convention known as "diatribe," which is a much more engaging style. It employs rhetorical questions, apostrophes, dialogues with imaginary interlocutors, refutations of objections and false conclusions, and so forth. In fact, Roman Christians would have understood the entire body of the letter as a "diatribe." Consequently, for Tobin, Paul's organization is governed not by a sequence of themes but by issues he was addressing between himself

18. Ibid., 86.

and the Roman believers by means of diatribe. These issues were not problems being faced by Christians in Rome, but issues and misgivings the Roman believers had with him.[19] And what were these misgivings? They lay below the surface of the letter's exhortations, but they were real nonetheless. They have to do with the value of the Mosaic law and its observance, how believers are to live their lives, and the status of the Jewish people and their relation to the gentiles. For Paul, these misgivings had to be dispelled if he expected to be greeted positively by them upon his arrival in Rome.

It is refreshing to see someone trying to follow the flow of Paul's thought, assuming that there was purpose behind his progression of thought other than merely presenting an outline of his gospel. While I may differ with Tobin as to what the issues were, I agree that Paul was addressing a specific situation within the Roman church itself. I do not view the whole of the body of the letter as diatribe. Nevertheless, Tobin is touching on an important point, the role of the engaging questions and dialogue often classified as diatribe. He finds these questions are used extensively throughout Romans, and so do I. How they are used by Paul is a major concern in this monograph.

Rhetorical Approaches

Other scholars attempt to discern the rhetorical structure of the letter. Robert Jewett agrees with Beker that Romans is a situational letter and not a doctrinal thesis. He states unequivocally that "since previous analyses of the letter have tended to reflect the thematic and theological interests of scholars, it seems apparent that we need a more impartial approach to following Paul's argument." He proposes "the rhetorical method" as the most promising resource as it allows us to grasp the structure of the argument in its oral setting. It also "counterbalances the tendency to follow the argument primarily from the viewpoint of contemporary theology."[20] The components in the

---

19. Ibid., 84–98; also 255.
20. Robert Jewett, "Following the Argument of Romans," in *The Romans Debate*, ed. Karl P. Donfried (Peabody, MA: Hendrickson, 1991), 265–77; for quote, see 265–66.

development of argumentation are found in rhetorical handbooks of antiquity, and there appears to be a similarity between the principles that were taught in those handbooks and the arguments found in Romans. Based on the classification of argumentation within the Hellenistic world of that time, Jewett puts forth this outline:[21]

> Part One: *Exordium* (1:1-12)—Paul introduces himself to a divided audience, plus his purpose
> Part Two: *Narratio* (1:13-15)—Paul describes background that has thus far been frustrated
> Part Three: *Propositio* (1:16-17)—Paul states major thesis of letter regarding the gospel
> Part Four: *Probatio* (1:18-15:13)—Paul provides four elaborate proofs of the thesis

- 1st: *Confirmatio* (1:18–4:25)—Paul confirms *propositio* by showing God provides righteousness for Jews and gentiles alike, by faith (in five major sections each with two pericopes)

- 2nd: *Exornatio* (5:1–8:39)—Paul deals with a series of objections to the doctrine of righteousness of God (in ten pericopes)

- 3rd: *Comparatio* (9–11)—Paul takes up the case of unbelieving Israel and the gospel (in ten pericopes that match the structure of the preceding proof)

- 4th: *Exhortatio* (12:1–15:13)—Paul lays out ethical guidelines for living in righteousness (in ten pericopes)

> Part Five: *Peroratio* (15:14–16:27)—Paul's conclusion (organized in five distinct sections)

Ben Witherington follows a path similar to Jewett's while at the same time making a distinction between epistolary elements in the frame of the letter and the rhetorical organization of the body.[22]

> Epistolary opening and greeting, 1:1-7

21. Ibid., 272–76; also Jewett, *Romans*, Hermeneia (Minneapolis: Fortress Press, 2007), pp. vii–ix (outline in abbreviated form). Jewett uses classical terminology of rhetoric that may be defined as follows: *exordium* (introduction), *narratio* (narration; presents facts that relate to issues), *propositio* (proposition; states the issues or themes to be proved), *probatio* (confirmation or argumentation; develops the arguments and proof), *confirmatio* (confirmation), *exornatio* (elaboration), *comparatio* (comparison), *exhortatio* (exhortation), and *peroratio* (conclusion; summarizes and evokes action).
22. Ben Witherington III, *Paul's Letter to the Romans: A Socio-rhetorical Commentary* (Grand Rapids: Eerdmans, 2004), 21–22.

Exordium/epistolary wish-prayer, 1:8-10

Narratio, 1:11-15

Propositio, 1:16-17

Probatio [Arguments I–II], 1:18–3:20

Recapitulatio [Arguments III–VIII], 3:21–8:39

Refutatio [Arguments IX–XII], 9:1–15:13

Peroratio, 15:14-21

Epistolary closing plans and greetings, 15:22-33

Concluding epistolary greetings and instructions, 16:1-16

Supplemental *Peroratio*, 16:17-20

Concluding epistolary greetings, 16:21-23

Final benediction, 16:25-27

These attempts to view the structure of the epistle from a rhetorical perspective are helpful in that they enable us to see how such oral argumentation influenced Paul's line of thought. Nevertheless, I have several concerns. First, in the examples just given, the only difference between these outlines and those thematically driven appears to be their nomenclature. They appear simply to be putting a rhetorical tag on outlines previously established by commentators. Of course, the response might be that Paul organized his argumentation according to the rhetorical patterns of his time. But was classical rhetoric really the controlling factor for how Paul organized the letter? Second, to identify rhetoric is simply that: to identify rhetoric. Such identification does not necessarily explain how the letter was designed. Moreover, in the examples just given, there is a lack of agreement in identifying the rhetoric. Jewett identifies all of 1:18–15:13 as *probatio* with different proofs in each of the smaller sections.[23] Witherington identifies

23. R. Dean Anderson Jr. (*Ancient Rhetorical Theory and Paul* [Leuven: Peeters, 1999], 192–93n7) argues that the ancient rhetorical terms used by Jewett in his outline lose much of their original meaning

1:18–3:20 as *probatio*, 3:21–8:39 as *recapitulatio*, and 9:1–15:13 as *refutatio*. Some scholars identify 1:16-17 as *propositio*, while others identify it as *transitus*. Some identify 1:18–3:20 as *probatio* while others as *narratio*, and so forth.

Third, one gets the impression that Paul's use of such patterns of argument was not so much deliberate ("Here is my *propositio*, now I need a *ratio*") as it was instinctive. He was his own unique person using the rhetorical tools of his time. We may identify components of Romans as *confirmatio* or *exhortatio*, which is fine, but it leaves us somewhat at sea as to what was actually guiding and driving the progression of thought. According to James Dunn,

> The key fact here is that the distinctiveness of the letter far outweighs the significance of its conformity with current literary or rhetorical custom. Parallels show chiefly how others wrote at that period; they provide no prescription for Paul's practice and no clear criterion by which to assess Paul; and the fact that no particular suggestion has commanded widespread assent in the current discussion suggests that Paul's style was as much or more eclectic and instinctive than conventional and conformist.[24]

Neil Elliott maintains, "I expect the ancient handbooks to be of only limited usefulness in determining the genre of Romans. The handbooks were designed, after all, for the fairly formal expectations of public oratory in the Greco-Roman world. But as scholars of classical rhetoric themselves have reminded us, many forms of speech cannot be fitted into the fairly rigid categories of the handbooks." He concludes by stating that they will be of limited assistance for understanding what he refers to as "an 'invasive' or disruptive rhetoric such as Paul's in Romans, a rhetoric that announces the revelation of 'God's wrath . . . against the impiety and injustice of those who by their injustice suppress the truth,' who although claiming to be wise, have been made fools by God's 'darkening' of their minds (Rom 1:18, 21-22)."[25]

as used in ancient theory. Anderson maintains that Paul "did not consciously think or write in rhetorical categories" (ibid., 290).

24. Dunn, *Romans 1-8*, lix.

25. Neil Elliott, *The Arrogance of Nations: Reading Romans in the Shadow of Empire* (Minneapolis: Fortress Press, 2008), 17-18. He writes, "Rhetorical-critical interpretations of Romans have often done

Elliott's description of Paul's rhetoric as "invasive" or "disruptive" is a bit unsettling. But on reflection, Elliott is right. Much of Paul's rhetoric is intrusive, and purposely so. It does not read as a nondescript essay, for Paul jumps almost immediately into depicting the judgment of God with the thrice recurring "God gave them over," and as quickly speaks directly to the person who would presume to judge another without recognizing his or her own culpability. Once Paul proclaims God's impartial judgment on the Jew first and also on the Greek, he starts making statements that are clearly "invasive," that the Jews have dishonored God by their works, that all are under sin, and that there is no room for boasting before God. All the while Paul raises questions relating to Jew-gentile relations and the role of the law of God in a sinner's life—What advantage has the Jew? Are we better than they? Where is boasting? Is God the God of the Jews only? Shall we sin because we are no longer under the law but under grace? Is the law sin? While expressing grief over Israel, he exhorts gentiles not to be arrogant, conceited, or high-minded toward them.

I have quoted only a few of the strong exhortations and questions that invade and at times disrupt the discourse of Romans. They obviously play an important role in the flow of thought of the letter. Paul himself confesses that he has written "very boldly on some points" as a minister of Jesus Christ to the gentiles due to the grace given him by God (15:15). Nevertheless, the outlines presented above do not appear to take into account that boldness. Rather, they seem to approach Romans more as an essay and may even be imposing their outlines on the text. Or they recognize the patterns of rhetorical argumentation in Hellenism, see similarities with Paul's discourse, and then frame Romans based on those patterns. That is fine if Paul's intention was to write an essay framed as a letter. But if Paul's intention was to write a letter, then there will of necessity be interaction with his readers, and that interaction will help guide the letter. Is there another, an alternative, surface structure that makes

little more than glean from the classical Greek and Roman rhetorical handbooks a novel technical nomenclature for an outline of the letter that has already been established, without the benefit of rhetorical categories, in dogmatic readings" (17).

sense of Paul's interaction with his audience and guides them through the letter?

We also need to give full weight to the insight of Beker, that Paul's letters are "words on target because of their contingency," that he wrote a variety of contingent letters, and that we should acknowledge the "epistolary integrity" of Romans. Beker is right on target regarding Paul's letters. For example, the structure of Galatians was determined by the situation he was addressing in Galatia. First he defends his authority as an apostle (Gal. 1:11–2:14); then he defends his gospel (2:15–5:1); and finally he defends the principle of Christian freedom (5:2–6:10). The structural sequence was based on dealing with the issues in Galatia, and both the opening and closing comments (1:1-10; 6:11-18) were written for that same purpose. In 1 Corinthians, Paul is responding to problems in that church heard through oral and written reports; and he addresses them seriatim (chapters 1–4, 5–6, 7, 8–10, 11, 12–14, 15, 16) throughout the letter. In Philippians, Paul is responding to the anxiety of his dear friends in Philippi and the structure is less formal. He first tells them of his thankfulness for them and his prayer for them. He seeks to alleviate their concern for him while in prison, reminding them of his purpose in life. He then encourages them to be "worthy" of the gospel, united in spirit, and so forth. The same may be said for all his letters. They are structured with his recipients in mind. If this is true of his other letters, we should expect it to be true of Romans as well. So what were the contingent factors in Rome? How do those contingent factors affect the structure of the letter? If Paul is addressing such issues, there should be evidence in the rhetoric.

Finally, we need to consider whether the letter is coherent. Do the parts of the letter relate to the whole, as well as to each other? Are the bookends vitally related to the body of the letter? Is there a surface structure that helps pull the whole letter together? We need to address all three issues for a proper understanding of the structure of Romans: (1) the invasive rhetoric of Romans and what guides the narrative; (2) the contingent factors in Rome that drive and govern the narrative; and (3) the coherence of the letter as a whole. But before we tackle these issues, we must first consider Paul's use of rhetoric and the nature of the letter itself.[26]

26. I will attempt to answer all three of these issues extensively in the following chapters: (1) in the chapters on the role of rhetoric and the surface structure of the letter, what guides the letter with its invasive rhetoric; (2) in the chapter on the circumstances in Rome, what drives and governs the content of the letter; and (3) in the final chapter, whether the letter is coherent.

3

The Rhetoric of Romans

In the hunt for the surface structure of Romans, I am assuming that it is a letter. A letter interacts with its readers, and its rhetoric serves to communicate throughout what is relevant for both writer and recipients, what J. Christiaan Beker calls "words on target." Nevertheless, while many commentators view Romans as a letter, they interpret it as an essay. Why is this? A major reason is its length. It is a very long letter.[1] Its length may be coupled with the view that Paul's primary motive was to write down his theology rather than send a personal letter. For some, there is a perceived lack of the epistolary and oral devices one normally finds in a letter. This may be coupled with the impression that Paul was not that familiar with the circumstances in Rome; therefore, why would he be addressing their concerns in

---

1. C. E. B. Cranfield (*A Critical and Exegetical Commentary on the Epistle to the Romans*, ICC [Edinburgh: T&T Clark, 1975], 1:46n2) informs us that, while Romans is similar to Greek letters, it is much longer than the great majority of ancient Greek and Latin letters. Private letters are seldom longer than what can be written on one side of one papyrus sheet, or approximately 150 to 250 words. He points out that the longest letter by Cicero was 4,530 words, but Romans includes over 7,000 words. E. Randolph Richards (*The Secretary in the Letters of Paul* [Tübingen: J. C. B. Mohr (Paul Siebeck), 1991], 213) notes that in the approximately 14,000 private letters we possess from Greco-Roman antiquity, the average length was about 87 words. Cicero's letters averaged 295 words per letter, Seneca averaged 995, while the thirteen letters bearing Paul's name average 2,495 words (from Philemon with 335 to Romans with 7,114).

a letter? There is also another underlying reason why some commentators hesitate to view the body of Romans as a letter, and this may be a surprising reason to add to the mix. The rhetorical questions in Romans are commonly viewed as diatribe and as a response to criticism in Rome of Paul's gospel, so that Paul is viewed more as defending his own gospel before coming to Rome and less as relating to circumstances in Rome. So there are assumptions to overcome if we are to persuade some that the body of Romans interacts as a letter. Nevertheless, this I will attempt to do.

Paul's Use of Epistolary Forms

Romans has been classified as a nonliterary letter,[2] a more literary *Lehrbrief* (or "didactic letter"),[3] an "ambassadorial letter of self-introduction,"[4] and a "letter-essay."[5] Richard Longenecker has surveyed the history of this discussion and agrees with the view that Romans is a "letter-essay."[6] In his view, the body of Romans lacks the "epistolary formulas" that are common in nonliterary letters. Epistolary formulas are common tools of communication between a writer and his or her reader. Longenecker provides a list of such forms.[7]

2. Whether Romans is an informal letter or a more carefully designed epistle has been debated since Adolf Deissmann's attempt to distinguish the two (*Light from the Ancient East: The New Testament Illustrated by Recently Discovered Texts of the Graeco-Roman World*, trans. Lionel R. M. Strachan [London: Hodder & Stoughton, 1927], 228–30, 239–41). Deissmann held that a letter was a private, nonliterary communication between persons, whereas an epistle was an artistic literary form intended for the public. For him, Romans was a nonliterary letter. Ernst Käsemann (*Commentary on Romans*, trans. Geoffrey W. Bromiley [Grand Rapids: Eerdmans, 1980], 3) pointed out that we cannot make a sharp distinction since Paul's letters were meant to be read by multiple people as instruction and proclamation. In Käsemann's view, Romans is not a simple letter. Nor is it a theological tractate as evidenced by the epistolary form found in the bookends of the letter. Abraham J. Malherbe (*Ancient Epistolary Theorists* [Atlanta: Scholars Press, 1988], 12–14) summarizes types and styles of ancient letters. In the present writer's view, there appears to have been a wide variety of types and styles, and we should be cautious about trying to box Romans into any particular style, or, conversely, trying to exclude Romans from the epistolary genre.

3. Otto Michel, *Der Brief an die Römer* (Göttingen: Vandenhoeck & Ruprecht, 1957), 5; Matthew Black, *Romans*, NCB (London: Marshall, Morgan & Scott, 1973), 18.

4. Robert Jewett, "Romans as an Ambassadorial Letter," *Int* 36 (1982): 5–20.

5. Martin Luther Stirewalt Jr., "The Form and Function of the Greek Letter-Essay," in *The Romans Debate*, ed. Karl P. Donfried, 147–74. Rev. and expanded ed. Peabody, MA: Hendrickson, 1991), 147–71. See also his work *Studies in Ancient Greek Epistolography* (Atlanta: Scholars Press, 1993), esp. 15–20.

6. Richard Longenecker, *Introducing Romans: Critical Issues in Paul's Most Famous Letter* (Grand Rapids: Eerdmans, 2011), 210–11; see also Karl P. Donfried, "False Presuppositions in the Study of Romans," in Donfried, *Romans Debate*, 121–25.

- Thanksgiving: "I give thanks that . . ."

- Prayer: "I pray for . . ."

- Expressions of grief or distress: "I am anxious because . . ."

- Disclosure formula: "I want you to know that . . ."; "For I know that . . ."

- Request formula: "I exhort you, brother . . ."

- Expression of joy: "I rejoice greatly that . . ."

- Expression of astonishment: "I am surprised how . . ."

- Reminder of past instruction: "as I have asked you . . ."

- Formulaic use of verb for hearing or learning: "I was grieved to hear/learn that . . ."

- Notification of a coming visit: "If the gods will, I will try to come to you . . ."

- Reference to writing: "You wrote that . . ."

- Verbs of saying and informing: "I say that . . ."; I have been informed that . . ."

- Expression of reassurance: "Do not think that . . ."

- Responsibility statement: "Do not neglect to . . ."

- Use of vocative of direct address: "I make known to you, brother . . ."

These are forms that interact with the reader and forms we would expect to find in a letter. According to Terence Y. Mullins, their use reflects more than any other element that a written document is a letter and not an essay.

> When dealing with epistolary forms, we must not lose sight of their epistolary nature. They were tools for communication between a writer and a specific reader or group of readers. They were not used by a writer as part of a purely literary project. They constitute a social gesture, not

---

7. Longenecker, *Introducing Romans*, 218–19. This list has been abbreviated for my purposes.

a thematic ploy. They show the writer's attitude toward the *audience* to which he is writing, not his attitude toward the *material* he is presenting. The use of epistolary forms, more than any other part of the letter, reflects the fact that it was a letter, not an essay or a theological tract, which was being written. The presence of one of these epistolary forms in an ancient Greek letter indicates a pause in a communication process, not a development in a literary process.[8]

Longenecker has analyzed the use of these forms in Romans. He finds "clusters" of epistolary formulas in the opening and closing of the letter (twenty-seven formulas), and a small cluster in 12:1, 3. However, he finds relatively few forms in the body of the letter (only thirty).[9] He also compares Romans to other Pauline letters and finds that the latter contain a relatively larger number of epistolary formulas in the middle sections of their letters, serving to introduce, connect, or close off sections of the letters. He logically concludes that Rom. 1:16–15:13 "should be understood as instructional and hortatory material set within an epistolary frame" and "analyzed more in terms of their rhetorical features," while the opening and closing should be analyzed according to their epistolary conventions.[10]

Ben Witherington says it is a mistake to overemphasize the epistolary character of Romans. Epistolary elements are confined primarily to "the outer edges of the discourse," the beginning and end of Romans. He quotes "Demetrius" in *On Style* 228–234, who cautions against viewing essays with brief epistolary openings and closings as letters. "If one writes logical subtleties . . . in a letter, one is writing, certainly, but one is not writing a letter. The aim of a letter is to be affectionate in brief, and to lay out a simple subject in simple terms. . . . The one who utters sententious maxims and exhortations seems to be no longer talking familiarly in a letter but speaking contrivance." Witherington then remarks that Demetrius would not have viewed Romans as a letter.[11]

---

8. Terence Y. Mullins, "Formulas in New Testament Epistles," *JBL* 91 (1972): 380–90 (here 388) (emphasis original).

9. Longenecker, *Introducing Romans*, 220–25.

10. Ibid., 223–24.

11. Ben Witherington III, *Paul's Letter to the Romans: A Socio-rhetorical Commentary* (Grand Rapids:

Most commentators today agree that there is a lack of epistolary conventions in the body of the letter. But are they underestimating the number? First, would we expect to find the same personal greetings, thanksgivings, and prayers expressed in the bookends repeated in the body of the letter? I suspect not. Second, would we expect to find proportionately more epistolary formulas in the opening and closing of the letter than in the body of a large letter? I suspect so. Third, would we expect Romans, due to its length, to retain the same intensity of epistolary formulas throughout the body as used in the introduction and conclusion? No. But more importantly, the case for the lack of epistolary forms in the body of Romans is not as strong as claimed. For example, Longenecker lists twelve "verbs of saying'" whereas another eleven may be added to that list. The same is true of disclosure formulas, eight added to his list of seven. Longenecker lists seven vocatives; I have found two more, plus seven articular participles serving as appositives to the subject of the sentence and hence as vocatives.[12] This more than doubles the number of forms in these three areas alone.[13]

However, I am hesitant to say that these additional finds are definitive, for Mullins alerts us that epistolary formulas must have a recognized structural rigidity to them, a stereotyped form that is repeated in ancient letters.[14] For example, the disclosure formula, "for I want you to know that . . ." is a stereotyped form; but would "for we know that" or "do you not know that" or "I know that" be included

---

Eerdmans, 2004), 17–18; also 18n41. Quotes by Demetrius are also found in Malherbe, *Ancient Epistolary Theorists*, 16–19.

12. Longenecker (*Introducing Romans*, 220–23) lists twelve "verbs of saying": 4:1; 6:1, 15; 7:1, 7; 8:31; 9:14; 9:30; 11:1, 11, 13; 12:3; add eleven more: 2:22; 3:3, 5, 8, 9; 4:9; 9:19; 10:18, 19; 11:19; 15:8. He lists seven "disclosure" forms: 6:3, 16; 7:1, 14; 8:22, 28; 11:25; add another eight: 2:2; 3:19; 6:6, 9; 7:18; 8:26; 11:2; 13:11. He lists seven "vocatives": 2:1; 7:1, 4; 8:12; 10:1; 11:25; 12:1; add two more: 2:3; 9:20; add another seven appositives serving as vocatives: 2:1 (×2), 3, 21, 21, 22 (×2) (there may be more appositives serving as vocatives).

13. See appendix 1 for my list of epistolary forms within the body of the letter. R. K. Rapa (*The Meaning of "Works of the Law" in Galatians and Romans*, [New York: Peter Lang, 2001], 218–23) lists some 77 epistolary conventions and formulaic features he finds within 1:18–11:36. He writes that "the disclosure formulae and the usage of verbs of speaking both occur, for the most part, in the argumentative section of the letter (1:16–11:36), and seem to indicate that Paul reasons through the defense of his gospel in a manner calculated to be as persuasive as it is well-articulated."

14. Mullins, "Formulas," 385.

as an epistolary form? According to Mullins, "It might seem . . . that any verb in the first person which is followed by ὅτι ["that"] can be considered a form—in which case the term 'form' would become meaningless."[15] That is a good point, but it adds to my skepticism about limiting epistolary formulas only to "fixed forms" agreed on by scholars who study ancient "nonliterary" letters. Are not many of these formulas common verbs or clichés that would normally be used to interact with readers? Could not these common verbs such as "to know" or "to say" be expressed in multiple ways, each of which could serve to interact with readers? What if similar words are used, but not the exact word in the exact form, such as "Where is boasting" rather than "What shall we say" (verb of saying)? The former is not an epistolary formula since it is not a stereotyped form repeated in ancient letters, but Paul clearly uses it to interact with his readers. The brief "disclosure" statements above are all attempts by Paul to interact with his readers and should count for something epistographically. So should verbs in the first-person singular such as "I hear that" or "I marvel that." Moreover, there is an ongoing discussion as to what is essential in a form, whether it be a thanksgiving, petition, or other form. Identifying forms is not an exact science. There is some subjectivity involved.

We also learn from Mullins that we can expect the following with epistolary forms. They almost always "punctuate a break in the writer's thought. . . . In a letter of any considerable length there will be places where a writer will pause and break the flow of his thought for a moment."[16] They may serve as breaks, turning points, or transitions in the argument of the letter. And when such a pause comes, it signals that the writer has shifted from conveying his personal ideas to dealing with his relationship to readers. In other words, epistolary forms serve both to guide the progression of thought and to interrupt the discourse for the purpose of interacting with readers. These guidelines, together

15. Ibid.
16. Ibid., 387–88.

with their interactive quality explained above, makes one wonder about Paul's use of expressions such as these:

- 2:3: "Do you suppose this, O man, when you pass judgment . . ."
- 2:4: "Do you think lightly of the riches of his kindness . . ."
- 3:9b: "For we have previously charged . . ."
- 5:2: "We exult [boast] in hope . . ."
- 5:3: "We exult in our tribulation, knowing that . . ."
- 6:11: "Consider yourselves to be dead to sin . . ."
- 6:17: "But thanks be to God that . . ."
- 7:7: "But I had not known sin except . . ."
- 7:22: "For I joyfully concur with the law of God . . ."
- 7:23: "Wretched man that I am! Who will set me free from the body of this death?"
- 7:25: "Thanks be to God through Jesus Christ our Lord . . ."
- 9:1: "I am telling the truth in Christ . . ."
- 9:2-3: "I have great sorrow and unceasing grief in my heart. For I could wish . . ."
- 10:1: "Brethren, my heart's desire and prayer to God for them is . . ."
- 10:2: "For I bear them witness"
- 11:13: "But I am speaking to you who are gentiles . . ."
- 11:18: "Do not be arrogant toward the branches . . ."
- 12:16: "Be of the same mind toward one another . . ."

These remarks are not listed as epistolary formulas, but they definitely punctuate the writer's thought and serve as turning points and transitions in the letter. They signal a pause in the argument of the letter for the purpose of engaging the reader. Perhaps I do not fully understand what Mullins is saying, and there is some question whether certain expressions are merely literary or editorial remarks by Paul. Some are viewed as Hellenistic diatribe or apostrophe and therefore dismissed as interactions with readers. (I will question that line of interpretation below.[17]) But their use was meant to accomplish what Mullins lists as essential qualities of epistolary forms. Hence, despite what may or may not be defined by researchers as forms (and I do respect those definitions), from my perspective, all statements in the body of Romans that interrupt the discourse and direct their attention to the readers may be considered epistolary in nature. For that reason, the number of epistolary interactions is significantly increased.[18]

Paul's Use of Rhetoric and Grammar

Another means of interacting with readers was Paul's use of rhetoric. He was an orator as well as a writer.[19] He dictated Romans with every expectation that it would be read orally to the various congregations in Rome.[20] Perhaps they all came together to hear it read, or more likely, it was read to individual congregations. It was read not just once, nor twice, but undoubtedly numerous times in multiple settings—in part or in whole—to various house churches, some predominantly gentile Christian and some predominantly Jewish Christian. Paul knew his letter would be read in this way, and so he used rhetorical devices

---

17. See chap. 5.
18. Some may not be convinced that all (or even most) of the above list of introductory remarks engages with or directs attention to the intended audience in any specific way, more than an essayist would. But they cannot be discounted as epistolary in nature if the writer's purpose is to address the readers in Rome about their circumstances.
19. It is interesting from Paul's perspective that when he writes to the Corinthian church, he mentions several times his writing and speaking to them (2 Cor. 2:3-4; 7:8, 12; 10:9-11; 11:6), including the statement: "For they say [whoever the "they" is], 'His letters are weighty and strong, but his personal presence is weak, and his speech contemptible'" (2 Cor. 10:10). Paul then adds this of himself in 2 Cor. 11:6: "But even if I am unskilled in speech . . ." (a simple fact condition). I doubt seriously that Paul was weak or contemptible in speech. His oral skills are evident even when he is writing.
20. Paul wrote Romans from the perspective that his audience in Rome would hear it orally being read. (Notice other references to Paul's letters being read and pondered [1 Thess. 5:27; Col. 4:16].) One cannot overestimate the importance of this insight. It affects how we view the progression of thought in Romans, and how Paul led his readers through such a long letter. According to George A. Kennedy (*New Testament Interpretation through Rhetorical Criticism* [Chapel Hill: University of North Carolina Press, 1984], 5), New Testament documents were orally conceived and retained a linear quality so that their audiences, hearing it read, could follow the argumentation. For this reason, we must read the letter as it would have been heard by its audience.

extensively. According to C. E. B. Cranfield, his use of these devices is "not self-conscious, but natural means to forceful and compelling expression of what he has to say."[21] Think of the acoustical impact Romans 1:16–2:29 would have on the hearers, one statement after another.

- "For I am not ashamed of the gospel" (1:16)

- "They exchanged the glory of the incorruptible God for an image in the form of corruptible man" (*ēllaxan* [1:23] . . . *metēllaxan* [1:25] . . . *metēllaxan* [1:26])

- "Therefore God gave them over" (the threefold repetition of *paredōken autous ho theos*)

- "Therefore you are without excuse, O man, everyone who judges" (2:1)

- "And do you suppose this, O man, when you pass judgment" (2:3)

- "Or do you think lightly of the riches of his kindness" (2:4)

- "Who will render to every man according to his deeds" (2:6)

- "To the Jew first and also to the Greek" (2:9-10)

- "For there is no impartiality with God" (2:11)

- "For all who sinned without the law will perish without the law" (2:12)

- "For the gentiles who do not have law. . ." (2:14)

- "But if you bear the name Jew . . ." (2:17)

- "For indeed circumcision profits if you practice the law . . ." (2:25)

Then consider the rhetorical conventions Paul used to express those statements, devices referred to in more technical terms as parallelism, anaphora, assonance, apostrophe, diatribe, chiasm, synonymous and antithetical parallelism, conditional sentences with questions serving

---

21. Cranfield, *Romans*, 1:26.

as the apodosis, followed by questions in a chiastic framework and brief responses. Through all of this, Paul was interacting with his readers and in multiple instances interrupting his discourse in order to direct his attention to them; and this sort of rhetoric is found consistently throughout Romans.

Longenecker's survey of oral, rhetorical, and epistolary conventions commonly used in the Greco-Roman world of Paul's day is most helpful for any analysis of Romans.[22] He notes that rhetorical conventions were part of the culture of Hellenism and that Paul did not have to be trained in rhetoric to use it effectively. There are diverse views as to the rhetorical genre of Romans, but Longenecker agrees with the growing number of those who view Romans simply as a "word of exhortation" (logos protreptikos). This differs from the usual genres of ancient rhetoric—forensic, deliberative, or epideictic.[23] A "word of exhortation" may include elements of exhortation, rebuke, and personal appeal, and Paul used all of them in Romans. His most prominent use of rhetoric may be his deliberate use of word chains and the structural techniques of parallelism and chiasm. The most evident modes of persuasion were his rhetorical questions, analogies, syllogisms, and supporting creedal formulations and Scriptures. One look at my appendix listing all the rhetorical devices he used demonstrates how significant their role was in communicating with readers.[24] It does not take long to realize that Paul was a master at oral persuasion. It is a primary tool he used to interact with his readers and to convey his thoughts, though it is not classified as epistolary.

Paul also had an ability to interact with readers through his use of grammar. One could almost list grammar as another rhetorical device due to (1) his deliberate placement of words, (2) the way he structures some of his sentences, and (3) his use of connectives, all meant for the ears of his audience. First, in his deliberate placement of words, there is the obvious example in 4:13. The Greek text looks like this:

---

22. Longenecker, *Introducing Romans*, 169–235.
23. Ibid., 196–200.
24. See appendix 2, "Rhetorical Devices in Romans." While listing all the rhetorical devices, the examples provided are not exhaustive.

Ou gar dia nomou hē epangelia tō Abraam ē tō spermati autou, to klēronomon auton einai kosmou, alla dia dikaiosynēs pisteōs.

Translations of the text are similar to this:

For the promise to Abraham or to his seed that he would be heir of the world was not through the law but through the righteousness of faith.

But when one looks at the order and placement of the words in the Greek, one realizes that the phrase "not through the law" (*ou dia nomou*) is placed in an emphatic position in front of the subject of the sentence, "the promise" (*hē epangelia*). This is not the normal word order of Greek. One also notes that the phrase "but through the righteousness of faith" (*alla dia dikaiosynēs pisteōs*) is placed at the very end of the sentence; and preceding both prepositional phrases is the strong *ou . . . alla* contrast, "for *not* through law . . . *but* through righteousness of faith." This is a deliberate placement of words that Paul knew would be heard clearly by his audience. Such a use of word order occurs regularly throughout Romans. Paul's use of sentence structure was a primary tool for interacting with his readers.

Second, regarding the structure of some of his sentences, this too is done for audible effect. For example, consider one of the major anacoluthons[25] of the letter—some view it as an anacoluthon, but the passage is written carefully and deliberately for audible effect. I am referring to 2:17-23, a conditional sentence with a prolonged protasis (the "if" clause) followed by rhetorical questions serving as the apodosis (the "then" clause). Allow me to translate the Greek in its literal word order, placing the protasis (with compound subclauses) in an indented position, and the apodosis consisting of rhetorical questions serving as the main clause (or clauses, since they are actually separate questions).

---

25. An anacoluthon is an incomplete sentence. Some think that on occasion Paul simply forgot to follow through with a complete sentence, but this is rarely if ever the case; a few say this could be attributed to his use of a scribe. Paul was very deliberate with how he structured his sentences. R. Dean Anderson Jr. (*Ancient Rhetorical Theory and Paul* [Leuven: Peeters, 1999], 197n26) writes, "The presence of an anacoluthon does not have to be considered 'violent,' nor a grammatical error. It may rather suggest a conversational style entirely appropriate to a letter."

^{17}But (*de*), if you bear the name Jew
    and rely on the law
    and boast in God
    ^{18}and know His will
    and approve things that differ,
        being instructed from the Law
    ^{19}and having persuaded yourself that you are
        a guide of the blind,
        a light of those in darkness,
        ^{20}an instructor of the foolish,
        a teacher of babes,
        having the form of the knowledge and the truth in the law,
^{21}Therefore [*oun*],[26]
    The one who teaches the other [*heteron*], do you teach yourself?
    The one who preaches not to steal, do you steal?
    ^{22}The one who says not to commit adultery, do you commit adultery?
    The one who abhors idols, do you rob temples?
    ^{23}You who boast in the law, through the trespass of the law do you
    dishonor God?

Some say the protasis ends in an incomplete sentence (an anacoluthon), and in terms of strict grammar they are right. But for Paul, in his mind, the apodosis is stated in the rhetorical questions. He deliberately frames the apodosis in this question format.[27] It is true that the apodosis of a conditional sentence may be in the form of a question (witness 2:26 below). However, here we have a series of rhetorical questions posed in response to the elongated protasis. Closer inspection reveals that the content of the questions in the apodosis matches the content in the protasis—"teaching the other" in 2:21 matches references to teaching in 2:19-20; references to stealing, committing adultery, and idolatry obviously reminiscent of the Ten Commandments in 2:21-22 would match the content of 2:18; and boasting in the law and dishonoring God in 2:23 matches resting on the law and boasting in God in 2:17. Actually, the questions seem to be addressing in reverse order (chiastically) the list in the protasis. Taken all together, "having the form of the knowledge and the truth

---

26. The Greek *oun*, translated "therefore" or "then," but having the nuance of "accordingly."
27. Some commentators agree. See John Murray, *The Epistle to the Romans*, NICNT (Grand Rapids: Eerdmans, 1965), 1:81; William Sanday and Arthur C. Headlam, *The Epistle to the Romans* (New York: Charles Scribner's Sons, 1897), 64, 66.

in the law" (2:20b) sums up what is stated in the protasis and projects forward to what is being addressed by the questions in 2:21-23. So, what are we to say about this supposed anacoluthon? Yes, technically, it is an anacoluthon. However, it is obviously a deliberate structuring of the apodosis by Paul. Ernst Käsemann calls 2:17-24 a "masterpiece of rhetoric."[28] My point is, Paul wrote in this manner for audible effect. It was interactive speech. It interrupted the narrative, even within itself, and was directed to readers. We should heed Paul Achtemeier's counsel that "we need to keep in mind the essentially oral communication of the written texts of the NT and shape our examination of those texts, and their interpretation, accordingly."[29]

Third, Paul's use of connectives plays a significant role in his interaction with readers. Cranfield stresses the importance of carefully watching the connectives linking the sentences. "Whereas in English it is not at all unusual for sentences to be set down one after the other without connexion, in ancient Greek it was normal to link each sentence with the preceding one by means of a connective of one sort or another."[30] This use of connectives to link sentences had two great advantages. First, it helped the writer think clearly and logically. Second, it enabled the reader to know the connection of thought that was in the writer's mind. One cannot overstress the importance of this insight. Much of Paul's discourse is deliberative, meant to persuade his hearers. As such, it requires causal and inferential connectives to follow the logic of his thought. He had no chapter or verse divisions, and a major means he had of leading his readers was through his use of connectives.[31] He chose them carefully, for they varied in strength and

---

28. Käsemann, *Romans*, 69. Regarding Paul's choice and management of grammar in Romans, Cranfield (*Romans*, 1:25) remarks that it is "perfectly competent" and that Paul "thought perfectly naturally in Greek." His use of anacoluthon in this passage was perfectly competent, and intentional for audible effect.

29. Paul J. Achtemeier, "*Omne Verbum Sonat*: The New Testament and the Oral Environment of Late Western Antiquity," *JBL* 109 (1990): 3; quoted by Longenecker, *Introducing Romans*, 171.

30. Cranfield, *Romans*, 1:27.

31. Nils A. Dahl (*Studies in Paul: Theology for the Early Christian Mission* [Minneapolis: Augsburg, 1977], 79) reminds us that in many manuscripts "not even the words are separated from one another. As the text was to be heard, rather than seen, the transition from one unit of thought to another had to be indicated by other means than by typographical or scribal arrangement." This is where the connectives are very important as the letter is being read.

intensity. His use of stronger connectives would especially resonate with the hearers as they sought to follow his line of thought.

For example, today we are debating whether a major section of the letter begins in 5:1 or 6:1, and we are not sure how 5:12-21 fits into the context.[32] But for the people listening in Rome, there would have been little confusion. They knew the difference between common and more intensive connectives, both causal and inferential.[33]

Therefore having been justified by faith . . .
5:1 Dikaiōthentes oun ek pisteōs . . .
For this reason just as through one man . . .
5:12 Dia touto ōsper di' henos anthrōpou . . .
Therefore as through the transgression of the one . . .
5:18 Ara oun ōs di' henos paraptōmatos . . .
What then shall we say? Are we to continue in sin . . .
6:1 Ti oun eroumen; epimenōmen tē hamartia . . .

In 5:1, Paul uses the common inferential oun, thereby making a normal inference from the prior discussion on justification by faith. Then in 5:12, Paul uses the stronger causal dia touto, signaling that he is about to provide the main reason or cause behind what has been previously stated. In 5:18, he uses the strong inferential ara oun to bring to a conclusion that reason, and immediately afterward in 5:20-21 he is clearly transitioning into the ti oun eroumen of 6:1, the idiomatic question that signals a new segment.[34] The audience would have heard

32. See my discussion below in chap. 5.
33. A "causal" clause gives the reason for a statement, whereas an "inferential" clause draws a conclusion from a truth just stated. But we should be quick to affirm that cause and inference are first cousins and at times one cannot tell them apart. (In the passages quoted, the Greek connectives together with their English translations are underlined.)
34. It is instructive to trace Paul's use of inferential and causal connectives throughout chaps. 4–5; ti oun (4:1), oun (4:9-10), dia touto (4:16), dio (4:22), oun (5:1), gar (5:6, 7 [×2]), oun (5:9), dia touto (5:12), ara oun (5:18), ti oun eroumen (6:1). Gar occurs regularly throughout chaps. 4–5 as a common causal conjunction. Dia touto is a combination of dia plus the demonstrative touto in the accusative, which makes it a stronger causal connective. Gar occurs 146 times in Romans, while dia touto occurs only 5 times. Oun is a common inferential and occurs some 49 times in Romans. Dio is said by H. E. Dana and Julius R. Mantey (A Manual Grammar of the Greek New Testament [New York: Macmillan, 1927], 245) to be the strongest inferential, and the compound ara oun is of similar strength. William D. Chamberlain (An Exegetical Grammar of the Greek New Testament [New York: Macmillan, 1952], 153) says that ara points to "a conclusion already apparent," and that compound illatives such as ara oun "have something of an intensifying effect on the conclusion." Dio occurs 6 times in Romans, while ara oun occurs 8 times. These intensives occur seldom, thereby accentuating their use. Of course, it is essential to weigh the intensity of conjunctions within their contexts;

this, being guided by the connectives. Paul is consistent and careful with his use of connectives. In this way, Paul is interacting with his readers and using grammar for audible effect.

Paul's Use of Questions

Thus far, we have found that Paul's interaction with his audience is much more evident than many grant. He uses sufficient epistolary forms to interrupt the narrative and provoke frequent interaction with his listeners. Paul's rhetoric and use of grammar should be valued as well for their interactive and oral qualities. But the most prominent way Paul guides the narrative and interrupts the discourse for the purpose of interacting with readers is through his use of questions. According to my math and interpretation, there are 78 specific questions in chapters 2–11. That is an average of 7.8 questions per chapter. That is a lot of questions. With 7.8 questions in ten chapters that average 31.5 verses, there is one question for every 4.1 verses. Obviously this has a strong impact on dialogue within the letter. Precisely what impact it has is yet to be determined. But that many questions should prompt us to reflect on how we understand the rhetoric of the letter.

Since counts may vary among commentators, allow me to explain my method of counting. First, I am counting questions specifically: 3:1-9a = 10 questions, not 5, plus we find one more question added in the response of 3:6; so to be specific means that even brief questions are counted (3:9a includes two questions with only three Greek words). Second, the exact number depends on the interpretation of several verses. Should 9:30b-31 not be viewed as a question, and 2:23, 9:22b-24a, and 11:15 viewed as questions, as I have interpreted them? There is a variant in 11:21 (*mē pōs*) that could make the sentence a question, but this is unlikely and not counted as such. In addition, there are four more questions in chapters 12–14 (13:3; 14:4, 10 [×2]), bringing

but the principle generally holds that Paul reserves his use of stronger connectives to signal to the audience the progression of his ideas. All of this demonstrates the importance of analyzing carefully Paul's use of connectives.

the total number of questions to 82. Interestingly, the questions in chapter 14 that serve to conclude the application of the letter raise the same issue as the questions that introduce the letter in 2:1-5, that of judging one another.

To press home the point of the extensive nature of these questions and their significance in the discourse of the letter, I list them below:

2:3: And do you reckon this, O man . . . that you shall escape the judgment of God?

2:4: Or do you think lightly of the wealth of his kindness . . . ?

2:21a: You who teach another, do you not teach yourself?

2:21b: You who preach not to steal, do you steal?

2:22a: You who say not to commit adultery, do you commit adultery?

2:22b: You who abhor idols, do you rob temples?

2:23: You who boast in the law, do you dishonor God through the breaking of the law?

2:26: Therefore if the uncircumcised keeps the righteous ordinances of the law, will not his uncircumcision be reckoned as circumcision?

2:27: And will not he, who is by nature uncircumcised and [yet] keeps the law, judge you who through the letter and circumcision transgress the law?

3:1: What then is the advantage of the Jew? Or what is the profit of circumcision?

3:3: What then if some did not believe? Their unbelief will not nullify the faithfulness of God, will it?

3:5: But if our unrighteousness commends the righteousness of God, what shall we say? The God who inflicts wrath is not unrighteous, is he?

3:6: Otherwise, how will God judge the world?

3:7-8: For if the truth of God abounded by my lie unto his glory, why am I still also being judged as a sinner? And why not [say] . . . , "Let us do evil that good may come"?

3:9a: What then? Are we better than they?

3:27: Therefore, where is boasting? . . . By what kind of law? Of works?

3:29: Or, is God the God of Jews only? Not also of gentiles?

3:31: Therefore, do we nullify the law through faith?

4:1: What then shall we say that Abraham our forefather according to the flesh has found?

4:3: For what does Scripture say?

4:9: Therefore, is this blessing upon the circumcision or also upon the uncircumcision?

4:10: How was it reckoned? While he was in circumcision or in uncircumcision?

6:1: What then shall we say? Shall we remain in sin that grace may increase?

6:2: We who have died to sin, how shall we still live in it?

6:3: Do you not know that as many of us as were baptized into Christ Jesus were baptized into his death?

6:15: What then? Shall we sin because we are not under law but under grace?

6:16: Do you not know that to whom you present yourselves for obedience, you are slaves to whom you obey . . . ?

6:21: Therefore, what fruit were you then having of which now you are ashamed?

7:1: Or do you not know, brothers . . . that the law rules over a man as long as he lives?

7:7: Therefore, what shall we say? Is the law sin?

7:13: Therefore, did the good become [a cause of] death for me?

7:24: Who will rescue me from the body of this death?

8:24: For why hope for what one sees?

8:31a: Therefore what shall we say to these things?

8:31b: If God is for us, who is against us?

8:32: The one who did not spare his own son, but delivered him for us all, how will he not also with him freely give us all things?

8:33: Who will bring a charge against God's elect?

8:34: Who is the one who condemns?

8:35a: Who shall separate us from the love of Christ?

8:35b: Shall tribulation or distress or persecution or famine or
     nakedness or peril or sword?

9:14: Therefore, what shall we say? There is no injustice with God, is
     there?

9:19: Why does he still find fault? For who has resisted his will?

9:20a: On the contrary, O man, who are you who answers back to God?

9:20b: Will the thing molded say to the molder, "Why did you make me
     like this"?

9:21: Or does the potter not have authority over the clay to make out of
     his lump one vessel for honor, and one for dishonor?

9:22-24: But what if God, willing to demonstrate his wrath . . . endured
     with much patience vessels of wrath . . . that he might make
     known the wealth of his glory upon vessels of mercy . . . [even]
     us whom he also called not only from the Jews but also from
     the gentiles?

9:30: Therefore, what shall we say?

9:32: Why?

10:8: But what does it say?

10:14a: Therefore, how shall they call on whom they have not believed?

10:14b: And how shall they believe whom they have not heard?

10:14c: And how shall they hear without a preacher?

10:15: And how shall they preach unless they are sent?

10:18: But I say, they have not heard, have they?

10:19: But I say, Israel did not know, did they?

11:1: Therefore, I say, God has not rejected his people, has he?

11:2: Or do you not know what Scripture says about Elijah?

11:4: But what is the response of God to him?

11:7: What then?

11:11: I say then, they did not stumble so as to fall, did they?

11:15: For if their rejection be the reconciliation of the world, what will
     their acceptance be except life from the dead?

11:34a: For who has known the mind of the Lord?

11:34b: Or who has become his counselor?

11:35: Or who has first given to him, and [so that] it will be paid back to him?

13:3b: But do you wish not to fear the authority?

14:4: Who are you who judges a servant of another?

14:10a: But you, why do you judge your brother?

14:10b: Or also you, why do you despise your brother?

More often than not, these eighty-two questions appear in groups. Within these groups, the questions are interrelated, often building off one another. In 3:1, you find synonymous parallelism, but in 3:3 you find synthetic parallelism, with the latter question building on the prior one. Some questions serve to complete or clarify prior questions or even answer the questions preceding them (8:31-35). For this reason, you even have three questions in 3:27 that are really only one, the latter serving to clarify and complete the former. Multiple questions in groups serve to draw attention to and strengthen the individual questions as well as frame the issues of the letter. There are as many as 18 groups depending on how you group them.[35]

These groups serve either to introduce or conclude major units of discourse. (Please bear with me on the specifics, for they are very important.) Groups introducing or continuing major units of thought are as follows: 2:3-4; 4:1-3; 4:9-10; 6:1-3; 6:15-16; 7:7, 13; 9:14; 9:30-32; and 11:1-4, 7. Occasionally only one question introduces a paragraph (7:1; 11:11); but even when there is only one question, that question is closely related to nearby questions (7:7, 13; 11:1-4, 7). Notice that an extended answer immediately follows these introductory questions. Groups at the conclusion of a major section or line of thought include 2:21-23 and 26-27; 8:31-35; 9:19-24;[36] 10:14-19; and 11:34-35. These are always joined at some point with support from Scripture (2:24; 8:36;

---

35. Groups are questions coupled together while standing alone, such as the two questions in 9:14 or the string of closely connected questions in 3:1-9a. I am classifying the following as groups: 2:3-4 (2 Q's); 2:21-23 (5 Q's); 2:26-27 (2 Q's); 3:1-9a (11 Q's); 3:27-31 (6 Q's); 4:1-3 (2 Q's); 4:9-10 (3 Q's); 6:1-3 (4 Q's); 6:15-16 (3 Q's); 7:7, 13 (3 Q's); 8:31-35 (7 Q's); 9:14 (2 Q's); 9:19-24 (6 Q's); 9:30-32 (2 Q's); 10:14-19 (6 Q's); 11:1-7 (4 Q's); 11:34-35 (3Q's); 14:4, 10 (3 Q's).

36. 9:19-24 serves multiple purposes. This group of questions serves both to continue a line of thought from 9:14 to 9:29, and to bring to a conclusion that line of thought. This is affirmed by the multiple references to Scripture that conclude that section (9:24-29).

9:25-29; 10:15-21; 11:34-35).[37] Then there is that group of questions that has stymied some scholars as to their presence and purpose—3:1-9a together with 3:27-31. Romans 3:1-9a is very carefully structured and has five pairs of two questions, each with very brief answers that do not even begin to cover the subject.[38] Their form is similar to Hellenistic diatribe, hence the inclination of some to interpret them as such, even viewing the entire question-and-answer of 3:1-9a as a digression of thought. However, they are significant questions followed by abbreviated answers. The same is true of 3:27-31, questions followed by brief answers. Why raise carefully structured questions only to answer them with short and incomplete responses? Are the readers left hanging, or do they have the benefit of having them answered elsewhere in the letter?[39]

Before answering these questions, I will make several observations about (1) the role of the questions, (2) what they may reveal about the contingency of the letter, and (3) their contribution to the coherence of the letter. First, about the role of the questions: it is important to observe that whether we concentrate on the eighty-two individual questions or on the eighteen groups of questions, they convey more than words in an essay. As mentioned above, they introduce and conclude sections of the letter. They serve to interrupt discourse for the purpose of interacting with readers. They raise substantive issues. They perform the function Mullins requires for a manuscript to be a letter. In fact, "epistolary forms" that are required for a manuscript to be a letter are embedded in the questions themselves. For example:

- 2:22: "you who say that" (verb of saying)

- 3:3: "What then [shall we say]?" (verb of saying)

---

37. The questions in 2:26-27 are in the context of verses that allude to Deut. 10:16 and 30:6.
38. There is an additional question in 3:6 that is part of the answer to the two questions raised in 3:5, an answer framed in the form of a question.
39. Seventeen groups account for seventy-one of the seventy-eight questions in chaps. 2–11. Of the remaining seven questions, six serve to continue the dialogue in some way (3:6; 6:21; 8:24; 10:8; 11:7; 11:15). The seventh, 7:24, serves the very important and prominent purpose of concluding the "speech in character" of 7:7-24 and transitioning into the expression of thanksgiving of 7:25 and the "now" of existence in chap. 8.

- 3:5: "What shall we say?" (verb of saying)

- 3:8: "And why not say . . ." (verb of saying)

- 3:9: "What then [shall we say]?" (verb of saying)

- 4:1: "What then shall we say?" (verb of saying)

- 4:9: "For we say . . ." – (verb of saying)

Of the epistolary forms embedded in or immediately attached to the eighteen groups of questions, there are, according to my count, at least fifty-six epistolary forms.[40] According to Mullins, the epistolary forms alone serve as a break or turning point in the argument of the letter, a pause that signals the writer has shifted from conveying his own ideas to directing his attention to his readers.[41] That is precisely what Paul was doing with these groups of questions with embedded epistolary forms. The groups are epistolary in function, for they serve as breaks or turning points in the argument of the letter and shift attention to the readers. There are also epistolary forms that stand independently of the questions, and questions that stand independently of epistolary forms. The sum of all the above for interactive purposes is indeed impressive and a further reason to consider the body of Romans to be a letter. Moreover, questions in this capacity, when they serve as breaks or turning points in the narrative, guide the narrative as well. For example, the questions in 9:14; 9:30-32; 11:1-4; and 11:11 are immediately followed by their answers, guiding the narrative in chapters 9–11. The same is true throughout chapters 3–8.

This is the primary role of the questions. They are used to interact with recipients and to guide the narrative. This raises the issue of whether we should view the questions as Hellenistic diatribe. Of course, those who view questions such as 3:1-9a as diatribe do not consider all questions in the same way. They focus on those that appear to them to be diatribal. Nor do they necessarily eliminate diatribal questions from being used to guide the narrative. (See my discussion

---

40. This count is based on my list of epistolary forms in appendix 1.
41. Mullins, "Formulas," 387-88.

below on Hellenistic diatribe.) However, I am suggesting that one has to consider Paul's extensive use of questions as a whole when viewing his use of particular questions. It is difficult to deny that the primary role of the majority of questions in Romans, if not all, was for interactive purposes and to guide the discourse of the letter.

Second, concerning the contingency of the letter, it is reasonable to suppose from the interactive nature of the questions that they are directed toward circumstances in Rome. By simply reading through the questions listed above, one senses that they serve to exhort and rebuke and appeal to believers. "Will he not judge you who through the letter and circumcision are the transgressor of the law?" "What advantage has the Jew?" "Are we better than they?" "Where then is boasting?" "Who are you to judge the servant of another?" "Why do you judge your brother?" Why do you despise your brother?" (2:27; 3:1, 9, 27; 14:4, 10). They are *logoi protreptikoi* (words of exhortation) directly engaging the church in Rome. This fits the emerging consensus that Romans was addressing a specific situation in Rome, that situation being tension between Jewish and gentile believers. This is my view as well, as I will demonstrate in the ensuing chapters.

Third, one may anticipate that the questions contribute to the coherence of the letter. If they serve to guide the discourse of the letter, they will inevitably be vital to the organization of the letter. I will argue that the flow of the letter is captured in Paul's rhetoric, especially in his extensive use of questions in 3–11. The questions served as an oral map for believers in Rome as they listened to the letter being read to them. Without that oral map, there would be no coherence in the letter.

4

The Surface Structure of Romans

We return to the question of whether there is an alternative surface structure that guides the discourse of the letter. In my opinion, Romans was intended by Paul to be a letter and not an essay. It comes across as a letter not only in the bookends but also in the body of the letter. There are sufficient epistolary forms in the body to confirm this judgment. The relational and acoustical effect of the rhetoric and grammar contributes to the interactive nature of the letter, along with all the invasive and disruptive rhetoric. But Paul's most prominent means of eliciting interaction from his listeners and guiding the discourse springs from his extensive use of questions, often embedded with epistolary formulas.

We found there are some eighty-two specific questions in Romans. These questions are generally found in groups, as many as eighteen groups of questions. Each group serves either to introduce or to conclude major units of discourse. For example, it is quite clear the groups of questions in 6:1-3; 6:15-16; 7:7; and 7:13 serve to introduce the subject matter that follows. They are joined by the individual questions in 7:1 and 7:24 that serve the same purpose, though 7:24 ("Wretched man that I am. Who will set me free from the body of this death?")

serves both to conclude and to transition into what follows. The final group of questions in 8:31-35 definitely serves to conclude what precedes. Consequently, all the questions in chapters 6–8 may be said, without question, to be guiding the discourse of that section of the letter. In chapters 9–11, the questions in 9:14; 9:30-32; 11:1-4; and 11:11 introduce, and those in 9:19-24;[1] 10:14-19; and 11:34-35 conclude, major units of thought. This is in line with the consensus of commentators that 9:14-29; 9:30-10:21; and 11:1-36 are distinct sections within chapters 9–11. Paul is clearly using these questions to guide the discourse of that portion of Romans. The same may be said for the groups of questions introducing and concluding Romans 2. The questions in 4:1-3 and 4:9-10 introduce the narrative that follows in chapter 4. All of the above groups of questions serve to guide the narrative and thus are part of the surface structure of Romans.

But how are we to understand the role of the two groups 3:1-9a and 3:27-31, about which there has been such a diversity of opinion? I will leave the issue of whether they should be interpreted as Hellenistic diatribe to the following chapter. First, we need to analyze for ourselves why Paul would include in rapid-fire such significant questions followed by abbreviated and incomplete answers. Are the questions momentary digressions of thought not serving in any way to guide the discourse of the letter? Do the questions simply stand alone, not as digressions but as abbreviated question-and-answer for whatever reason Paul may have had in mind? Or is there some connection with the discourse that follows? Do they anticipate what follows? Let us first examine 3:27-31.

The Group of Questions in 3:27-31

This group contains six specific questions along with their brief answers. The six actually represent three primary sets of questions.[2]

---

1. The questions in 9:19-24 may be viewed as continuing the discourse as well as concluding the section. However, these questions are joined with supporting Scripture, suggesting that they serve more to conclude the section.
2. For a direct comparison of these sets of questions with the Greek, see appendix 3.

First Set of Questions:

> Q1: [27]Therefore, where is boasting? A: It is excluded.
> Q2: By what kind of law?[3] Q3: Of works?

> A: No [ouchi], but [alla] by a law of faith.
> [28]For we reckon that a man is justified by faith apart from works of law.

Second Set of Questions:

> Q1: [29]Or, is God the God of Jews only?
> Q2: Not also [ouchi kai] of gentiles?
> A: Yes also [nai kai] of gentiles, [30]if indeed God is one,
> who will justify the circumcision by faith and the uncircumcision through faith.[4]

Final Question:

> Q1: [31]Therefore, do we nullify the law through faith?

> A: May it not be [mē genoito], but [alla] we establish the law.

Several observations may be made. First, the questions rise naturally from the preceding context (3:9b-26) that one is not justified by works of law but apart from law through faith in Christ. The focus on boasting stems from the questions on "judging one another" (2:1-5), boasting in God and the law (2:17, 23), whether the uncircumcised have the right to judge the circumcised (2:27), whether Jews have any advantage (3:1) and whether "we" are better than "they" (3:9)—a major issue that resurfaces in chapters 11 and 14–15. Second, in this rapid series of questions and answers, one is struck by the use of strong adversatives: Q1: "No, but . . ." (ouchi, alla); Q2: 'Not also. . . . Yes also . . ." (ouchi kai . . . nai kai . . .); Q3: "May it never be, but . . ." (mē genoito, alla . . .).[5] These serve to accentuate as well as identify the issues Paul

---

3. C. E. B. Cranfield contends (A Critical and Exegetical Commentary on the Epistle to the Romans, ICC [Edinburgh: T&T Clark, 1975], 1:220) that "by what kind of law" is referring to the OT law. I would suggest that "law" (nomou) in this specific instance has the sense of "principle." Paul uses nomos in this same sense in 8:2. Moreover, the interrogative pronoun poiou in this phrase stresses the qualitative nature of the question.

4. I agree with C. E. B. Cranfield (Romans, 1:222), who views the variation between "by faith" (ek pisteōs) and "through faith" (dia tēs pisteōs) as purely rhetorical.

wishes to address. They are issues of superiority (boasting, judging one another), inclusiveness (Jew and gentile), and the role of the law. Third, the content of the question-and-answer is quite specific: Q1: there is no room for *boasting* based on *works* of *law*, for a person is *reckoned* to be *justified* by *faith* apart from works of law; Q2: God is not only the God of the Jews, for he is one God who *justifies* both *circumcision* and *uncircumcision* through *faith*; and Q3: the *law* is not *nullified* through *faith*, but rather established. (My use of italics is to demonstrate that the questions and answers in 3:27-31 are not isolated statements standing alone; they are repeated and expanded in what immediately follows in chapter 4.)

Group of questions introducing 4:1-8:

> Q1: ¹What then shall we say that Abraham our forefather according to the flesh has found?
> E: ²For if Abraham was justified by works, he has reason to boast, but not before God.
>
> Q2: ³For what does Scripture say?
> A: Abraham believed God and it was reckoned to him as righteousness.

These questions are reiterating the question-and-answer on boasting in 3:27-28, using the example of Abraham. Abraham had no room to boast before God based on works, for he was justified by faith. The multiple repetitions of word roots and concepts between 3:27-28 and 4:1-8 are obvious: "boast" (1×), "works" (4×), "justify" (5×), "faith" (3×), and "reckon" (5×) (compare with the italicized words above). The subject matter of 4:1-8 is clearly the subject matter of 3:27-28 and provides an extended answer. So we may conclude that the question-and-answer introduced in 3:27-28 was meant by Paul to anticipate the question-and-answer in 4:1-8.[6] Together they guide the narrative.

---

5. *Ouchi . . . alla* in 3:27 represents a very strong contrast, especially with Paul's use of the more intensive form of *ouk* (*ouchi*). This same intensive form is used in 3:29 in a question expecting a positive answer; and the answer includes the response, *nai*, yes! *Mē genoito* is used by Paul always after a rhetorical question to stress a very strong denial (3:6, 31; 6:2, 15; 7:7, 13; 9:14; 11:1, 11).
6. The view of Stanley K. Stowers (*The Diatribe and Paul's Letter to the Romans*, SBLDS 57 [Chico, CA: Scholars Press, 1981], 168) that 3:27 and 4:1 form an *inclusio* and that they structurally frame the

Group of questions introducing 4:9-12:

Q1: [9]Therefore, is this blessing upon the circumcision or also upon the uncircumcision?
E: For we say, "Faith was reckoned to Abraham as righteousness."

Q2: [10]Therefore, how was it reckoned? While he was in circumcision or in uncircumcision?
A: Not in circumcision but in uncircumcision.

These questions along with their extended answers expand on the brief question-and-answer in 3:29-30, that God justifies both circumcision and uncircumcision by faith. In 4:9-12, the following word roots occur in these numbers: "circumcision" (6×), "uncircumcision" (6×), "faith" (3×), "reckon" (2×), making the argument that Abraham was the father of "all" who believe, both circumcised and uncircumcised.

There are no further questions in 4:13-25 that address the issue raised in 3:31 of faith "nullifying" the law. However, 4:13-15 does speak to that issue. It stresses that the promise God made to Abraham and his seed was not through the *law* but through the righteousness of *faith*; and that if those who were of the *law* were heirs, then *faith* would be made void,[7] and the promise "*nullified*" (*katērgētai*[8]), the same terms used in 3:31.[9] This is the same argument Paul used in Galatians 3:15-29, that the law does not nullify the promise previously ratified. However, while Paul discusses what is *not* nullified in 4:13-15, he reserves discussion of the role of the law for chapters 7–8.[10] He asks in 7:7 and 13: "Is the law sin?" and "Did that which is good [the law] become a cause of death for me?" His answers are that the law is holy and

dialogue in between them fails to recognize that 4:1 is introducing the extended answer to 3:27-28, not concluding 3:27–4:1.

7. *Kekenōtai* ("made void" in 4:14) is a perfect passive indicative third singular verb, meaning to make empty, to render void, destroy, or of no effect (William F. Arndt and F. Wilbur Gingrich, *A Greek Lexicon of the New Testament* [Chicago: University of Chicago Press, 1957], 429).

8. *Katērgētai*, a perfect passive indicative third singular verb, means to nullify, abolish or destroy, cancel, do away with, render ineffective. Paul uses this term advisedly in Rom. 3:3; 6:6; 7:2, 6; Gal. 3:17, 5:4, 11, to distinguish what is not abolished (the promise), the sin that enslaves us (that should be abolished), and the law, which is holy and righteous and good. The sin within us is the culprit (7:7-13), not the law.

9. In 4:13-15, "law" occurs four times, "faith" two times, and "nullify" one time.

10. E.g., Douglas Moo, *The Epistle to the Romans*, NICNT (Grand Rapids: Eerdmans, 1996), 253–55.

righteous and good (7:12), and spiritual (7:14); and that God sent his Son in the likeness of sinful flesh to condemn sin in the flesh so that the righteousness of the law might be fulfilled in those who walk not according to the flesh but according to the Spirit (8:3-4). Thus one can legitimately argue that the question initially raised in 3:31 is answered in chapters 7–8. What is or is not nullified through faith is satisfactorily answered in more length.

This group of rapid-fire questions and answers in 3:27-31 anticipates the discourse in chapter 4 by providing a preview or outline of that discourse for the listener. They differ from questions that serve to introduce portions of the letter precisely because they are *not* followed by extended answers. The purpose of this abbreviated question-and-answer is to alert the audience orally to the extended question-and-answer that immediately follows in chapter 4. This was by design. The questions and answers in 3:27-31 find their extended answers respectively in 4:1-8, 4:9-12, and 4:13-15 (and 7:7–8:17).

A. 3:27-28: brief question-and-answer
 B. 3:29-30: brief question-and-answer
  C. 3:31: brief question-and-answer
A. 4:1-8: extended question-and-answer
 B. 4:9-12: extended question-and-answer
  C. 4:13-15: extended answer (also 7:7–8:17)

May the same be said for the question-and-answer in 3:1-9a, that these brief questions and answers anticipate discourse that follows?

The Group of Questions in 3:1-9a

Virtually all commentators seek to interpret these verses within the context of 1:18–3:20. Indeed, there is hardly a contemporary commentator who does not view all of 1:18–3:20 as a unit of material;[11]

---

11. For example: Colin G. Kruse (*Paul's Letter to the Romans*. PiNTC. [Grand Rapids: Eerdmans, 2012], viii):

   A. Humanity under the Power of Sin and Exposed to Wrath, 1:18–3:20
    1. Primary Focus on the Sins of the Gentile World, 1:18-32
    2. Primary Focus on the Sins of the Jewish World, 2:1–3:20

   Moo (*Romans*, 33):

then they view 3:1-9a as some form of diversion within that unit. Matthew Black writes of this passage, "His mind is typically diverted."[12] Ernst Käsemann says that Paul writes this passage as if he were "taking a breath" before adding his conclusion to 1:18-3:20.[13] Of course, it is well known that C. H. Dodd did not think much of this passage. He felt constrained to say: "The fact is that the whole argument of iii:1-8 is obscure and feeble. When Paul, who is normally a clear as well as a forcible thinker, becomes feeble and obscure, it usually means that he is defending a poor case. His case here is inevitably a poor one, since he is trying to show that, although *there is no partiality about God*, yet *the Jew's superiority* is, somehow, *much in every way*." Then he concludes, "It is no wonder that he becomes embarrassed, and in the end dismisses the subject awkwardly. The argument of the epistle would go much better if this whole section were omitted."[14] Aside from the dubious statement that Paul elsewhere may be defending "a poor case," and I

A. The Universal Reign of Sin, 1:18-3:20
    1. All Persons Are Accountable to God for Sin, 1:18-32
    2. Jews Are Accountable to God for Sin, 2:1-3:8
    3. The Guilt of All Humanity, 3:9-20

James D. G. Dunn (*Romans 1-8*, WBC 38A [Waco: Word, 1988], vii-viii):

    II. The Wrath of God on Man's Unrighteousness, 1:18-3:20
       A. God's Wrath on Humankind—from a Jewish Perspective, 1:18-32
       B. God's Wrath on Jew First As Well As Gentile, 2:1-3:8
       C. Conclusion, 3:9-20

Ernst Käsemann (*Commentary on Romans*, trans. Geoffrey W. Bromiley [Grand Rapids: Eerdmans, 1980], ix):

    II. The Need for the Revelation of the Righteousness of God, 1:18-3:20
       A. The Revelation of God's Wrath on the Gentiles, 1:18-32
       B. Judgment on the Jews, 2:1-3:20

Cranfield (*Romans*, 1:28); his outline is more descriptive, but in the same vein:

    I. In the light of the gospel there is no question of men's being righteous before God otherwise than by faith, 1:18-3:20
       i. Man under the judgment of the gospel, 1:18-32
       ii. Jewish man is no exception, 2:1-3:20

12. Matthew Black, *Romans*, NCB (London: Marshall, Morgan & Scott, 1973), 62.
13. Käsemann, *Romans*, 78. Dunn (*Romans 1-8*, 129-30) views the entire section as transitional with the question-and-answer format at first advancing the discussion, but then beginning to reflect Paul's own issues, and he could only respond in slogans and axioms. Dunn refers to them as "the unsatisfactory character of Paul's response."
14. C. H. Dodd, *The Epistle of Paul to the Romans* (London: Fontana, 1970), 70-71 (bolded text in original changed to italics).

would question where that might be, my position is quite the opposite. To omit 3:1-9a is to omit questions that anticipate what is to follow.

Many view these verses polemically as in some way responding to issues Jews might have had with what Paul had just written in 2:17-29. However, I would propose that the questions in 3:1-9a are a major turning point in the letter, as they introduce the subject matter that lies at the heart of the letter in 3:9b–11:36.[15] How is this possible? This I intend to resolve by first analyzing the questions themselves, then asking how they anticipate what follows in 3:9b–11:36. I will also show how they serve as a crossroads for what precedes in chapters 1–2. First, an analysis of 3:1-9a.[16]

Section 1
Q: [1]What then [Ti oun] is the advantage of the Jew?
Or what [tis] is the benefit of circumcision?

A: [2]Much in every way.
Foremost, that they were entrusted with the words of God.

Section 2
Q: [3]For what if [ti gar ei] some did not believe?[17] [mē] Their unbelief will not nullify the faithfulness of God, will it?
A: [4]May it never be [mē genoito]!
But may God be true, and every man a liar,
as it is written,[18]
"That you may be justified in your words
and vindicated while you are being judged."[19]

---

15. It is interesting to note that there are eighteen questions within eighteen verses, 2:21-3:9. The seven questions in 2:21-29 lead up to the eleven major questions in 3:1-9a. (I view 2:23 as a question.) There is no other passage like it in Romans that has such a cluster of questions in such a brief space. Orally, that would certainly gain the attention of the recipients of the letter. Also, we should note what is obvious: 2:25-29 flows naturally into 3:1; the same is true of 3:9a into 3:9b. If one were to omit (as a diversion) the question-and-answer in 3:1-8, 3:9 does not flow naturally from 2:25-29.

16. For a direct comparison of these sets of questions with the Greek, see appendix 4.

17. Some view the first question as consisting simply of the ti gar (e.g., the Nestle-Aland text). I choose to place the question mark after tines, with mē serving to introduce the second question. The same is true of 3:5, with mē serving to introduce the second question in that verse. However, in either case, the second question builds on the first and the content of the two questions remains the same.

18. Paul uses kathōs gegraptai ten times in Romans to highlight that the OT text about to be stated supports the point he just made.

19. God's "word" is true, especially as it relates to his promises; the truth of God is further defined by his faithfulness, his righteousness, and his judgments.

Section 3

Q: [5]But if [*ei de*] our unrighteousness commends the righteousness of God, what shall we say [*ti eroumen*]? [*mē*] The God who inflicts wrath is not unjust, is he?

(I am speaking according to man.)[20]

A: [6]May it never be [*mē genoito*]!
Otherwise how will God judge the world?

Section 4

Q: [7]For if [*ei gar*] the truth of God by my lie abounded to his glory, why [*ti*] am I also still being judged as a sinner?

[8]And [*kai mē*] why not say (as we have been slandered and as some say that we say),[21] "Let us do evil that good may come"?

A: Whose judgment is just!

Section 5

Q: [9a]What then [*Ti oun*]? Are we better than they?

A: [9b]Not at all.
For we have already charged that both Jew and Greek are all under sin.

The structural analysis of these questions is fascinating. (1) There are ten specific questions, better understood as five pairs of two questions each. Each pair is interrelated and is asking one major question, followed by a brief answer. The pairing of questions serves to accentuate them for the listener. (2) There is a consistent pattern to the questions. The first and last pairs of questions (sections 1 and 5) are both introduced by *Ti oun* ("What then?") and ask similar questions; both their answers are abrupt followed by a brief explanation.[22] The middle three pairs of questions (sections 2, 3, and 4) are all similarly structured. All three are introduced by the particle *ei* (if) introducing a type 1 simple fact condition clause, together with the particle *ti* raising the questions; and all three include the particle *mē* used in questions expecting a negative answer, which all three get respectively: 'May it never be!" "May it never be!" "Whose judgment is just!" In sections

---

20. Parentheses are added for clarification.

21. Parentheses are added for clarification.

22. I view 3:1-9a as a unit. Joseph A. Fitzmyer (*Romans: A New Translation with Introduction and Commentary*, AB 33 [New York: Doubleday, 1992], 326) notes that those who take 3:1-8 as a unit fail to see the *inclusio* involved in the use of *ti oun* in both 3:1 and 3:9a. I would also note the clear relation of the content of the question in 3:9a with 3:1 and the rest of the questions.

2 and 3, the negatives are followed by a brief response in which God is the subject. In section 4, there is no brief response, leaving only the negative, "Whose judgment is just!"[23] So this group of questions is very carefully and deliberately structured. Yes, they are brief and to the point, with answers that are abrupt and incomplete, but there is a measured and thoughtful formation to them. (3) This becomes even more evident when we realize that there are nine *hapax legomena* (words used nowhere else by Paul) in this brief group of questions; and all nine are very significant words within this group: *ōpheleia*[24] (benefit) in 3:1, *logia* (words) in 3:2, *apisteō* (disbelieve) in 3:3, *adikos* (unjust) in 3:5, *epipherō* (inflict) in 3:5, *pseusma* (lie) in 3:7, *endikos* (just) in 3:8, *proechō* (excel) in 3:9, and *proaitiaomai* (accuse beforehand) in 3:9.[25] Does the presence of so many *hapax legomena* mean that Paul did not write these questions? This is what many conclude when considering confessional formulas such as Rom. 1:3-4.[26] Rather, this is a further indication that Paul was choosing his words carefully, going beyond his normal vocabulary to articulate these questions. There is a consistent pattern to the questions. They are carefully and deliberately structured. They are significant questions that cry out for more complete answers. Do more complete answers follow?

Before proceeding to answer that question, it is important to point out that a prevalent view among commentators is to view 3:1-4 as one set of questions, and 3:5-8 as another. The primary rationale has to

---

23. One might ask whether in section 4 there are two related but separate questions. My view is that the first question logically leads into the second, and that the accent falls on the latter question introduced by the negative particle *mē*. If this is accepted, then section 4 is seen to be a unit of thought similar in structure to both sections 2 and 3, with one major question being raised: "Why not say . . . let us do evil that good may come?" There is the additional parenthetical note, "as we have been slandered and as some say that we say." Being parenthetical, it does not disrupt the parallel structures of the three sections. For a careful analysis of 3:7-8 together with a listing of all the possible ways of interpreting the verses, see Cranfield, *Romans*, 1:185-87.

24. The noun *ōpheleia* is found elsewhere, in Jude 16. The verb form *ōpheleō* is found in Rom. 2:25 and is no doubt the reason that *ōpheleia* is used in 3:1. Paul also uses the verb form in 1 Cor. 13:3, 14:6 and Gal. 5:2.

25. Of these nine *hapax legomena*, three are found nowhere else in the NT, and three occur only once. The numbers are based on W. F. Moulton and A. S. Geden's *A Concordance of the Greek Testament* (Edinburgh: T&T Clark, 1970).

26. In this passage, I am not prepared to say that due to the large number of *hapax legomena*, these questions were not written by Paul. That would be folly. Perhaps this should caution us about rushing to judgment that Paul could not have written certain confessional formulas based on the presence of *hapax legomena*.

do with the shift from "Jewish advantage" to "our unrighteousness," and from "their unbelief" to "my lie."[27] However, the grammatical structure of the sentences as demonstrated above negates that understanding and enables us to see the relation of the sentences. Moreover, one can sense the step-like approach to the questions and their relation to each other. The questions proceed from "Jewish advantage" to "their unbelief" to "our unrighteousness" to "my lie" and "being judged as a sinner" and sinning, to the final question of judging, "Are we better than they?" The answers proceed from "the words of God" to "the faithfulness of God" to "the righteousness of God" to "the truth and glory of God" to the final answer of "Not at all! For all are under sin." But more importantly, there appears to be a step-like progression in the question-and-answer as evidenced by prominent word chains. The answer in 3:2, "that they were entrusted [episteuthēsan] with the words of God," appears to lead into the question in 3:3 that continues the word chain ēpistēsan, apistia, and pistin. Likewise, the answer in 3:4 with its Old Testament quotation, "That you may be justified [dikaiōthēs] in your words and vindicated while you are being judged [krinesthai]," appears to lead into the question-and-answer in 3:5-6 that continue these word chains adikai, dikaiosynē, adikos, and krinō. Likewise, the answers in both 3:4 and 3:6 that introduce the word chains for "truth," "lie," and "to judge" are picked up in the question-and-answer of 3:7-8. These word chains are striking and demonstrate the interrelation of the questions. But the questions-and-answers still beg for extended answers. Do the abbreviated questions-and-answers in 3:1-9a anticipate the content to follow in 3:9b–11:36?

First, we should acknowledge the remarkable resemblance of questions that occur later in the letter with those in sections 2–4 above.

---

27. Some commentators divide the text into two parts: 3:1-4 responding to Jewish objections, and 3:5-8 responding to charges of libertinism. For example, Fitzmyer (Romans, 325) states that Paul is pitting his teaching against "the Torah fidelity of the contemporary Jew." In 3:1-4, Paul is setting out the Jews' advantage due to God's fidelity to his covenant promises, and in 3:5-8 he is handling the objection of antinomianism. Similarly, Cranfield (Romans, 183) writes that in 3:5 Paul's thought takes an unexpected turn. He remembers how his doctrine of grace was misunderstood by Jewish opponents in the past and thus digresses from 3:1-4 to guard against charges of antinomianism in 3:5-8.

They appear to be reiterating the questions initially raised in 3:3-8 while providing more extended answers. Considering them seriatim, the question in 3:3-4 is restated in chapter 11.

> 3:3: Their unbelief will not nullify the faithfulness of God, will it? May it never be!

> *mē hē apistia autōn tēn pistin tou theou katargēsei? mē genoito!*

> 11:1: I say then, God has not rejected his people, has he? May it never be!

> *Legō oun, mē apōsato ho theos ton laon autou? mē genoito!*

> 11:11: I say then, they did not stumble so as to fall, did they? May it never be!

> *Legō oun, me eptaisan hina pesōsin? mē genoito!*

Notice the similarity of the questions, including the structural similarities. The negative *mē* is used in all three passages to introduce a question expecting a negative answer; and all three end with *mē genoito!* The context of 3:3 is that among the advantages of the Jews, they were entrusted with the words of God (3:2), but some did not believe. Would their unbelief nullify[28] the faithfulness of God in fulfilling his "words"? *Mē genoito!* God remains true to his words, and anyone who supposes that God will not accomplish what he sets out to do is a "liar." In 11:1, the context is the unbelief of Israel (9:30-10:21). They heard "the word [*to rhēma*] of faith that was proclaimed," the "gospel," the "word [*rhēma*] of Christ" (10:8, 16, 17), but they did not believe. The question is then raised in 11:1. Has God rejected his people? The answer is a resounding *mē genoito*. God has not rejected his people whom he foreknew. Even now,[29] there is "a remnant according to God's gracious choice" (11:5). Well then, did they stumble so as to fall (11:11)? *Mē genoito!* Rather, there is a partial hardening of Israel until the fullness of the gentiles has occurred. Thus all Israel will be saved, as stated in his word (11:26-27). From the vantage point of God's choice,

---

28. *Katargein* means "to render ineffective" or "to cancel," though it may carry the stronger sense of "to abolish" or "to destroy" (7:2; Gal. 5:4; Eph. 2:15). See footnote 8 above.
29. *En tō nyn kairō* ("in the now time").

"the gifts and the calling of God are irrevocable" (11:28). God is faithful to his words. In other words, the abbreviated question-and-answer in 3:3-4 is reiterated and expanded in the discourse of 9:30–11:36.

A similar reiteration takes place in chapter 9, with 9:14 restating the question in 3:5.

> 3:5: What shall we say? The God who inflicts wrath is not unjust, is he? May it never be!
>
> *Ti eroumen? Mē adikos ho theos ho epipherōn tēn orgēn? . . . Mē genoito!*
>
> 9:14: What then shall we say? There is no injustice with God, is there? May it never be!
>
> *Ti oun eroumen? Mē adikia para tō theō? mē genoito!*

The entire question-and-answer in section 2 (3:5-6) reads: "But if our unrighteousness commends the righteousness of God, what shall we say? The God who inflicts wrath is not unjust, is he? (I am speaking according to man.) May it never be! Otherwise how will God judge the world?" The general nature of this question with its immediate response is a bit unclear. To whom is Paul referring when he refers to "our" unrighteousness? Is Paul identifying himself with the Jews or the gentiles in that remark, or with both? How does our unrighteousness "commend" the righteousness of God? And if that is true, is the Judge of all the earth a just judge? There are a lot of rather significant and related questions in play here. The issue has shifted from "their" (Jewish) unbelief to "our" (gentile?) unrighteousness, and from God's faithfulness to God's righteousness. Is Paul seeking to address a perceived disparity between the way God deals with Jewish unbelief and gentile unrighteousness? Will all this be resolved in what follows?

Again we find that the question raised in 3:5-6 is repeated and expanded in 9:14-32. First, the similarity of the questions is indisputable. The presence in both of the *ti eroumen* and *ti oun eroumen*, the negative *mē* introducing a negative question, the cognate forms *adikos* and *adikia*, the references to God, and the *mē genoito* is striking. Second, we may compare the reluctance of Paul in 3:5 even to raise a question about the justice of God, with his emphatic denial in 9:19-20 of the right for anyone to ever question the justice of God: "You will say to me then, 'Why does he still find fault? For who resists his will?' On the contrary, who are you, O man, who answers back to God?" Third, this exchange is then followed by reference to the "wrath" of God and the withholding of his wrath so that God might make known "the riches of his glory upon vessels of mercy" (9:22-24). Fourth, all this leads into the question-and-answer of 9:30-32. I have already raised the issue of whether "our unrighteousness" in 3:5 refers to the gentiles in contrast to the unbelief of the Jews in 3:3. This same contrast between gentile unrighteousness and Jewish unbelief is found in the questions of 9:30-32: "What shall we say then? That gentiles, who did not pursue righteousness attained righteousness, even the righteousness that is by faith; but Israel, pursuing a law of righteousness, did not arrive at that law. Why? Because they did not pursue it by faith, but as though it were by works." It is important to observe that the questions in 9:14 begin the line of questioning that continues in 9:19-24 and transitions into 9:30-32, all of which serve to provide an extended answer to 3:5-6.[30] I conclude, then, that there is a definite correspondence of the questions and content in 9:14-32 with the initial question-and-answer in 3:5-6.

A third reiteration is found in chapter 6, which repeats the question raised in 3:7-8. Here is the comparison:

3:8: And why not [say] . . . "Let us do evil that good may come"? Whose judgment is just!

Mē [ti] . . . Poiēsōmen ta kaka hina elthē ta agatha? hōn to krima endikon estin!

6:1: What then shall we say? Are we to continue in sin that grace may increase? May it never be!

Ti oun eroumen? epimenōmen tē hamartia, hina hē charis pleonasē? mē genoito!

6:15: What then? Shall we sin because we are not under law but under grace? May it never be!

---

30. One should note that the questions in 9:30–32 lead into the subject matter of the 'unbelief of Israel' in 10:1-21, which in turn leads into the questions in 11:1 and 11:11.

Ti oun? hamartēsōmen hoti ouk esmen hypo nomon alla hypo charin? mē genoito!

The two questions in chapter 6 are introduced by the epistolary formulas *ti oun eroumen* and *ti oun* and conclude with a *mē genoito*. They are the first in a sequence of questions that guide the narrative—6:1-3, 15-16; 7:1, 7, 13, and 24[31]—from 6:1 to 8:17.

6:1: Are we to continue in sin that grace may increase? *Mē genoito!*

6:15: Shall we sin because we are not under law but under grace? *Mē genoito!*

7:1: Do you not know, brothers . . . that the law rules over a man as long as he lives?

7:7: Is the law sin? *Mē genoito!*

7:13: Did that which is good become a cause of death for me? *Mē genoito!*

7:24: Who will rescue me from the body of this death?

Within this sequence, we find transitional statements in 6:14 and 7:5-6. Romans 7:1 introduces an analogy that transitions into the questions of 7:7 and 13. The question in 7:7 is introduced by the epistolary formula *ti oun eroumen*, and both 7:7 and 13 conclude with *mē genoito!* Romans 7:24 serves both to conclude the previous discourse in 7:7-23 and to pivot to the positive answer of the gospel in 7:25–8:17. Romans 6:1–8:17 is, in toto, the extended answer anticipated in 3:7-8.[32] We may also view chapter 7 as an extended answer anticipated in 3:31.

What seems to be quite evident is that the questions initially raised in brief in 3:3-8 are reintroduced later in the letter with extended answers. There is a clear correspondence between 3:3-4 and 9:30–11:36, 3:5-6 and 9:14-32, and 3:7-8 and 6:1-8:39. In addition to restating and even repeating at times word for word the initial questions, Paul used words that caught the attention of those listening. All the restated questions begin with the words *ti oun eroumen* or *ti oun* or *legō oun;* all conclude with *mē genoito;* and all include embedded epistolary

---

31. The single question in 6:21 is there to support the dialogue of the narrative.
32. As for the presence of 8:18-39, see my thoughts in the concluding portion of chapter 6.

formulas.[33] All are part of a group of questions that serve to introduce their respective sections of the letter. All include extended answers. In other words, all are carefully and deliberately structured to capture the attention of the audience orally and to guide them through the narrative. It is also interesting to observe that there is a chiastic pattern to the questions.

> A. 3:3-4: brief question-and-answer
>   B. 3:5-6: brief question-and-answer
>   C. 3:7-8: brief question-and-answer
>   C. 6:1, 15: extended question-and-answer: 6:1–8:39
>   B. 9:14: extended question-and-answer: 9:14-32
> A. 11:1, 11: extended question-and-answer: 9:30–11:36

Such correspondence does not take place by coincidence. Paul is purposely guiding his listeners through the letter by first raising questions in 3:3-8 and then reiterating them later in reverse order with extended answers. Hence, they must be regarded as part of the "surface structure" of the letter. If one asks, is Paul capable of doing this? The answer is yes. His rabbinic mind and years of experience and proclamation of the gospel made him perfectly capable of structuring the letter in this way. If one asks, why should we accept this view of the surface structure of the letter? the answer is, a rhetorical analysis in which we find a predominant group of questions followed by corresponding questions all embedded with epistolary formulas guiding the narrative of a long letter. Why is this difficult for us to accept? We are not accustomed to analyzing a long letter framed to catch the ear of a listening audience. We are not used to viewing either grammar or rhetoric from this perspective. Also, we have been conditioned to view Romans as a letter-essay. The idea that it is a theological treatise runs deep. Our interpretation is hampered by former outlines as well as by chapter and verse divisions. They were

33. The following particles are reserved for the major questions I am referencing in chaps. 3–11. Of the major questions, and only of the major questions, *ti oun eroumen* or *ti eroumen* are found in 3:5; 4:1; 6:1; 7:7; 8:31; 9:14, 30, and *ti oun* in 3:1, 9; 6:15; 9:19; 11:7. *Mē genoito* is found only in 3:4, 6, 31; 6:2, 15; 7:7, 13; 9:14; 11:1, 11. *Tis/ti* is also used to introduce the following major questions: 3:1b, 3, 7; 4:3; 7:24; 8:33, 34, 35; 9:30, 32; 10:16; 11:4, 34, 35.

not there originally, and yet they have inevitably influenced how we view Paul's flow of thought. We should follow Paul's rhetoric as it leads us, not as we perceive it should be. Our approach to the grammar and rhetoric of the letter must be inductive. This is especially important in Romans, where the argument is cumulative. The dependence of new lines of thought on prior material as well as the progression of word chains is characteristic of this letter. Yet all this has to be organized by Paul in some audible way if the audience is to follow his discourse and if there is to be any coherence in the progression of thought of the letter. All this to say that one must take pains to follow the flow of thought as the rhetoric and grammar and text dictate. There are multiple rhetorical devices, but the most dominant of these is that of raising questions and pursuing answers to those questions.

Second, we need to consider the role of the question-and-answer in 3:1-2:

Q: What then is the advantage of the Jew? Or what is the profit of circumcision?

A: Much in every way. Foremost, that they were entrusted with the words of God.

The synonymous parallelism of the two questions gives weight to the issue of whether there is any benefit to being a Jew.[34] The prior context leads up to those questions. After placing all under sin (1:19-32) and all under the impartial judgment of God (2:1-11), Paul explains how the gentiles will be judged by the law of God (2:12-16). He then writes in heightened detail how the Jews, who have the law and rely on the law and love to instruct others out of the law, have broken the law (2:17-29). Circumcision is of profit (ōpheleō) only if you keep the law. A true Jew is not to be defined in terms of his name or mark of being a Jew, but "he is a Jew who is one inwardly; and circumcision is that

---

34. Both *to perisson* (translated "advantage") and *hē ōpheleia* (translated "profit") could be translated by "advantage." Circumcision was a mark of being a Jew, hence synonymous parallelism in these two questions.

which is of the heart, by the Spirit, not by the letter, and his praise is not from men but from God." In the words of J. W. Doeve,

> Whoever has some idea how strongly the Jew was convinced of his exceptional status compared with the Gentiles, through the very fact of belonging to the people who had received the Law and through being circumcised, will understand that to the Jewish mind the question must unavoidably follow: "What advantage then hath the Jew, or what is the profit of circumcision?" (Rom. iii.1). For indeed, it would seem that in Rom. ii Paul denies that the Jew has any advantage, or any exceptional status as compared with the nations at large.[35]

The same question will present itself to the gentile mind as well. This then becomes a turning point in the letter as Paul raises the question in 3:1, "What then is the advantage of the Jew? Or what is the profit [ōpheleia] of circumcision?" The unexpected answer is, "Much in every way." This in turn introduces the question-and-answer that follows in step-like sequence in 3:3-9a.

A number of scholars have already observed the relation between 3:1-2 and chapters 9–11.[36] In a helpful article devoted to this entire passage, S. Lewis Johnson writes: "It is axiomatic, of course, that the full treatment of the question of Israel and her promises is found in chapters nine through eleven."[37] In his extended analysis, he refers to the catalog of blessings listed in 9:4-5.

> It is as if Paul were writing an answer to the question, "What is the advantage of the Jew" (3:1)? Here is his advantage and his profit, and it is "much every way" (3:2), but particularly in his possession of the messianic revelation,—national election (adoption, covenants), educational preparation for the Messiah's coming (the Law and the service), the

---

35. J. W. Doeve, "Some Notes with Reference to τὰ λόγια τοῦ θεοῦ in Romans III, 2," in *Studia Paulina in honorem Johannis de Zwaan septuagenarii* (Haarlem: Bohr, 1953), 111.

36. Nils A. Dahl (*Studies in Paul: Theology for the Early Christian Mission* [Minneapolis: Augsburg, 1977], 139): In chaps. 9–11, Paul answers the questions he failed to answer in 3:1-5. Fitzmyer (*Romans*, 325): "What Paul discusses in these verses is in reality a preparation for what he will take up in chaps. 9–11." John A. Ziesler (*Paul's Letter to the Romans* [London: SCM, 1989], 94–95): "Paul develops his argument by debate with an imaginary or typical interlocutor and with the problems to be dealt with in 9–11 already in view." R. Dean Anderson Jr. (*Ancient Rhetorical Theory and Paul* [Leuven: Peeters, 1999], 229) remarks that "it seems as if in chapters six to eleven Paul intentionally returns in detail to the two objections briefly raised in 3.1-8."

37. S. Lewis Johnson Jr., "Studies in Romans, Part VII: The Jews and the Oracles of God." *Bibliotheca Sacra* 130 (1973): 235–49 (here 236–37).

messianic hope (promises), the typical messianic figures (the fathers), and the Messiah Himself. It is difficult not to believe that Paul had these things in mind when he said that Israel was entrusted with the oracles of God.[38]

I concur with Johnson, but with this major caveat. The text in 3:2 reads, "Much in every way. Foremost,[39] that they were entrusted with the words of God." The catalog of blessings in 9:4-5 appears to be expanding on the remark, "much in every way." But what was "foremost" among the blessings? To what does *ta logia tou theou* refer? Some believe that it is restricted to the law.[40] One may suppose the law would have been "foremost" on the minds of most Jews. But if this were the case, why didn't Paul simply use the phrase "the law of God"? John Murray holds that it refers to the Old Testament in its entirety, not simply to oracular utterances.[41] William Sanday thinks it includes both the utterances of the law as spoken at Mt. Sinai and the messianic promises.[42] Douglas Moo focuses on the promises of God.[43] But, again, if Paul were referring solely to the promises of God, why did he not simply use that phrase? On the other hand, one can hardly exclude those promises. Johnson makes a strong case that *ta logia* refers to "the promises of the OT and their fulfillment in Christ."[44] *Ta logia* may be translated literally as "words," "utterances," "oracles," or "messages," and appears to reflect the oral nature of God's revelation. James Dunn

---

38. Ibid., 244.
39. The Greek (*prōton men*) can be translated "first of all" or "foremost." The former suggests "first in a sequence," which obviously does not occur here. There is no second or third. I opt for the latter nuance meaning primarily or chiefly (pro Calvin, Kruse, Jewett; contra Moo, Barrett, Cranfield). Paul uses this adverbial expression in the same way in Rom. 1:8. Kruse (*Romans*, 159) writes, "Paul was not intending to provide a comprehensive list of Israel's privileges but rather was highlighting what was most important: Israel's privilege in having received the words of God."
40. Adolf Schlatter, *Gottes Gerechtigkeit: Ein Kommentar zum R?merbrief* (Stuttgart: Calwer, 1959), 113–14.
41. John Murray, *The Epistle to the Romans*, NICNT (Grand Rapids: Eerdmans, 1965), 1:92–93; also C. K. Barrett, *A Commentary on the Epistle to the Romans* (London: Black, 1957), 62; Charles Hodge, *A Commentary on the Epistle to the Romans* (1886; repr., Grand Rapids: Eerdmans, 1950), 107.
42. William Sanday and Arthur C. Headlam, *The Epistle to the Romans* (New York: Charles Scribner's Sons, 1897), 70.
43. Moo (*Romans*, 182–83): "That the promises of God are included in 'the oracles' is, of course, obvious; and Paul has probably chosen to use this word, rather than, for example, 'the Scriptures,' because he wants to highlight those 'sayings' of the OT in which God committed himself to certain actions with reference to his people." Käsemann (*Romans*, 79) says *ta logia* refers to "the promise of the gospel." Kruse (*Romans*, 160) concurs that preeminent among the words of God entrusted to Israel would have been the preaching of the gospel by Jesus Christ and continued by the apostles.
44. Johnson, "Studies in Romans," 240–45.

views the phrase as referring to the utterances of God given through Moses and the Prophets, and that we should not try to restrict them.[45] C. E. B. Cranfield says that we must view *ta logia* in "its widest sense."[46] This comports with the findings of Doeve, who wrote a definitive study on *ta logia*.[47] He demonstrates how it was used by Hellenistic writers of divine utterances and oracles, and by Jewish authors not only of divine utterances but also of Scripture, which would include both the law and the promises of God. The fact that Paul in this context did not specifically identify the promises, law, or Scripture tends to affirm its widest possible sense. Romans 3:2 says the Jews were "entrusted" with *ta logia tou theou*. "Entrusted" conveys the sense of something committed for safe keeping. It also conveys the sense of a "trust" so that others would benefit from them as well. Obviously such a trust would include God's messianic promises, his promises to Israel but also his utterances about all humankind preserved in the Scriptures. Cranfield notes that the Jews alone had the privilege of being entrusted with God's self-revelation and message of salvation, "to treasure it and to attest and declare it to all mankind."[48] This would demand fidelity on their part.[49] In terms of the immediate context, notice how their being entrusted with the *logia* of God feeds into the second set of questions about the Jews in 3:3, "What if some did not believe? Their unbelief will not nullify the faithfulness of God, will it?"

It is important to observe that chapters 9–11 are basically an enlargement on (1) the advantages of the Jew, and (2) *ta logia tou theou* as understood above. First, the advantage for Israel of being chosen by God to be his children and for this promise not to be vacated but

45. Dunn, *Romans 1-8*, 130–31.
46. Cranfield, *Romans*, 1:179.
47. Doeve, "Some Notes," 111–23. Arndt and Gingrich (*Lexicon*, 477) affirm that in Hellenism *logia* was "used mostly of short sayings originating from a divinity." In the OT, it is used of Balaam's "oracle" in Num. 24:4, 16, and occurs some twenty-four times in Psalm 119 to refer to the revelation of God generally and to God's law. In the NT, it is used only three other times (Acts 7:38; Heb. 5:12; 1 Pet. 4:11), and only in Acts 7:38 is the reference clearly referring to the law of Moses.
48. Cranfield, *Romans*, 1:179.
49. Brendan Byrne, SJ (*Romans*, SP [Collegeville, MN: Liturgical Press, 1996], 108–9) writes that *ta logia* was given to the Jews "in trust" so that others, the gentiles, would benefit from them as well. So that, while the oracles contained God's pledge of faithfulness to bring in salvation, their entrustment implied a corresponding fidelity on their part.

ultimately fulfilled is an unbelievable advantage. The introductory litany in 9:4-5 is for all intents and purposes the subject matter of chapters 9–11—the advantages of their being Israelites and adopted as sons, historically being in a covenant relation with him and receiving his instruction (the law), belonging to the lineage of the fathers and thereby heirs of the promises especially pertaining to Christ. They are the first in line, and their calling is not to be contested. They are the olive tree to which the gentiles have become attached, and the gentiles are to appreciate them as such. This aligns with the repeated statement "to the Jew first, and also to the Greek." This also aligns with the prominence Paul gives to the "fathers" and God's promises to them.[50] Chapter 4 is devoted to the promises of God to Abraham (4:13, 14, 16, 20). These promises to the fathers form an *inclusio* in chapters 9–11 (9:8-9 and 11:27-29). They also form a *conclusio* for the entire body of the letter regarding the mercy of God on Israel: "that Christ has become a servant to the circumcision . . . to confirm the promises given to the fathers" (15:8). This is a major theme of Romans.

Second, *ta logia tou theou* is to a great extent the subject matter and focus of chapters 9–11. Romans 9:6 begins with the statement, "But it is not as though the word [*ho logos*] of God has failed." Then Paul records God's "words of promise" (9:8, 9) to the fathers, with three specific utterances (9:7, 9, 12). Chapters 9–11 expand to include God's words through Moses and the Prophets regarding both Jews and gentiles in God's plan. In fact, one is struck by the multiple examples of the utterances of God quoted in chapters 9–11 pertaining to both ethnic groups, some twenty-nine quotations plus Old Testament analogies such as the potter and clay (Jeremiah 18) and the olive tree (Jer. 11:16). James Dunn finds that 30 percent of chapters 9–11 consists of Old Testament quotations, more than half of all the quotations in Romans. They draw from all portions of Scripture, but especially from Isaiah (40 percent). These quotations are used especially to support the answers to the questions in 9:6-29; 9:30–10:21; 11:1-10; and 11:11-36.[51] They

---

50. The term *epangelia* occurs in 4:13, 14, 16, 20; 9:4, 8, 9; [11:28–29]; 15:8.
51. Dunn, *Romans 9–16*, 520.

include promises to Israel as well as God's words about the inclusion of the gentiles. In chapter 10, they focus on the promise of the Messiah using the word *rhēma*, the spoken "word of faith," or "word of Christ," also referred to as the "gospel" (10:8 [×2], 9, 17, 18). But would Israel's unbelief cause God to reject them (11:1)? *Mē genoito!* The "word of promise" spoken initially to Abraham and Rebekah in 9:6-13 is affirmed at the end of chapter 11, "for the gifts and the calling of God are irrevocable" (11:29).[52] It would seem evident that chapters 9–11 are a fuller treatment of the question-and-answer of 3:1-2. And as 3:1-2 serves to introduce the questions in 3:3-9, so it anticipates the fuller treatment in 9–11. Hence, 3:1-2 is a (if not the) primary question in the letter, and chapters 9–11 are central to the discourse.

The final consideration is, what does the question-and-answer in 3:9a introduce?

Q5: What then? Are we better than they? Not at all!

Romans 3:9a leads rhetorically into 3:9b–5:21. What follows are the fundamental truths of the gospel that underlie the unity of Jew and gentile in Christ. Using inclusive language throughout, Paul progressively details how all are under sin and cannot be justified by works of law (3:9b-20); how all are justified through faith in Christ Jesus apart from law (3:21-26); how all those justified are now reconciled to God through the death of Christ (5:1-11); and how all are made right before God based on the righteousness of Christ (5:12-19). In the center of this gospel narrative, using the question-and-answer format (as explained above), Paul highlights that all who believe in Christ, both circumcised and uncircumcised, apart from works of law are children of Abraham.[53] Abraham is the father of us all! We are one

---

52. Doeve ("Some Notes," 117) observed that of the thirty-five occurrences of *ta logia* in the LXX, twenty-eight were translations of the Hebrew words *'ēmer* or *'imrâ* (speech, word, utterance); five were translations of *dābār* (word, speech); and two were of *ḥesed* (kindness, mercy). He comments that this might give the impression that in the LXX *logion* is the more or less accepted translation of *'ēmer* and *'imrâ*. However, conversely, these two Hebrew words are also translated three times by *logos* (word), six times by *rhēma* (spoken word), and one time by *legein* (to say). What I find interesting is that both *logos* (3× in chap. 9) and *rhēma* (5× in chap. 10), together with *legein* (19× in chaps. 9–11) are used regularly in chaps. 9–11 as is the concept of mercy, perhaps confirming the view that *ta logia tou theou* in its widest sense is the subject matter of chaps. 9–11.

body in Christ. The truth of the gospel, the inclusive rhetoric, and the highlighted example altogether serve as the extended answer to 3:9a.

One may ask whether 3:9a is properly translated and interpreted, "Are we better than they?" To begin with, there is a similarity between the first and last questions in 3:1-9a. Romans 3:1 asks about the advantage of the Jew, and 3:9a asks whether we are better than they. But while both raise similar questions, the answers are not the same. In 3:2 we read, "Much in every way!" The brevity of this response in lacking a verb and including a brief idiomatic prepositional phrase adds force to this reply; the Jews enjoyed every advantage. In 3:9b, the answer is, "Not at all!"[54] Again, the brevity is startling, adding force to Paul's next statement that both Jew and Greek are all under sin. Now if both these verses refer to the Jews, there is an obvious contradiction. (For the record, most commentators hold that both 3:1 and 3:9a refer to Jews.[55] Some translations even go so far as to add the word "Jew" in 3:9a, which is neither helpful nor proper.[56]) The Jew cannot at the same time have every advantage and then have no advantage at all. The answer lies in the focus of the questions. They are not addressing the same issue. Romans 3:1 is clearly addressing Jewish advantage, with the extended answer being chapters 9–11. Romans 3:9a is addressing

---

53. Romans 3:27–4:25 is an example, a *paradeigma*, parenthetically inserted between 3:21-26 and 5:1-11. It highlights the truth that gentile believers are joined together with Jewish believers as seed of Abraham, hence their unity. See my extended discussion below in chap. 6.

54. Bruce M. Metzger (*A Textual Commentary on the Greek New Testament* [New York: United Bible Societies, 1971], 507) points out that *ou pantōs* is used here in a sense normally reserved for *pantōs ou*, meaning "not at all," or "by no means." Cranfield (*Romans*, 1:190–91) prefers the translation "not altogether" or "not in every respect" contending that it suits the context better by not conflicting with 3:1-2, where the Jew has an advantage "much in every respect." Cranfield is assuming that the "we" in 3:9 continues to refer to the Jew, a view I consider mistaken. Most commentators agree that the expression *ou pantōs* must mean "not at all."

55. Stanley K. Stowers ("Paul's Dialogue with a Fellow Jew in Romans 3:1-9," *CBQ* 46 [1984]: 707–22 [here 709–10]) argues that 3:1-9 only makes sense as a dialogue with an imaginary Jewish interlocutor. He criticizes the translation of the RSV as "using a collective 'we' referring to humanity in v.5, an exemplary or generalizing first person singular in v.7, a first person plural referring to Paul himself or Paul and his fellow workers in v. 8, a first person plural in v.9a meaning 'we Jews' and another first person plural in v. 9b, which is read as an 'authorial we' and translated as 'I.'" He asks, how could anyone follow this diverse use of pronouns? You would have to assume a priori that Paul had the Jews, Christians, and Libertines all in mind at once. Rather, Stowers says that the answer lies in the diatribal model, where the entire conversation flows more naturally as dialogue between Paul and his imaginary dialogue partner, the Jew. The vast majority of commentators follow his lead. See also Stowers, *A Rereading of Romans: Justice, Jews, and Gentiles* (New Haven: Yale University Press, 1994), 161.

56. NEB, RSV, REB, the Oxford Study Bible, the Moffatt translation.

another issue, one that serves to divide the recipients of the letter. It is the attitude that one is better than the other. Neither Jew nor gentile were immune to that condescending attitude (as will be shown in chapter 6). But the primary focus in chapters 9–11 is on the arrogance of the gentiles toward their Jewish brothers and sisters. In 3:9a, Paul is identifying with the recipients of his letter who were predominantly gentile. Romans 3:1 raises the question of Jewish advantage, while 3:9a raises the question of gentile condescension toward their Jewish brothers and sisters.[57]

First, consider the use of the pronouns and personal endings of the verbs throughout 3:1-9a. In section 1, the Jew is referred to specifically in the third person in the verb *episteuthēsan* (they were entrusted with). For the Roman believers (composed of a gentile majority), Paul was demonstrating that "they," the Jews, had every advantage. In section 2, the pronouns *tines* and *auton* are used. Again Paul is reminding those in Rome that "their" (the Jews') unbelief does not make void the faithfulness of God. In section 3, the focus changes to the first-person plural, "our" unrighteousness (*hēmōn*) and what shall "we" say (*eroumen*). By changing his focus to the first-person plural, Paul is taking attention away from Jews as a group to his listeners with whom he is identifying. Hence, "our unrighteousness" is not referring to Jewish unrighteousness, but to the unrighteousness of his listeners in general as reflected in the gentile majority.[58] In section 4, the first-person singular and plural are again the focus in his use of *emō*, *kagō*, *krinomai*, *blasphēmoumetha*, *hēmas*, and *poiēsōmen*; and there is tension between what we, the Roman or gentile believers, might do and what we assume others may accuse us of saying and doing.[59] Finally, in

---

57. For an extended discussion of Paul's "oppositional rhetoric" regarding Jews and gentiles, see chap. 6. In Romans, Paul is especially concerned about the gentiles' display of arrogance and pride toward their Jewish brothers and sisters (Romans 11, 14). This was a divisive issue, hence the extended answer to the question in 3:9a focuses on what gentiles have in common with Jewish believers (3:9b–5:21). They are now one with the Jews by lineage to their father Abraham.

58. In 3:5-6, Paul is speaking of "our unrighteousness" (*adikia*) commending "God's righteousness" (*dikaiosynēn*) and raising the question of God exercising his wrath and judging the world. This is picking up on Paul's prior discourse in 1:18-32 of God's wrath and justice being revealed due to humanity's unrighteousness (*adikia*), gentiles included.

59. Paul's use of the first-person plural in "as *we* are blasphemed . . . let *us* do evil that good may come" makes sense if speaking of actual gentile antinomianism. The question is whether Paul was

78

section 5, Paul continues with the first-person plural. To interpret this as though a Jew were asking, "Are we Jews then better than the gentiles?" is to isolate it completely from its context and to fail to consider the use of the personal pronouns and verbal endings throughout the section. This use of pronouns is consistent with Paul's use of pronouns throughout Romans. He uses the third person when referring to gentiles or Jews as a group or party to be considered (e.g., 2:17-24 and 2:14-16 respectively), and he uses the first-person plural when identifying with his readers (e.g., 4:23–5:11; 9:24; 15:1-2). But he is also distinguishing between "we" and "they": "Are *we* better than *they*?" These separate pronouns reflect the oppositional pairings that dominate the rhetoric throughout chapters 1–4: Jew/Greek, in law/without law, gentile/Jew, circumcision/uncircumcision (1:16; 2:9-10, 12-13, 14-16/17-24, 25-27; 3:1, 9, 29-30; 4:9-10). This is the broader context of the question-and-answer in 3:1-9a.

Before proceeding to a second consideration, allow me to repeat what I have just said above. There are commentators who would have us think that when Paul switches from the third-person plural in 3:1-4 to the first-person plural and singular in 3:5-8, he is continuing his dialogue about the same group of people, the Jews.[60] The "they" refers to the Jews, and the "we" refers to the Jews. The passage is interpreted as a debate with a Jew with either Paul raising and answering their objections or a "Jewish interlocutor" raising or answering objections. But let's think about this. According to this view, Paul is debating with a Jew, about Jews, while using the third person plural "they," rather than "you." Then while having dialogue with the Jew, he switches to

responding to Jewish criticism of his gospel or to actual gentile antinomianism. The words "as we are blasphemed" suggests the former option; but the extended answer in chaps. 6–8, which speaks of continuing in sin and being enslaved to sin and being sold under sin appears to be addressing the issue of actual gentile antinomianism (which is why it was blasphemous for some to suggest that his gospel implied otherwise).

60. For example, Fitzmyer (*Romans*, 325) speaks for many when he states that 3:1-9 is a dialogue with an imaginary Jewish interlocutor, and the first-person plural in 3:5-9 should be understood as Paul conversing with his Jewish interlocutor. Neil Elliott (*The Rhetoric of Romans: Argumentative Constraint and Strategy and Paul's Dialogue with Judaism*, JSNTSup 45 [Sheffield: JSOT Press, 1990], 141) identifies the "we" in 3:5, 8, and 9, as "Jews," "reflecting the belief that Paul maintains the diatribal fiction throughout this pericope." Interestingly, he concedes that 3:6 could apply to gentiles as well ("the world").

the first person and talks with the Jew about "*our* unrighteousness" and "*we* are blasphemed as *some* say that *we* say, Let *us* do evil that good may come." Do any of these statements in the first person make sense if Paul is dialoguing and identifying with his Jewish partner? Are the Jews being blasphemed for saying, "Let *us* do evil that good may come"? Would Jews identify with the phrase "*our* unrighteousness" or being under condemnation as a sinner? The answer is not difficult. Paul is writing to a predominantly gentile-Christian community of congregations in Rome, identifying with them. The entire letter is written to this audience. He does not change his audience in midstream.

Why is this idea of a dialogue with Jews so prevalent in Romans interpretation? This view rests on a strong tradition which holds that Paul is debating Jews in Romans. This tradition was fortified especially by Werner G. Kümmel, who spoke of the "double-character" of the letter as essentially a debate with Judaism though written to gentiles. Then there is the ingrained idea of a Jewish "interlocutor" objecting to Paul's statements made in 2:17-29. If the entire passage is viewed in this way, then the same interlocutor is viewed as continuing his objecting throughout the passage. We need to dispense with the Jewish interlocutor and the underlying assumption that Paul is having a dialogue with Jewish opponents. He is not. Paul is asking questions that raise issues pertinent to Rome. He is purposely guiding the dialogue of the letter so that these questions are front and center and will receive extended answers in what follows. We can also dispense with any remnants of the double-character idea, for Paul is not having a big debate with Judaism in Rome. That was not an issue there. The issues are defined by the questions Paul raises. In the following chapter, we will return to the issue of the double-character of Romans as well as the presence of a fictitious Jewish interlocutor.

The second consideration is the verb *proechometha* in 3:9. It is difficult to gain a consensus on how to interpret this verb. Its basic meaning is "to hold before" or "to excel." The voice is either middle or passive. The middle voice would ask, "Are we excelling?" The passive would ask, "Are we being excelled?" Therefore, if the gentiles are the primary subject of the first-person plural ending, there are two alternatives—the middle voice, "Are we gentiles excelling the Jews? Not at all!" or the passive voice, "Are we gentiles being surpassed by the Jews [since they received the promises of God]? Not at all!" I choose the former alternative and find in this concluding question an allusion to gentile pride in relation to their Jewish brothers and sisters in Christ.[61]

The Resulting Surface Structure of Romans

What then do we find regarding the surface structure of Romans? We find that the brief question-and-answer raised in 3:1-9a is anticipating the discourse that follows in 3:9b–11:36. The question-and-answer in 3:1-2 receives fuller treatment in chapters 9–11. The three questions-and-answers in 3:3-8 receive fuller treatment in chapters 6–11, in reverse order; and it is important to note that each of the three is at times repeated almost verbatim; and when they are repeated, they conclude with a *mē genoito!* The question-and-answer in 3:9a leads naturally into the discourse that follows in 3:9b–5:21. Paul apparently raised the initial questions with the full intention of answering them in reverse order in 3:9b–11:36.

3:1-2: brief question-and-answer introducing the group of questions
   A. 3:3-4: brief question-and-answer
     B. 3:5-6: brief question-and-answer
       C. 3:7-8: brief question-and-answer
         D. 3:9a: brief question-and-answer with extended answer:
           3:9b–5:21
       C. 6:1, 15: extended question-and-answer: 6:1–8:39
     B. 9:14: extended question-and-answer: 9:14-32
   A. 11:1, 11: extended question-and-answer: 11:1-36, with context of
     9:30–10:21

This correspondence of questions with extended answers did not take place by chance. The questions were intentionally raised to guide the

---

61. For an excellent analysis of this verb and the options for its interpretation, see Cranfield, *Romans*, 1:187–91.

narrative of the letter. The question-and-answer in 3:1-9a not only anticipates what follows but is also an "oral map," so to speak, for the listeners in Rome. They also served as a mental outline for Paul as he wrote the letter.

The questions-and-answers could also be referred to as the "crossroads" of the letter, for they provide the major transition of the letter from the introduction and underlying principles stated in chapters 1-2 to the heart of the letter expressed in 3:9b-15:13.[62] A contextual analysis reveals that the questions-and-answers in 3:1-9a are premised heavily on the preceding discourse of 1:16-2:29, which is only to be expected.[63] The initial question regarding Jewish advantage (3:1) flows naturally from the discussion in 2:17-29, especially 2:25-29. The initial question also stems from Paul's signature use of the phrase "to the Jew first" (1:16; 2:9-10; 3:9b). Paul is bringing the issue of Jewish priority to the forefront in these questions. The concluding question-and-answer explicitly states that he has already charged both Jew and Greek to be under sin, obviously referring to what has been written in 1:18-2:29, especially 1:18-32.[64] As we review the questions in the intervening sections 2, 3, and 4, we find they are replete with concepts derived from the first two chapters. The underlying principle had already been expressed that humankind in its unrighteousness has

---

62. Dunn (*Romans 1-8*, 130) notes that Paul uses 3:1-8 "not only to point forward to subsequent discussion (particularly chapters 6 and 9-11), but also to tie his discussion back into the first part of his indictment: note particularly 3.3—1.17; 3.5—1.17-18; 3.7—1.25. 3:1-8 therefore is something of a bridge between earlier and later parts of the letter, or like a railway junction through which many of the key ideas and themes of the epistle pass."

63. Consider these links between 3:1-8 and chaps. 1-2: 3:1a: *perisson* is premised on repetition of "to the Jew first" (1:16; 2:9-10; and refs. to those without law and under law; 3:1b: *ōpheleia* and references to Jew and circumcision are word chains from 2:25-29; 3:2: *ta logia tou theou* includes ref. to their possession of the law in 2:17-20 (also anticipates refs. to *epangelia* in 4:16-17 and chaps. 9-11); 3:4a: *alēthēs* and *pseustēs* refer back to their use in 1:18, 25; 2:2, 8, 20; 3:4b: ref. to God's judgments and justice is premised on 2:1-3, 6-11, 12, 16; 3:5: our *adikia* is based on 1:18-19, 29; 2:8; 3:5b: God's *orgē* is premised on 1:18, 2:5, 8; 3:6: question of God's judging the world is the subject matter basically of 1:18-2:24; 3:7: the repetition of God's *alēthēs* and humanity's *pseusma* as well as the *krima* of God has already been noted; 3:8: the issue of doing good or evil is premised in the multiple verses referencing either practicing or doing evil in 1:18-2:29 as well as the impartial judgment on good or evil deeds in 2:6-11.

64. Some scholars fail to find where Paul has already charged in chaps. 1-2 that all are "under sin." A good example of that is Charles H. Cosgrove, "What If Some Have Not Believed? The Occasion and Thrust of Romans 3:1-8," *ZNW* 78 (1987): 90-105. I would suggest that 1:18-32 is all-inclusive and not only provides the origin of sin in all people (1:19-23) but lists the sinful consequences as well (1:24-32). The catena of OT references in 3:10-18 serves to support what was previously stated.

suppressed the truth of God and exchanged the truth of God for the lie, that God will judge both Jew and Greek impartially according to truth, and that his wrath will be rendered to those who do not obey the truth. These are fundamental concepts informing the intervening question-and-answer: "may God be true and every man a liar" (3:4); "if our unrighteousness commends the righteousness of God . . . the God who inflicts wrath is not unjust, is he?" (3:5); "how will God judge the world" (3:6); "if the truth of God by my lie abounded to his glory" (3:7); "Let us do evil that good may come" (3:8). It is often overlooked that the questions in 3:1-9a are heavily premised on the preceding discourse. Consequently, if the group of questions in 3:1-9a does indeed anticipate the discourse that follows, as I claim that they do, then it will be proper to refer to them as the crossroads of the letter.

We need to revise the idea that 3:1-9a is a brief digression within 1:18-3:20. Rather, 3:1-9a provides the major transition from 1:18-2:29 to the remaining portion of the body of the letter.[65] In 3:1, for the first time in the letter, Paul raises the question *Ti oun*, "What then?"[66] This has the effect of breaking into the discourse for the purpose of directing the way forward. *Ti oun* is followed by what Romano Penna calls "a relentless series of questions" unlike any other in the letter. These questions anticipate what is to come.[67]

All of this accounts for the surface structure of 3:1-11:36. However, there is one more factor. That pertains to the two major breaks of discourse that serve to accentuate one block of material, chapters 9-11. While Paul was providing extended answers to the question-and-answer in 3:1-9a, he purposely set apart those answers that pertained

---

65. This transition is highlighted by all the questions that are raised in that transition, eighteen questions in all. There are seven questions in 2:21-29 concluding the prior discourse and leading into the question-and-answer of 3:1-9a. There are eleven questions in 3:1-9a anticipating the discourse to follow in chaps. 3-11. This use of eighteen questions in such short order is unparalleled in Romans. It captures the attention of the listeners and helps them focus on what is turning out to be the major subject matter of the letter. See note 14 above.

66. *Ti oun* (or *ti oun eroumen*) reoccurs in 3:5, 9; 4:1; 6:1, 15; 7:7; 8:31; 9:14, 19, 30; 11:7. One must note the inferential and causal connectives leading up to *ti oun* in 3:1: *dioti* (1:19), *dioti* (1:21), *dio* (1:24), *dia touto* (1:26), *dio* (2:1), the relative *hos* (2:6), *gar* (2:11, 12, 13, 14), *oun* (2:21), *gar* (2:24, 25), *oun* (2:26), *gar* (2:28), *Ti oun* (3:1).

67. Romano Penna, *Paul the Apostle: A Theological and Exegetical Study*, vol. 1, *Jew and Greek Alike*, trans. Thomas P. Wahl (Collegeville, MN: Liturgical Press, 1996), 72-73.

to the question of Jewish advantage. Paul opens chapter 9 by expressing his strong feelings of affection for Israel and reminds his audience of God's choice of Israel. By blocking off the discourse in chapters 9-11, Paul is saying, here is the heart of the matter. "I do not want you to be ignorant, brethren, concerning this mystery...." (11:25-32). God's calling and gifts to Israel are irrevocable. God will extend his mercy to them as he has to you. Therefore, reconsider your pride or arrogance toward them, and join me in my desire for their salvation.

Were we to attempt to outline the surface structure of Romans, here is the essence of it.[68]

> 1:1-18: Opening of the Letter
> 1:19-2:29: Premise of the Letter
> 3:1-15:13: Heart of the Letter
> > 3:1-9a: Main Questions Raised
> > > 3:9b-5:21: Extended Answer to 3:9a
> > > 6:1-8:39: Extended Answer to 3:7-8
> > > 9:1-11:36: Extended Answer to 3:1-6
> > 12:1-15:13: Exhortations That Apply
> 15:14-16:27: Closing of the Letter

Paul's opening remarks express his desire to come and proclaim the gospel to them (1:1-18). Then, after demonstrating the impartial justice of God toward both Jew and Greek (1:19-2:29), Paul raises the issues he wishes to discuss regarding both Jew and gentile (3:1-11:36), blocking off in a deliberate way his explanation of Israelite advantage (9-11). This is followed by exhortations applicable to both (12:1-15:13), and Paul concludes with his desire to come to Rome along with his final greetings (15:14-16:27).

---

68. Chapter 7 will provide a rationale for the opening of the letter extending through 1:1-18, and for 1:19-2:29 being viewed as the premise of the letter leading up to the questions in 3:1-9a.

5

Issues to Be Resolved

This approach to the surface structure of Romans is not new. The present writer has relied heavily on those who have gone before, especially the research of William Campbell.[1] Campbell holds that Romans 3 is the structural center of the letter. "In search for clues to the organization of the letter, the question-answer sections especially 3:1-8, offer useful guidelines for discerning the structural centre out of which the entire letter is developed."[2] He references Hans Lietzmann, Adolf Schlatter, and Ulrich Luz as scholars who have drawn attention to the high correspondence between the questions in chapter 3 and the later material in the letter.[3] Campbell's structure differs somewhat from the present author's, but the underlying principle is the same,

---

1. William Campbell, "Romans III as a Key to the Structure and Thought of the Letter," in *The Romans Debate*, ed. Karl P. Donfried, rev. and expanded ed. (Peabody, MA: Hendrickson, 1991), 251–64; see also Campbell, "Revisiting Romans," *ScrB* 12 (1981–1982): 2–10; Campbell, "The Freedom and Faithfulness of God in Relation to Israel," *JSNT* 13 (1981): 43–59; Campbell, "Why Did Paul Write Romans?," *ExpTim* 85 (1974): 264–69. Romano Penna (*Paul the Apostle: A Theological and Exegetical Study*. Vol. 1, *Jew and Greek Alike*, trans. Thomas P. Wahl, [Collegeville, MN: Liturgical Press, 1996], 60–89) also views chaps. 9–11 as a delayed response to the question-and-answer in 3:1-4, and chaps. 6–8 as a delayed response to the question-and-answer in 3:5-8. He argues for the coherence of themes, that chaps. 6–8 develop logically from 3:21–5:21, which in itself is the positive alternative to 1:18–2:29 and 3:9-20, and that chaps. 9–11 presuppose all that precedes.
2. Campbell, "Romans III," 257.
3. Ibid., 252n8.

that the question-and-answer in 3:1-8 and 3:27-31 serve to guide the letter. He holds that

- 3:1Q is developed in 9:4-5,

- 3:3Q is answered in 9:6-7,

- 3:5Q is answered in 9:14-5,

- 3:8Q is answered in 6:1–7:6, and

- 3:27-31 is the outline for 4:1-25.

His surface structure is also a bit more complicated in that he holds that "the questions in 3:1-8 link this section with 6–7 and 9–11, whilst those in 3:27-31 link 3:21f. with ch. 4."[4] Stylistically, all these sections are linked by use of the diatribe style. Other sections are linked by a declarative style. These include 3:21-26 and chapters 5 and 8.

- Diatribal style: 3:1-8; 3:27–4:25; 6–7; 9–11

- Declarative style: 3:21-26; 5; 8

For Campbell, the diatribal sections point to the real theme of the letter and the problems in Rome about which Paul is writing, while the declarative sections are designed to provide answers to those problems. In addition, Campbell acknowledges the common themes that link chapters 1–4 with 9–11—Jews, gentiles, the gospel, together with extensive scriptural support. He points out that the linkage of these themes tends to isolate chapters 5–8. However, if chapters 6–7 are viewed separately as diatribe style, then 5 and 8 may be viewed as declarative and linked with 3:21-26.

I mention Campbell's views because I am indebted to his insights and believe he is pointing us in the right direction regarding the surface structure of Romans. The principle that the questions in 3:1-9a offer guidelines for the organization of the content that follows is correct. However, Campbell's structure is a bit too complicated to follow, and

---

4. Ibid., 259–60.

I think it would be for the listeners in Rome as well. His distinction between the declarative and the diatribal is not uncommon among commentators. For example, Horace E. Stoessel[5] distinguishes between the declarative and the argumentative. He views Paul as oscillating between two moods and methods as he writes the letter. When his mood is dogmatic and he wants to set forth his normative theology, his method is declarative. When his mood is argumentative and he wants to explain the logic of his theology, his method is reasoning. Declarative verbs control the tone of the theological passages, while questions govern the reasoning passages; all one has to do to distinguish between them is to chart the incidence of questions, and you can quickly discern the two types of passages.

Passage	Number of Questions	Type of Passage
1:18-32	0	Declarative
2:1–3:8	17	Argumentative
3:9-20	2	Declarative
3:21-26	0	Declarative
3:27–4:25	13	Argumentative
5:1-21	0	Declarative
6-7	27	Argumentative
8:1-30	1	Declarative
8:31-39	8	Argumentative
9–11	11	Argumentative

Stoessel's analysis has been a forerunner for many who view Romans from the perspective of two styles of writing. (Remember the outline of Thomas Tobin above distinguishing the expository from the argumentative.)[6] I appreciate Stoessel's focus on questions and their number. But is Paul really in an argumentative mood when raising these questions? Are the questions-and-answers in 8:31-39 there for

5. Horace E. Stoessel, "Notes on Romans 12:1-2," *Int* 17 (1963): 161–75, esp. 168.
6. Tobin's outline is discussed above, in chap. 2, "The Structure of Romans."

argument? In fact, can any of the above sections best be designated as argumentative? More importantly, is the structure of Romans really dependent on contrasting two styles of writing as though Paul were fluctuating from one style (or mood) to another? The two-style approach fails to show the coherence of the letter or its progression of thought. It fails to consider the guiding function of the questions.

Campbell's separation of chapters 5 and 8 from 6–7 is also common among commentators. An example is that of Nils Dahl, who finds all the major themes of 5:1-11 reappearing in chapter 8: "Justification and a restored relationship to God as the basis for the hope of future salvation and glory, in spite of present sufferings; the gift of the Holy Spirit, the death of Christ, and the love of God as warrants for this hope; a note of exultation."[7] Once he lists them, he declares that "this synopsis speaks for itself"; the themes of 5:1-11 are repeated and more fully developed in chapter 8.[8] In his view, chapters 6 and 7 (actually 6:1-8:13) are two digressions about sin and the law that do not directly develop the themes from 5:1-11. Hence, we should view chapters 5 and 8 as thematically connected, and chapters 6 and 7 as digressions. In Dahl's view, we should also find a clear break between chapters 4 and 5, not between chapters 5 and 6, as the older commentators did. They did so because of their views of justification and sanctification or juridical and mystical-ethical lines of thought. Those views are to be set aside due to the obvious relation between 5:1-11 and chapter 8.[9] Dahl has served us well by demonstrating the similarity of themes,

---

7. Nils A. Dahl, *Studies in Paul: Theology for the Early Christian Mission* (Minneapolis: Augsburg, 1977), 89, cf. 88–90; also found in Dahl, "Two Notes on Romans 5," *ST* 5 (1951): 37–42; See also Richard Longenecker, *Introducing Romans: Critical Issues in Paul's Most Famous Letter* (Grand Rapids: Eerdmans, 2011), 370–71; Joseph Fitzmyer, *Romans: A New Translation with Introduction and Commentary*, AB 33 (New York: Doubleday, 1992), 96–99.

8. According to Dahl ("Two Notes," 37–42), reference to the Holy Spirit in 5:5 is more fully developed in 8:10-11, 13-17; the themes of suffering and glory in 5:3-4 are developed in 8:18-28; and the love of God in Christ in 5:5-8 is developed in 8:31-39. He views 5:12-21 as closely related to 5:1-11, while chaps. 6–7 contain digressions that are related to the themes but do not directly develop the themes in chap. 5. The end result is the close relation established between chaps. 5 and 8. Campbell's response to Dahl ("Romans III," 256) is that the vocabulary of 5:1-11 is actually more like that of chaps. 1–4, whereas the vocabulary of chap. 8 is set against the background of 5:12-7:25. Thus chaps. 5 and 8 are a continuation of the themes of 3:21-26, and all three successively develop the theme of the eschatological fulfillment in Christ Jesus.

9. Dahl, "Two Notes," 39–41.

but there is more than one possible conclusion. Dahl suggests a form of *inclusio*, with chapters 5 and 8 enclosing chapters 6-7. They could also be viewed as *conclusio*, with chapter 5 concluding chapters 1-4, and chapter 8 concluding chapters 6-7. If one agrees with Dahl that the themes of 5:1-11 are more fully developed in chapter 8, one need not align chapter 5 with chapters 6-8.

The views of Campbell, Stoessel, and Dahl remind us that there are issues yet to be resolved regarding the surface structure of the letter. These issues are important as they effect the interpretation of the letter. The first issue is the role of chapter 5. Does 5:1 introduce a new section in the letter, providing a shift to more personal and ethical content, or is chapter 5 a sequel to chapters 1-4? The second issue regards the role of "diatribe" in the letter. Is the entire body of the letter structured around objections raised by imaginary interlocutors responding to propositions in the letter? The third issue is related to the second issue. In the letter, is Paul actually carrying on a debate with Jews? All these issues are crucial for understanding the progression of thought of Romans.

The Role of Romans 5

Traditionally, it was often held that chapter 5 concluded chapters 1-4.[10] More recently, a few have viewed 5:1-11 as belonging with what precedes, with 5:12-21 belonging with what follows.[11] But most commentators today view all of chapter 5 as introducing a new unit of material, chapters 5-8.[12] My own understanding is, as stated above, that 3:9b-5:21 is a unit, that 5:20-21 transitions into the questions that

10. E.g., John Calvin, Sanday and Headlam, Godet, Lagrange; more recently, James D. G. Dunn, *Romans 1-8*, WBC 38A (Waco: Word, 1988), 242-44.

11. See Franz J. Leenhardt, *The Epistle to the Romans: A Commentary* (London: Lutterworth, 1961), 131n1; Theodor Zahn, *Introduction to the New Testament* (Edinburgh: T&T Clark, 1909), 1:358-59; Matthew Black, *Romans*, NCB (London: Marshall, Morgan & Scott, 1973), 81. Black views chap. 5 as transitional with 5:12-21 constituting a "bridge" to the theme of life in Christ.

12. Douglas J. Moo, *The Epistle to the Romans*, NICNT (Grand Rapids: Eerdmans, 1996), 290-95; Longenecker, *Introducing Romans*, 367-72; C. E. B. Cranfield, *A Critical and Exegetical Commentary on the Epistle to the Romans*, ICC (Edinburgh: T&T Clark, 1975), 1:252-54; Fitzmyer, *Romans*, 96-97. For exhaustive sources for all three positions, see J. Christiaan Beker, *Paul the Apostle: The Triumph of God in Life and Thought* (Philadelphia: Fortress Press, 1984), 377n43.

follow in 6:1 and 6:15, and that those questions are anticipated by the question-and-answer in 3:7-8. As charted above:

A. 3:3-4: brief question-and-answer
  B. 3:5-6: brief question-and-answer
    C. 3:7-8: brief question-and-answer
    C. 6:1, 15: extended question-and-answer: 6:1-8:39
  B. 9:14: extended question-and-answer: 9:14-29
A. 11:1, 11: extended question-and-answer: 9:30-11:36

However, if chapter 5 actually introduces chapters 6-8, then that would basically dismiss the idea that the surface structure of the letter is guided by the questions in 3:1-9a. A number of arguments have been put forth to prove that chapter 5 begins a new section in the letter that extends through chapter 8. These need to be examined if we are to form any conclusions about the surface structure of the letter. First, I will list some of their primary arguments (five of them), and then respond to them seriatim.[13]

First, the opening phrase of Rom. 5:1, "Therefore, having been justified by faith," is transitional, serving to summarize what precedes and introduce what follows. Thus Richard Longenecker calls 5:1 a "literary hinge."[14] In addition, it is argued that the example of Abraham being "proof from Scripture" for justification by faith serves to conclude chapters 1-4;[15] that the supposed confession in 4:25 serves the same purpose;[16] and that 5:1-11 functions as "thesis material" for what follows.[17] Longenecker also notes the two forms of "therefore" in 5:1 and 5:12 (*oun* and *dia touto* respectively). He views them as problematic in that they both seem to reach back to what was argued in 1:16-4:25. He rightly points out,

---

13. This list is dependent on arguments put forth by Moo in *Romans*, 290-95, and Longenecker, *Introducing Romans*, 367-72. It also relies on a number of other commentators.
14. Longenecker, *Introducing Romans*, 371.
15. Ibid., 370-71. Ernst Käsemann (*Commentary on Romans*, trans. Geoffrey W. Bromiley [Grand Rapids: Eerdmans, 1980], 131) writes, "Our understanding of ch. 4 as a proof from Scripture does not allow us to attach 5:1-11 to the preceding section."
16. Cranfield (*Romans*, 1:254) views the confession in 4:25 as a "solemn formula" that concludes the preceding.
17. This view is broadly held; e.g., Dahl, *Studies in Paul*, 82-91; Fitzmyer, *Romans*, ix-x, Arabic numbers 17-30.

What one concludes regarding these seemingly minor linguistic points has a profound effect on how one relates 5:1-11 (also, perhaps, 5:12-21) to the flow of the argument from chapters 1-4 to chapters 5-8—that is, whether it is the conclusion to what precedes in 1:16-4:25, whether it serves as transitional material between 1:16-4:25 and 5:12-8:39, or whether it functions as an introduction to what follows in 5:12-8:39.[18]

This writer cannot find where Longenecker returns to that subject, except to argue from other grounds that chapter 5 goes with chapters 6-8. Personally, I would not call them "minor linguistic points." It is of considerable importance to a listening audience how Paul uses causal and inferential connectives throughout chapters 4-5 and the marked emphases and/or conclusions some of them bring.

Second, there is a shift of tone in Romans 5-8. There is, it is said, a noticeable shift from a polemical tone in chapters 1-4 to a more confessional tone in chapters 5-8. The polemical tone stems from Paul's rhetoric against the viewpoint of Jews. The confessional tone is seen in his participatory style and use of the first-person plural—"we have peace with God" and "we shall be saved."[19] This stands in concert with the idea of some that Paul is directing the gospel to the Jew first in chapters 1-4 and then to the gentile in chapters 5-8; then he addresses questions about the gospel being to the Jew first in chapters 9-11, and offers a paraenesis for his largely gentile audience in chapters 12-15.[20] Likewise, the tone shifts from theological to ethical, from the righteousness of God to the love of God and hope and joy. In the words of Joseph Fitzmyer, "1:16-4:25 is dominated by juridical, forensic notions, but in 5:1-8:39 the emphasis is put on the ethical, even the mystical, in that it affects human behavior and union with God; mild polemics give way to hope and exhortation."[21] The distinction is made

---

18. Longenecker, *Introducing Romans*, 368.
19. Moo, *Romans*, 292n9; cf. Beker, *Paul the Apostle*, 83.
20. Ben Witherington III, *Paul's Letter to the Romans: A Socio-rhetorical Commentary* (Grand Rapids: Eerdmans, 2004), 20; Richard Longenecker, "The Focus of Romans: The Central Role of 5.1-8.39 in the Argument of the Letter," in *Romans and the People of God*, ed. Sven K. Soderlund and N. T. Wright (Grand Rapids: Eerdmans, 1999), 61, 67. Longenecker holds that chaps. 5-8 is a distinctive message to the gentiles.
21. Fitzmyer, *Romans*, 97.

that in chapters 1-4 justification is viewed as status, whereas in chapters 5-8 it has an ethical connotation.

Third, there is a shift in the form of address, from rhetorical to personal. In chapters 1-4, Paul uses rhetorical devices, not personal forms of address; for example, in 2:1 he says, "O man!" and in 4:1, "What then shall we say?" There are thirteen first-person-plural verb endings in chapters 1-4, but forty-eight in chapters 5-8. Those in chapters 1-4 are for editorial or stylistic purposes, whereas those in chapters 5-8 are more relational. Longenecker contends that "Paul—for the first time since the salutation of 1:1-7 and the thanksgiving of 1:8-12—speaks directly to his addressees in 5-8."[22] The use of "us" and "our" in 4:24-25 transitions to that personal mode of address.

Fourth, there is a shift in the frequency of words—from "faith" and "believe" to "life" and "live" (in chaps. 1-4, "faith"/"believe" occurs thirty-three times and "life"/"live" two times; in chaps. 5-8 "faith"/"believe" occur three times and "life"/"live" twenty-four times). Romans 1:16-4:25 centers on Jew and Greek, but they are not mentioned in chapters 5-8. By contrast, 5:4 contains the first mention of the Holy Spirit since 1:4, a subject developed in chapter 8. In addition, it is noted that the "in/through the Lord Jesus Christ" is repeated in 5:1, 11, 21; 6:23; 7:25; and 8:39, while virtually absent in chapters 1-4. C. E. B. Cranfield suggests that Paul's use of this phrase at the end of each chapter serves to bind the four chapters together.[23] Add to this the observation of Longenecker that while Scripture is quoted frequently in chapters 1-4 and 9-11, it is quoted only twice in chapters 5-8 (7:7; 8:36).[24] Regarding this last point, it should be noted that the discourse on Adam and Christ in 5:12-19 is grounded in Scripture, and all of chapter 7 is devoted to the relevance of the Old Testament law of God. Nevertheless, Longenecker's point is with regard to citations of Scripture, not the discussion of biblical themes.

Fifth, Romans 5 and 8 form an *inclusio*. Douglas Moo states, "This

---

22. Longenecker, *Introducing Romans*, 369.
23. Cranfield, *Romans*, 1:254; also Fitzmyer, *Romans*, 96-98.
24. Longenecker, *Introducing Romans*, 369.

theme, the 'hope of sharing in God's glory' (cf. 5:2 and 8:18, 30), 'brackets' all of chaps. 5–8."[25] Longenecker adds that the phrase "in/through the Lord Jesus Christ" also serves as an *inclusio* (5:1 and 8:39).[26] This is in line with the view of Dahl (detailed above) that all the major themes of 5:1-11 reappear in chapter 8.[27] This is a common theme among commentators, that chapters 5 and 8 form an *inclusio*. Moo also views chapters 5–8 as chiastic in structure, 5:12-21 having much in common with 8:1-17, and chapters 6 and 7 sandwiched in between these passages.[28]

A. 5:1-11: assurance of future glory
  B. 5:12-21: basis for this assurance in work of Christ
    C. 6:1-23: The problem of sin
    C. 7:1-25: The problem of the law
  B. 8:1-17: Ground of assurance in the work of Christ, mediated by the Spirit
A. 8:18-39: assurance of future glory

While these arguments for combining chapter 5 with chapters 6–8 are considerable, they are not all that compelling. First, regarding the transitional function of Rom. 5:1, the issue is whether 5:1 really does serve to introduce a new major section of Romans. Actually, what follows is not a new subject. Yes, 5:1-11 introduces a few new terms, as many paragraphs do. However, 5:1-11 repeats even more what precedes. Even Dahl admits that 5:1-11 is closely linked to chapters 1–4 in terminology and seems to bring those chapters to a conclusion. References to justification by faith, the grace of God, the concept of "boasting," our being under the wrath of God, the blood of Christ, and salvation—all connect with what precedes.[29] I would add, references in 5:12-19 to Adam, sin, the law, and justification also connect to chapters 1–4. The example of Abraham in chapter 4 is just that, an example from Scripture supporting the truth that justification is by faith, not

---

25. Moo, *Romans*, 293.
26. Longenecker, *Introducing Romans*, 371.
27. Dahl, *Studies in Paul*, 88–90. See also Longenecker, *Introducing Romans*, 370–71; Fitzmyer, *Romans*, 96–98.
28. Moo, *Romans*, 293–94.
29. Dahl, *Studies in Paul*, 89–90.

works; and 4:23-25 can be viewed as transitioning from the example of Abraham and justification by faith to its corresponding effect in 5:1, peace with God. "Therefore, having been justified by faith, we have peace with God. . . ." Consequently, there is every reason to assume from the terminology of 5:1-11 that it is a continuation of the discourse of 3:21-26.[30]

The point is often made that 5:1-11 is "thesis material" for 5:12–8:39. How is it thesis material for chapters 6 and 7? Moo himself refers to these chapters as parenthetical,[31] Dahl as digressions.[32] The problems raised in chapters 6–7 do not appear to be an exposition of 5:1-11. Actually, they seem to have more of a connection with the ideas Paul introduced in condensed versions in 3:7-8, 19-20, 31. Longenecker speaks of 5:1 as a literary hinge, whereas Paul Achtemeier treats 4:23–5:11 as a single paragraph.[33] A lot of it has to do with how you view Paul's grammar and his use of inferentials. This is an important point and drives us back to the issue of how Paul guides his listening audience. For us, the inferentials in Paul's letter may be of minor consequence. But for the listening audience in Rome, this was not the case. They were dependent on Paul's choice of inferential and causal connectives—*oun, ara, dio, dioti, ara oun,* and *dia touto.* They were guided by his choice. These connectives differ in strength from normal to strong, *oun* being the normal inferential used more for continuous flow of discourse. That is how it is used in 5:1, as a normal inferential following what precedes and not marking a major break with the past. (Remember, there were no chapter divisions. Those listening would

---

30. The text of 5:1 must also be taken into consideration. Does it read *echomen* (we have peace with God), or *echōmen* (let us have peace with God)? If we choose the former, then there is a clear carryover from the former dialogue. If we choose the latter, it might suggest a clear break with the past. According to Bruce M. Metzger (*A Textual Commentary on the Greek New Testament* [New York: United Bible Societies, 1971], 511), the latter has better external textual support, but scholars prefer the former reading for internal reasons.

31. Moo, *Romans,* 294.

32. Dahl, *Studies in Paul,* 82–91. Dahl maintains that the problems raised in chaps. 6–7 are not directly related to the main positive argument raised in chaps. 5 and 8. These intervening chapters are not to be placed in a rigid logical structure, but viewed as an "excursus." Fitzmyer (*Romans,* 96–98) says 5:12-21 appears as an isolated unit but is related to chapters 6–7.

33. Paul J. Achtemeier, *Romans,* IBC (Atlanta: John Knox, 1985), 89–90. Achtemeier views 4:23–5:11 as a unit, with the themes in 4:23-25 (righteousness in 4:23-24, Christ's death for sins, 4:25a, and Christ's resurrection, 4:25b) as the themes for 5:1-5, 6-8, and 9-11, respectively.

have to depend on markers such as the strength of inferentials.)[34] The stronger connectives are found in 5:12 (*dia touto*) and 5:18 (*ara oun*). These serve to conclude the entire declarative discourse of 3:9b–5:19.[35] The true transition to a new section is found in 5:20-21, the themes of which are taken up in the questions of 6:1, 15, and 7:7, 13.[36]

Second, as for the shift of tone from polemical to confessional and from theological to ethical, it simply does not reflect what is happening. First, it assumes that all the questions are devoted to being polemical. It overlooks their function of guiding the discourse of the letter. I have surveyed above various views of commentators identifying some passages as polemical and others as confessional, and they are not all in agreement. If you hold that chapters 6 and 7 are polemical, that would negate the whole of chapters 5–8 as being confessional. Rather than isolating the supposed polemical from the confessional, should we not be asking how they complement each other and together contribute to the flow of the letter? Instead of alternating from one audience to another—from Jew to gentile to Jew to gentile—should we not be asking how the entire discourse is directed to all believers in Rome?[37] Moreover, to suppose that 5:1-11 or 5:12-19 is any less theological than 3:21-26 is mistaken. Just because Paul uses the pronoun "we" in 5:1-11 does not diminish its theological tone. Actually, chapter 5 is as carefully constructed theological discourse as is 3:21-26. In 5:1-11, Paul is not talking about an ethical peace of mind, but rather a "state" of being at peace with God, reconciled to God by the death of his Son.[38] In 5:12-19, Paul is not

34. It should be noted that 12:1 begins with the inferential *oun*. Romans 12:1 represents a major break in the letter. One might have expected Paul to use a stronger inferential such as *dio* or *ara oun*. Perhaps the reason for his selection lies in the fact that the doxology in 11:33-36 ends the prior section with such finality that the use of a stronger inferential was not necessary.

35. I should add that Paul's use of strong inferentials leading up to 5:1 are found in 4:16 (*dia touto*) and 4:22 (*dio*). These must also be taken into account in considering the entire flow of thought in chaps. 4–5. All of this is enlarged above on p. 46n34, relating to Paul's use of grammar.

36. According to Dunn (*Romans 1–8*, 242–44), 5:12-21 is cosmic in scope and spans human history, and contains the whole course of the argument of 1:16–5:11, from the rule of sin in 1:18–3:20, to the rule of grace and justification by faith in 3:21–5:11. The prominence of the *dikaioō* language in 5:15-19 is also a fitting summary for the prior chapters. Then 5:20-21 provides a "springboard" for what follows.

37. See my discussion of the audience of the letter in chap. 1.

38. The concept of "reconciliation" suggests "estrangement," parties being reconciled who were

making an ethical distinction between Adam and Christ, but is contrasting two positions—that which has resulted through Adam and ends in condemnation and death, and that which comes through Christ and results in justification of life. If you want to see a shift from the theological to the ethical, you could argue that shift really takes place in 6:1-14, which begins with the question, "What then shall we say? Are we to continue in sin that grace might increase?" Then the passage continues to state how our position in Christ enables us to walk in newness of life. That is where the so-called ethical may begin—in Romans 6!

Third, regarding a shift in the form of address from rhetorical to personal, there is clearly an increase in the use of personal pronouns in chapters 5–8. According to my count, personal pronouns in the first- and second-person singular and plural occur sixteen times in 1:18–4:22, and fifty-three times in 4:23–8:39. This count does not include the nineteen times "I" or "me" is used in chapter 7, a particular use that many would view as "literary," not "personal," though it certainly is applied personally. So the fact that Paul uses a form of address in a literary or rhetorical way is not to be denied. However, are we to assume that the "you's" and "we's" in chapters 1–4 are entirely "literary" devices, devoid of any relation of Paul to his audience, totally impersonal and editorial? If so, then truly 1:18–4:25 is set apart as a doctrinal thesis. But I doubt recent commentators would fully agree to this. When Paul says, *ti eroumen* ("What shall we say"), are we to suppose that his use of this expression in 3:5 and 4:1 is literary and therefore impersonal, whereas his use of the same expression in 6:1,

formerly enemies or hostile toward one another. In Paul's writings, "reconciliation" is contrasted many times with "enmity" and "alienation" (Rom. 5:10; Eph. 2:12-16, 19; Col. 1:21). Positively, it is associated with "peace" and speaks of "access" to God (Rom. 5:1-2, 10; Eph. 2:14-18; Col. 1:20). In all these passages (including 2 Cor. 5:17-21), God is the subject and humanity is the object. Reconciliation is based not in the subjective change that takes place in the hostile minds of humans, but in the death of Christ. "He [Christ] has now reconciled you in his fleshly body through death" (Col. 1:22); he "made peace through the blood of the cross" (Col. 1:20); "we were reconciled to God through the death of his Son" (Rom. 5:10). Accordingly, George Eldon Ladd (*A Theology of the New Testament* [Grand Rapids: Eerdmans, 1993], 493–94) writes: "Reconciliation is not primarily a change in humanity's attitude toward God; it is, like justification, an objective event that is accomplished by God for humanity's salvation." Romans 5:1-11 is not referring to the peace of heart and mind that results from being reconciled to God, but to the state of being at peace with God. The passage (5:1-11) is profoundly theological.

7:1, and 8:31 is relational? When Paul says "but we know" in 2:2 and 3:19, is this expression any less relational than when used in 7:14 and 8:22? It is unclear how one can declare that all personal pronouns in chapters 1-4 are only editorial or literary. We may disagree on how personal his use of these pronouns is, but one could easily argue that they are not as impersonal as some suppose. We should also note that while 5:1-11 uses the first-person plural quite often, 5:12-21 shifts back to the third-person singular and is reminiscent of chapters 1-4. Aside from 4:23-5:11, the pronouns in chapters 5-8 are found primarily in chapter 6 and 8:18-39.

Fourth, as for the shift in the frequency of words in chapter 5, one can easily demonstrate that there are just as many words continued from chapters 1-4 as there are new ones leading into chapters 6-8. Consider, for example, the words "justification," "faith," "wrath," "sin," "death," "boasting," "grace," "glory," "in his blood," "ungodly," "now," and so on. Even the words of grace and glory find prior mention in chapters 1-4. James Dunn states that "the backward links are too many and deliberate."[39] As for the introduction of new words, that occurs in virtually every paragraph in Romans! One can gain a sense of this from the very opening chapters, where Paul deliberately introduces one concept after another, in successive paragraphs in planned sequence. One should not say, as did William Sanday and Arthur Headlam,[40] that one section of Romans is more "primary" than another, since any part depends on the whole of the parts, in sequence one after the other. There is always a shift in the frequency of certain words, depending on the content of the section of the letter. That is to be expected. You can prove all kinds of things by counting words. Douglas Moo himself notes statistics are easily abused.[41] But the reason why counting words proves so little is that Paul constantly introduces new lines of thought in which he uses new or repeated terms to further his ideas. Word chains begin, continue, or stop constantly in Romans.[42]

---

39. Dunn, *Romans 1-8*, 242.
40. William Sanday and Arthur C. Headlam, *The Epistle to the Romans* (New York: Charles Scribner's Sons, 1897), xliv-xlv.
41. Moo, *Romans*, 292.

The reoccurrence of the phrase "through/in our Lord Jesus Christ" in 5:1, 11, 21; 6:23; 7:25; and 8:39 is important, but not for determining the role of chapter 5. The phrase begins to occur precisely where it does in chapter 5 due to the content preceding chapter 5. Paul begins his letter by arguing that those under the law will be judged *"through* the law" (2:12) and that *"through* the law" comes the knowledge of sin (3:20).[43] However, *"apart from* the law" there is a righteousness of God, which is *"through* faith in Christ Jesus" to all who believe (3:21-22), being justified freely by his grace[44] *"through* the redemption which is in Christ Jesus . . . *through* faith in his blood" (3:24-25). Then 3:27–4:25 serves to clarify from Old Testament Scripture the truth that there is no room for boasting since the promise of God comes "not *through* law . . . but *through* the righteousness of faith" (4:13). All this precedes and leads up to 5:1-11, which is framed by the phrase italicized in the following:

> 5:1-2: Therefore, being justified by faith, we have peace with God *through our Lord Jesus Christ, through whom* . . .
> and we boast in hope of the glory of God.
> 5:11: We boast in God *through our Lord Jesus Christ, through whom* we have now received the reconciliation [i.e., peace with God].[45]

---

42. Concerning word chains beginning in chap. 5, James Dunn (*Romans 1–8*, 244) makes the point: "It is primarily because chaps. 6–8 have the function of working out the conclusions drawn in chap. 5 that we find so many thematic and verbal links between them, particularly in the twin themes of sin and grace, and death and life. But this is simply to recognize once again that Paul makes it his regular practice in Romans to set out his conclusions in such a way as to lead into the next stage of the discussion." According to Bruce Norman Kaye (*The Thought Structure of Romans with Special Reference to Chapter 6* [Austin: Schola Press, 1979], 7 and nn25–30), "The mere listing of words used in Rom 5 does not necessarily indicate anything, but there are certain patterns of usage of words in relation to Rom 5, as compared with the rest of the letter, which are interesting." He then documents words used only in chap. 5 (16), those used for the first time in chap. 5 (7), those that begin significant use in chap. 5 (8), those dropped after chap. 5 (4), those used later in the letter but not in chaps. 6–8 (5), and he adds that there are a number of words that appear before, during, and after chap. 5.

43. I am pursuing the use of the instrumental phrase *dia* genitive.

44. "By His grace" is an instrumental dative.

45. As indicated above (n26), Longenecker views the use of the phrase in 5:1 and 8:39 as an *inclusio*. In light of the obvious chiastic structure of 5:1-11 and the parallelism of 5:1 and 11, if there is any *inclusio*, it is here in 5:1 and 11. Regarding its chiastic structure (5:1-5 [A], 6-8 [B], 9-11 [A]), note the repetition of *dikaiōthentes* in 1 and 9; *kauchasthai* in 2, 3, and 11; the *ou monon de, alla kai* in 3 and 11; and the terms for reconciliation in 1-2 and 9-11 (peace, access, wrath, enemies, reconcile, reconciliation). In 5:6-8, note the repetition of the *hyper* phrases and the verb 'to die.' Romans 5:1-11 is carefully constructed rhetoric. Achtemeier (*Romans*, 89–90) concurs.

Moreover, 5:9-10 includes these phrases "*in* his blood . . . *through* him . . . *through* the death of his son . . . *in* his life." The progression of thought leading up to 5:1-11 as well as the content of 5:1-11 prompts the placing of this phrase in 5:1 and 11. The same can be said for 5:12-19, which uses the phrase "*through*" nine times, contrasting what happened "*through* the disobedience of the one" with "*through* the obedience of the one." The same can be said in chapter 6, which declares that we have been united with Christ in his death, burial, and resurrection and therefore are alive "*in* Christ Jesus" (6:11), hence the final verse that ends with "the gift of God is eternal life *in* Jesus Christ our Lord" (6:23). Again, the same can be said in chapter 7. The initial illustration conveys the idea that "*through* the body of Christ" you died to the law (7:4). Then Paul proceeds to convey what happens "*through* the law . . . *through* the commandment . . . *through* the good" (7:5, 7, 8, 11 [×2], 13 [×2]). Then comes the doxology, thanking God "*through* Jesus Christ" (7:25). The phrase "through/in our Lord Jesus Christ" does reoccur in chapters 5-8. However, its placement is elicited by Paul's progression of thought and not simply for the purpose of separating chapters 5-8 from 1-4.[46] Thus it is quite clear that by chapter 5, this has become a phrase pregnant with meaning due to the preceding chapters. This little tangent in my study reminds us that Paul is carefully developing his letter in a way that guides his listeners to understand the gospel and its application to their lives. It also reminds us of the significance of word chains in Romans.

Fifth is the view that the themes of Romans 5 and 8 form an *inclusio*. Nevertheless, the same themes of hope, glory, Spirit, and endurance in the face of persecution found in 5 and 8 are also found in 15:1-13, while the themes of glory, salvation, and God's love and mercy are found in 11:25-36.[47] So a case for *conclusio* can be made as well. In fact, if

---

46. Interestingly, Paul does not seem to use this formula elsewhere in the Pauline corpus to conclude a paragraph or section (cf. 1 Cor. 15:57; 1 Thess. 5:9; Titus 3:6), only here in Romans. This would seem to indicate that Paul's use of the phrase in Romans is intentional in its placement.

47. Terms that occur in 5:1-11 that also occur at the end of chaps. 8, 11, or 15:1-13: *elpizō/elpis*—5:2, 4, 5; 8:20, 24, 25; 15:4, 12, 13 (×2); *doxa*—5:2; 8:18, 21; 11:36; 15:7; 16:27; *pneuma*—5:5; 8:14, 15, 26, 27; 15:13; *sōzō/sōtēria*—5:9, 10; 8:24; 9:27; 10:1, 9, 10, 13; 11:11, 14, 26; *hypomonē*—5:3, 4; 8:25; 15:4, 5; *agapē* (of God/Christ)—5:5, 8; 8:35, 37, 39.

one considers 5:12-19; 8:31-39; 11:25-36; and 15:7-13 as concluding their respective sections, each one ends rather persuasively and with some finality.[48]

- 5:12-19, with its series of antithetical parallel statements highlighting a God of grace who has made 'the many' righteous through the obedience of Christ Jesus;

- 8:31-39, with its series of seven rhetorical questions highlighting a God of love who preserves His own;

- 11:33-36, with its doxology to a God who shows mercy to both Jew and gentile;

- 15:9-13, with its catena of OT scriptures of gentiles glorifying God along with Israel, concluding with a benediction from the God of hope.

As for the chiasm that Moo finds in chapters 5–8, a similar claim could be made for a chiasm in chapters 1–5.

> A. 1:18–3:20: All are under sin (indictment of Adamic humanity in 1:19–32)
> B. 3:21-26: All are justified by faith
> C. 3:27–4:25: All are children of Abraham (*paradeigma* of Abraham)
> B. 5:1-11: All who are justified by faith are also reconciled
> A. 5:12-21: All are either in Adam or in Christ

There is a difference of opinion whether the Adam motif is found in 1:18-23[49] Longenecker finds the Adam motif only in 5:12-19 and 7:7-13.[50] But the Adam motif does appear to be behind Paul's use of terminology from the creation narrative in Romans 1:18-23. Dunn calls it "the obviously deliberate echo of the Adam narratives."[51] It is more of

---

48. Also, 5:12-19 ends with a very clear transition (5:20-21) into the questions in chap. 6; and 8:31-39; 11:33-36; and 15:9-13 all end quite clearly their respective sections.

49. Pro: Dunn, *Romans 1-8*, 53; Morna D. Hooker, "Adam in Romans 1," *NTS* 6 (1960): 297–306; A. J. M. Wedderburn, "Adam in Paul's Letter to the Romans," in *Studia Biblica 1978, III: Papers on Paul and Other New Testament Authors*, ed. Elizabeth A. Livingstone, JSNTSup 3 (Sheffield: JSOT Press, 1980), 413–30.

50. Longenecker, *Introducing Romans*, 369.

51. Dunn, *Romans 1-8*, 53.

a stretch to see it behind Paul's reference to "coveting" in 7:7, though that may also be the case.

We arrive, then, at the conclusion that the arguments in favor of joining chapter 5 with chapters 6–8 are not all that formidable. In regard to the surface structure of the letter, it is better to view 3:9b–5:21 as a unit with 5:20-21 transitioning into the questions that follow in 6:1–8:17. This is not to discount the research of Bruce Kaye, who views Romans 5 as a "bridge" between chapters 1-4 and 6-8. He argues that much of the vocabulary, grammar, and argumentation in chapter 5 serves to transition into chapters 6–8.[52] He is correct in his findings. But this may be said about many paragraphs throughout Romans, that they demonstrate continuity both with what precedes and with what follows. Of course, Romans 5 does that on a broader scale. It definitely serves to conclude what precedes while transitioning to what follows.

The Role of Diatribe

Another important issue to resolve has to do with the extent to which Paul employed the style of diatribe in Romans. The tendency has been for commentators to assume Paul employed both the form and function of Hellenistic diatribe when writing Romans. Whether he used a diatribal style at times is not an issue. He did. But to what degree does his style conform to its use in Hellenism? How much did diatribe as it was used in philosophical circles of that day influence Paul and the way he used it in the letter? That is the issue, and it involves further questions. Are the primary features of Paul's dialogue (1) address to an imaginary interlocutor and (2) objections from that interlocutor? Does Paul periodically pause to address an imaginary interlocutor in an indicting tone? Is the body of the letter (chaps. 1–11) structured around objections and false conclusions from such interlocutors? Is 3:1-9 meant to be understood as a response to a Jewish interlocutor who is objecting to propositions just made in 2:17-29? Is Paul relating

---

52. Kaye, *Romans 6*, 7–13, and notes on 150–51. It would be well worth one's time to look carefully at his research.

to his readers in Rome as a "philosopher or religious-ethical teacher" would to his students, seeking to transform them through an "indictment-protreptic" process of teaching? These are questions that come in response to the research of Stanley Stowers, who would answer all of them in the affirmative. It is his influential thesis on diatribe that is informing current interpretations and to which I am responding.[53] Not all interpreters agree with all of Stowers's views; but to the degree that I disagree with them, to that extent I raise the question of Paul's dependence on Hellenistic diatribe.

Terence Y. Mullins offers this principle of how to go about analyzing New Testament forms in the context of Paul's letters:

> The way to go about analyzing the NT forms is first to establish the fact that certain forms which were in common use around the first century appear in the NT. Then you analyze points of agreement and disagreement between the common use and the NT use. Where the forms have a distinctive shape in the NT, you seek to determine how the instinctive shape came about. And finally you seek the interpretive significance of the form, following the common significance as far as possible, but taking into account the meaning of the changes which produced a distinctive shape in NT use.[54]

This I will attempt to do.

It is interesting to note that two dissertations inform one's approach to the subject. The first is the dissertation of Rudolf Bultmann published in 1910.[55] His thesis was that Paul's style of writing Romans reflected his diatribe-like style of preaching in synagogues or the marketplace, especially when confronted by objectors. It was marked by a lively dialogue in which an unidentified interlocutor interrupts Paul's line of thought, usually with an objection in the form of a question, to which the speaker responds either with a rejection or

53. Stanley K. Stowers, *The Diatribe and Paul's Letter to the Romans*, SBLDS 57 (Chico, CA: Scholars Press, 1981).

54. Terence Y. Mullins, "Formulas in New Testament Epistles," *JBL* 91 (1972): 380–90 (here 390).

55. Rudolf Bultmann, *Der Stil der paulinischen Predigt und die kynischstoische Diatribe* (Göttingen: Vandenhoeck & Ruprecht, 1910). This was his doctoral thesis, and it became the standard work for decades. It was never translated but has been described by numerous scholars. Stowers (*Diatribe*) provides a careful analysis of Bultmann's views on diatribe on pages 17–26 as well as throughout his book. Karl P. Donfried ("False Presuppositions in the Study of Romans," in Donfried, *Romans Debate*, 112–19) offers a critique of Bultmann's thesis.

by countering with another question. From this understanding, then, it was natural for commentators to view the questions as hostile in nature, raised by Jews who were offended by what Paul was saying (or in this case, writing). Paul was stating their objections in his own words and then rejecting them in order to advance his own line of thought. It was understood that the questions raised particularly in Romans 2–4 and 9–11 came from or were directed toward Jewish opponents of his gospel.

The second dissertation is that of Stanley Stowers, published in 1981. Stowers sought to reconsider the role of diatribe in Paul. In his dissertation, Stowers describes the formal characteristics of diatribe as found in writers such as Seneca, Epictetus, and Plutarch. They include a sudden turning in the narrative to address a fictitious interlocutor in the vocative, this in response to a preceding objection and/or false conclusion by the interlocutor, often accompanied by a series of rhetorical questions or statements in didactic or indicting tone, and replies to the interlocutor suggesting a lack of perception on his part ("Are you ignorant . . ." or "Do you not see . . ."). Stowers allows that there are variations of the theme, but these are some of the formal characteristics that occur over and over again.[56] Hence, one can speak of diatribe as a "rhetorical genre."[57] The model is that of a classroom in which a teacher would employ

> the "Socratic" method of censure and protreptic. The goal of this part of the instruction was not simply to impart knowledge, but to transform the students, to point out error and to cure it. Our review of the sources suggests that the dialogical element of the diatribe was an important part of this pedagogical approach. The two major categories of dialogical features are address to the interlocutor and objections from the interlocutor.[58]

56. Stowers, *Diatribe*, 85–93.
57. Ibid., 76.
58. Ibid., 76–77 (emphasis original). Stowers expands his analysis of Hellenistic diatribe at some length. At one point (140), he notes that in diatribe, there were two levels of intent of the author, one speaking to his real audience and the other speaking to a fictitious person. He says there was a unique ambiguity of this double focus, in that you had one speaker with two sets of addressees, one real and one fictional. The author slips back and forth between these two audiences, and the real audience is caught up in this simulated dialogue, this question-and-answer with its indictment-protreptic process. First they identify with the indictment and then align with the

Stowers then turns his attention to Romans.[59] First, he identifies certain texts as addressing an imaginary interlocutor (2:1-5, 17-24; 9:19-21; 11:17-24; 14:4, 10). In these texts, Paul stops addressing the actual recipients of the letter and abruptly directs his comments to a fictitious person in a brisk and censorious tone. As Stowers describes these texts, they include indicting statements, rhetorical questions, supporting quotations, with anticipated objections and consequent warnings. Paul uses terms such as "O man . . . do you know . . . do you think, etc."[60] His use of apostrophe (the interruption of discourse to address a person) is especially analogous to the pedagogy used in philosophical schools where the instructor would interrupt his discourse to address an imaginary interlocutor whose behavior was pretentious and arrogant and needed to be censured. According to Stowers, Paul uses the same pedagogy in 2:1-5 where he censures a pretentious or arrogant gentile (or all men), in 2:19-24 the pretentious Jew, in 11:17-24 the pretentious or arrogant gentile Christian, and in 14:10, 14, the pretentious Christian.[61] However, these imaginary interlocutors are not opponents whom Paul is censuring, but students or "fellow discussion partners." The discourse is not polemic, but indictment for the purpose of leading to truth.

Second, Stowers identifies certain texts as having objections and false conclusions (3:1-9; 3:31; 4:1-2; 6:1-3, 15-16; 7:7, 13-14; 9:14-15, 19-20; 11:1-3, 11, 19-20).[62] Either an interlocutor is objecting to something Paul has said, or he is reaching a false conclusion. Commentators frequently interpret the objections as a polemic against Jews or Judaizing opponents. But according to Stowers, the objections are not directed toward Jews as opponents, but toward Christians as

---

protreptic. This is how diatribe brings about transformation. And this, he suggests, is what we see happening in Romans where Paul addresses an imaginary interlocutor.

59. My discussion of the role of diatribe is focused on Stowers's research because it has become the immediate source of much of our understanding of Hellenistic diatribe. Commentators use Stowers as their primary reference. For example, Robert Jewett, *Romans*, Hermeneia (Minneapolis: Fortress Press, 2007), 25, 240; Brendan Byrne, SJ, *Romans*, SP (Collegeville, MN: Liturgical Press, 1996), 108; Fitzmyer, *Romans*, 91, 325.

60. Stowers, *Diatribe*, 79–118.

61. Ibid., 116–17; cf. 79–81.

62. Ibid., 119–54.

disciples; and rather than being an occasion of hostility, it is a time of learning. Paul is not being argumentative, but persuasive.[63] Stowers explains that the formal features of objections and false conclusions in Hellenistic diatribe include the following: They are introduced by short exclamations (e.g., *ti oun, ti de*), by connectives such as *oun* and *alla*, and introductory formulas such as words of saying (*phēsi, legeis*, and *ereis*). False conclusions are predominantly questions, and statements are usually objections. Reactions to objections and false conclusions can be abrupt and indicting; Epictetus often uses *mē genoito*. Rejections may be supported by examples, analogies, and quotations.[64] Also, the imaginary interlocutor is pictured as colorless and without identity in these sources. Likewise in Romans, Paul uses similar introductory formulas (*to oun, ei de, oun*) as well as the negative *mē genoito*; and he supports his diatribe with examples, analogies, and quotations from Scripture.[65]

Stowers concludes: "The similarities between Paul and the diatribe in the forms associated with objections and false conclusions are rather striking. This is especially true when Paul and Epictetus are compared, since not only the general forms or the same categories of elements are present, but many times even the exact expressions." Then he adds this qualifier: "The differences between Romans and the diatribe in this area are also striking, but not unexpected in view of Paul's vastly different background. There is no question of clumsy combination of unrelated styles and traditions, but rather there is an assimilation of diatribal forms into the apostle's exposition and exegesis."[66] Stowers also qualifies his thesis by admitting that each author has his own

---

63. Achtemeier (*Romans*, 75) summarizes this position well: "If the reality underlying the diatribal form was not so much confrontation as education, then Paul was using it in his letter to the churches in Rome to further the knowledge of Christians who already shared Paul's major presuppositions, rather than to confute those who opposed them. Paul thus includes the kind of questions he does, as for example in 3:1-8, not so much to show the way he meets hostile objections as to answer the kinds of questions his experience as a missionary has taught him people tend to raise who want a better understanding of their faith. That of course fits in precisely with what Paul says about the reason for this letter as well as for the long-desired visit he would now at last be able to undertake (see 1:11-12)."
64. Stowers, *Diatribe*, 125-32.
65. Ibid., 133-37.
66. Ibid., 137.

peculiar pattern of formal usage, and notes what we would all affirm, that we need to do justice to that diversity. The peculiarities of individual authors should not be ignored.[67]

Paul is clearly familiar with this form of question-and-answer. It was a useful tool for teaching stretching back at least to the time of Plato, who wrote the dialogues of Socrates. The question is, how was Paul using this style? That has to be determined from the text itself. We should not automatically say, this is how it was used by Epictetus and therefore this is how it is used by Paul. (By the way, we should remind ourselves that Epictetus, ca. 55–135 CE, was only a little child when Paul wrote Romans in ca. 57–58).

Variance of Form

What one finds interesting in Stowers's research are some of the examples of variance with Hellenistic diatribe. Paul's frequent use of *ti oun eroumen* to introduce false conclusions appears to be unique to Paul, as is his frequent use of the first-person plural when stating an objection.[68] This inclusive style of using the first-person plural is interesting because it appears to be excluding a personal conversation with an external interlocutor. In 2:1-5, you have the first example of apostrophe with Paul addressing an imaginary interlocutor. Yet Stowers notes three features not found in the diatribe: addressing the fictional person using the adjective *pas* in an attempt to include both Jews and gentiles (again an inclusive term);[69] using an articular participle to specify further the interlocutor (making him less "colorless"); and using the first-person plural *oidamen* (inclusive first-

---

67. Ibid., 125. R. Dean Anderson Jr. (*Ancient Rhetorical Theory and Paul* [Leuven: Peeters, 1999], 243) argues that there is no real consensus in defining the precise contours of *diatribe* as used in various philosophical writings of antiquity. He notes that "the style of individual authors concerned does indeed vary, and this is only to be expected. It is of course true that these popular philosophers have much in common, but the wisdom of using such a term as *diatribe* to describe what is common in their style is questionable."

68. Stowers, *Diatribe*, 133–34. *Ti gar* in 3:3 is also peculiar to Paul. What is not found in Paul but is frequently found in sources is an objection with a formula of saying that begins with the connective *alla*.

69. When *pas* is followed with an articular participle as occurs in Rom. 2:1, *pas ho krinōn*, it is translated "everyone" who judges.

person pl.)[70] Consequently, one does not have to posit an imaginary interlocutor for that passage to make sense. Paul speaks generally of "every man who passes judgment," and returns in 14:4 and 10 to address in the same manner the strong and the weak. As Paul Minear points out, "The behavior which Paul singles out for special attention is that of judging and condemning others. The key word is *krinō* which appears ten times here (2:1, 3, 12, 16, 27; 3:4, 6, 7). It appears nowhere else in Romans except in ch. 14 (vv. 3, 4, 5, 10, 13, 22)."[71] Is all of this being addressed to a fictional character, or is this protreptic discourse and part of Paul's exhortation to those in Rome? Does one have to posit an imaginary interlocutor for the references in 14:4, 10, to make sense?

Moreover, what Stowers refers to as an imaginary interlocutor in chapters 9–11 is not all that imaginary. For example, in both 9:19 and 11:19, Paul uses the second-person singular *ereis* ("you will say") to quote a supposed imaginary interlocutor in his own words. Not only is this exact expression (*ereis*) not found in Hellenistic sources of diatribe, but also Paul in using this expression identifies them both. In 9:19-24, he identifies him as "O man, who answers back to God," and then becomes more specific with the pronoun *hēmōn* ("us"), including both Jew and gentile believers. In 11:19, Paul identifies the interlocutor by using the analogy of the wild olive tree and speaking directly to the gentiles.[72] These are not minor variations. They may both be viewed as protreptic discourse, direct exhortations to believers. Paul has his own distinctive style, and the question is still open as to what degree Paul has assimilated diatribal forms. Could it be that Paul was simply dependent on rhetoric that was common in his day, the use of questions to engage his audience? The variations in form oblige us to raise this question.

Returning to 3:1-9, Stowers argues that this cluster of questions and answers has all the characteristics of diatribe—an imaginary Jewish

---

70. Ibid., 93–94. Notably, articular participles are also found in the apostrophe of 2:21-2.
71. Paul S. Minear, *The Obedience of Faith: The Purposes of Paul in the Epistle to the Romans*, SBT 2/19 (London SCM, 1971), 46.
72. These observations come from Stowers's own analysis in *Diatribe*, 125–37.

interlocutor in dialogue with Paul, raising objections that are then countered by strong rejections including the negative *mē genoito*.[73]

3:1: Objection in form of questions implying a false conclusion from what precedes
3:2: Response to the objection
3:3: Objection in form of question combined with false conclusion
3:4: Rejection, and reason for rejection
3:5: Objection in form of question combined with a false conclusion
3:6: Rejection, and reason for rejection
3:7: Objection in form of question
3:8: Objection in form of question combined with false conclusion
3:8: Reply in form of ad hominem retort
3:9: False conclusion repeated from 3:1
3:9: Rejection, and reason for rejection

Stowers interprets the objections and rejections in this way: the first objection is raised by the Jewish interlocutor with Paul giving the response in 3:2. But then, from 3:3 on, Paul is raising the objections with the interlocutor responding in 3:4 and 6. Then in 3:9a, the interlocutor asks the final question, "What then? Are we Jews at a disadvantage?"[74] In this approach, the imaginary Jewish interlocutor not only raises the initial objection in 3:1 but is also credited with responding with strong rejections including the use of the Old Testament quotation in 3:4b (a bit unusual). The questions in 3:3, 5, 7, and 8 are not objections by the interlocutor but Paul's own probing questions meant to lead the dialogue partner to the proper answer. Commentators may not agree as to who is saying what, but they still hold to this diatribal exchange. They argue over whether certain objections and/or responses are words of the Jewish opponent or of Paul. Could the answer simply be that Paul is writing his own thoughts down in dialogical style?

Again, there is a variance of forms in 3:1-9. The presence of *ti gar*

---

73. Ibid., 119–53, esp. 119–20 and 134–37. Käsemann (*Romans*, 78) holds that there are only two Jewish objections: the first is whether the advantage of Jews in salvation history has been canceled by Paul's discourse in 2:17-29 (3:1-4); the second is whether Paul's doctrine of justification pushes one into libertinism (3:5-8). Some commentators follow his lead.

74. Stanley K. Stowers, "Paul's Dialogue with a Fellow Jew in Romans 3:1–9," *CBQ* 46 (1984): 707–22 (here 715).

in 3:3 and the use of the first-person plural when stating objections (3:5, 7-8) are unique to Paul, as has already been noted. But the use of the first-person plural, for example, in the formula *ti eroumen*, "what shall we say?" in 3:5, is clearly not introducing an external objection by an imaginary interlocutor, but an internal debate. David Hall notes that it need not be introducing an objection at all, but rather asking the question, "What conclusion shall we draw from the preceding argument"?[75] Elsewhere in the letter, the same formula serves to introduce new sections that arise naturally from the flow of preceding argumentation (4:1; 6:1; 7:7; 8:31; 9:14; 9:30). Why is that not the case here? Also in 3:5b, the rhetorical question, "Is God unjust . . ." is questionable as an objection since it is introduced by the negative *mē*, expecting a negative answer. As Cranfield observes, "If it were intended as an objector's question, it would of course have been introduced by *ouk*, 'Is God not unjust?'"[76] Frédéric Louis Godet states, "It is certainly the apostle who is speaking and not an opponent."[77] Not only may the question in 3:5 be attributed to Paul, but also in 3:3. Cranfield asks how much of 3:3 should be attributed to an imaginary objector. His answer: "It seems best to take the whole verse as Paul's own thought; for, while it seems to carry on quite naturally the thought of v.2, neither the verse as a whole nor the first part of it by itself seems particularly natural at this point as an objection."[78] Furthermore, the questions in 3:7-8 are probably to be attributed to Paul. As Hall has observed, the parenthetical statement "'as we are falsely accused of saying,' in which 'we' refers to 'Paul and his colleagues,' comes very awkwardly in the middle of a sentence attributed to an objector."[79] All the questions in 3:3-8, therefore, could

75. David R. Hall, "Romans 3:1-8 Reconsidered," *NTS* 29 (1983): 183–97 (here 184). Robert H. Mounce (*Romans*, NAC [Nashville: Broadman & Holman, 1995], 103–4n153) appears to agree with Hall's position, that Paul is having an inner debate with himself and that there are questions about the diatribal interpretation of 3:1-9.

76. Cranfield, *Romans*, 1:184.

77. Frédéric Louis Godet, *Commentary on St. Paul's Epistle to the Romans*, trans. A. Cusin (Edinburgh: Funk & Wagnalls, 1883), 136.

78. Cranfield, *Romans*, 1:179–80.

79. Hall, "Romans 3:1-8 Reconsidered," 192. Hall also notes that while objections are stated in detail in 3:1-9, the rejections are brief, even dismissed on one occasion (3:7-8) without any argument in five words in 3:8b. His view is that this does not reflect Hellenistic diatribe.

be attributed to Paul rather than objections by a Jewish interlocutor.[80] If this is the case, then why do we have to view 3:1-9 as diatribe with objections raised by a Jewish interlocutor? Can we not view all the questions, including 3:1 and 9, as questions (!) that flow logically from preceding statements and raise issues that are pertinent to Roman believers?[81] Hall recalls the opinion of Godet: "It is obvious that the reasoning is consecutive, even very compact, and that there is no need of expressly introducing an opponent, as many commentators have done."[82] These formal differences are not minor; they question the need to posit an imaginary interlocutor with objections from that interlocutor. They question Stowers's statement that 3:1-9 has all the characteristics of diatribe. They clearly do not have "all" the characteristics. Rather, there may be as much, if not more, reason to view all of 3:1-9 as Paul's own questions and answers. And while there may be some affinities stylistically with philosophers, that does not mean Paul's use of that style of writing carries with it the same force it had when used by philosophers with their students.

Apart from questions of form, does interpreting 3:1-9 from the vantage point of diatribe really make sense? Here you have a dialogical exchange supposedly between Paul and an imaginary Jewish interlocutor about diverse matters—Jewish advantage, God's

---

80. This view contrasts with that of many who insist that Paul is having a dialogue with an imaginary Jew throughout 3:1-9. Romans 3:1-4 begins with a Jewish objector, and it is assumed that the dialogue continues with the same objector through to the end. Thus both 3:5-6 and 3:7-8 must be related to questions raised by a Jewish antagonist; and 3:9a, "Are we better than they?" must be interpreted as a question raised by a Jew. My view is that the content of 3:5-8 does not support that view. Paul speaks of "our unrighteousness" commending God's righteousness and asking "What shall we say?" (3:5); Jews were not known for admitting their own unrighteousness. He uses the inclusive "we" as being charged with antinomianism (3:7-8); Jews were never aligned with Paul on the charge of antinomianism.

81. Just as the question in 3:3 carries over the thought of 3:2, so also it is quite natural for the question in 3:1 to carry over the thought of 2:25-29. Moreover, I have already demonstrated above that the question-and-answer in 3:1-2 was intentionally raised by Paul in anticipation of the extended answer in chaps. 9–11. The same may be said of all the questions in 3:3-9a, that they carry over the thought of the preceding questions and that they intentionally anticipate the extended answers to come later in the letter.

82. Hall, "Romans 3:1-8 Reconsidered," 184, quoting from Godet, *Romans*, 131. C. K. Barrett (*A Commentary on the Epistle to the Romans* [London: Black, 1957], 61) leaves the matter open. He notes that the style of the paragraph is that of the diatribe, and behind the literary form there may be real debates. However, it is possible that to some extent it was Paul's own mind that formulated the objections, which he proceeds then to brush aside.

faithfulness, God's righteousness, God's judgments, Jewish disadvantage—limited to nine verses, very important questions being raised with very limited answers, all to be dismissed by an ensuing discourse. Which is more likely, that Paul all of a sudden reverts to a questionand-answer with an imaginary Jewish interlocutor, or that Paul is leading us through his own sequence of ideas as he anticipates discourse that follows in chapters 3–11? Which is more likely, that Paul is diverted by a concern that some Jews might object to what he has just stated, or that he is leading his readers up to the point where these questions could be raised? Actually, the brevity of the questions and answers as they stand serves only an immediate purpose from the diatribal perspective. By treating them as a brief diatribal exchange within the larger section of 1:18–3:20, the interpreter basically relegates them to relative insignificance. In fact, a number of commentators label 3:1-8 in their outlines with the caption "Objections."[83] F. F. Bruce labels it "Objections Answered";[84] Fitzmyer, "Objections to This Thesis about the Jews";[85] John Stott, "Some Jewish Objections";[86] Matthew Black, "The Alleged Advantage of Being a Jew";[87] Paul Jewett, an interlocutor attempting "to find apparent flaws in Paul's argument";[88] Sanday and Headlam views it as parenthetic and describes it as an "answer to casuistical objections from Jewish stand-point";[89] Stowers himself refers to it as a "dialogical flourish" and "Paul's Dialogue with a Fellow Jew."[90] In other words, the role of 3:1-8 is diminished; it is an aside from Paul's discourse. A Jewish teacher interrupts Paul's narrative, and it takes nine verses to get back on track. If this is all there is to the passage, perhaps C. H. Dodd has won the argument that the whole section is not worth much. The

83. E.g., Peter Stuhlmacher, *Paul's Letter to the Romans*, trans. Scott J. Hafemann (Louisville: Westminster: John Knox, 1994), 14; Käsemann, *Romans*, ix.
84. F. F. Bruce, *The Epistle to the Romans*, TNTC (Nottingham: Inter-Varsity Press, 1985), 67.
85. Fitzmyer, *Romans*, viii.
86. John R. W. Stott, *The Message of Romans* (Downers Grove, IL: InterVarsity Press, 1994), 94.
87. Black, *Romans*, 61.
88. Jewett, *Romans*, 26.
89. Sanday and Headlam, *Romans*, xlviii.
90. Stowers, *Diatribe*, 134; Stowers, *A Rereading of Romanss: Justice, Jews, and Gentiles* (New Haven: Yale University Press, 1994), 159.

alternative is to view the questions as leading questions that flow naturally from the discourse and are being used by Paul orally to guide the flow of thought. In the words of Douglas Moo, "Chapters in Romans develop according to the inner logic of Paul's own teaching. Even the questions and objections that periodically interrupt the argument arise naturally from the flow of Paul's presentation."[91]

Focus on Objections

In diatribe, "objections" play a major role. For Stowers, the entire body of the letter is structured around objections.[92] Objections occur at the beginning of major sections of argument (3:1; 6:1; 7:7; 9:14; 11:1), and objections introduce subsections as well (3:9; 6:15; 7:13; 9:19; 11:11). The latter objections are closely related to the objections that precede them (3:1 and 3:9; 6:1 and 6:15; 7:7 and 7:13; 9:14 and 9:19; 11:1 and 11:11).[93] Moreover, the dialogical progression of 3:1-9 moves without a break in the discourse, for it functions as an indictment of false inferences from 1:18-2:29 and serves as a program for what follows in chapters 3–11.[94] These observations could be viewed as supporting my surface structure of Romans. But there is a primary difference. Stowers views all the questions as "objections" that are reacting to basic propositions preceding them.[95] Objections "usually arise when the argument has reached a point where some important thesis, basic principle or claim is sharply stated and false inferences might logically be drawn."[96] In other words, *objections* govern the discourse. First comes the preceding

---

91. Moo, *Romans*, 14–15.
92. Stowers, *Diatribe*, 154: "As is often the case in the diatribe, the objection or false conclusion is an important part of the structure of the discourse. When Romans is outlined simply on the level of ideas, this natural flow of the argument, where elements such as objections and false conclusions are significant, is obscured. Exegesis of Romans must come to terms with the weight Paul places on these objections and false conclusions and their importance for the structure of the letter and manner of argument."
93. Stowers, *Diatribe*, 148.
94. Ibid., 149. While acknowledging that 3:1-9 serves as a program for what follows in chaps. 3–11, he says it does not help to say that Paul raises questions he will treat adequately in later chapters; he views them as a diversion that inadequately accounts for its place in the letter's argumentation. Cf. Stowers, *Rereading of Romans*, 160–61.
95. Stowers, *Diatribe*, 149. Romans 3:1 is reacting to 2:28-29; 6:1 to 5:20-21; 6:15 to 6:14; 7:7 to 7:5-6; and 7:13 to 7:12.
96. Ibid., 177.

proposition that arises from preceding argumentation; then comes the objection followed by a rejection and argumentation for rejection, which then sets up a new proposition followed by another objection and rejection. He argues that Paul intentionally employed the diatribal style throughout the body of the letter, that the structure is dependent on the objections raised, and that this sets Romans apart from all his other letters.[97]

This focus on objections governing the discourse has been adopted by many. Paul first affirms a proposition, and then follows with an objection in the form of a question. The reality is the opposite order. The questions come first, not as diatribal objections, but as leading questions that arise naturally from preceding narrative, questions that define the issues Paul wishes to address. Propositions and argumentation contribute to the narrative, but they are not what guides the narrative or the driving force behind the narrative. What drives the narrative are the underlying issues Paul is addressing, and what guides the narrative are the questions he raises. It is not that propositions give rise to the questions, but that they flow from the questions; the questions dictate the progression of themes and choice of rhetoric. Stated another way, the progression of thought in Romans is dependent on the questions that are raised, and those questions are focused on the needs of the recipients. If we want to know the circumstances to which Paul was writing, then look to the questions and the answers to those questions. If we are at all serious about the rhetorical and literary structure of Romans, we need to face the reality of the great number of questions raised throughout the letter and ask as to their purpose. We are caught up in the idea that their usefulness is limited to diatribal rhetoric that serves only to defend Paul's gospel against an imaginary Jewish objector. Quite the opposite is the case. The question-and-answer in Paul, rather than answering criticisms, is providing answers; rather than confronting an imaginary interlocutor,

---

97. Ibid. Stowers points out on p. 179 that objections and false conclusions occur fifteen times in Romans but elsewhere only in 1 Cor. 15:35 and Gal. 2:17 and 3:21. *Mē genoito* is used nine times in Romans but only twice elsewhere (Gal. 2:17 and 3:21) to reject false conclusions. Paul addresses an imaginary interlocutor elsewhere only in 1 Cor. 15:36.

113

the question-and-answer is informing and exhorting believers. In any interpretation of Romans, the interpreter should always remember three things: (1) that the letter is primarily directed to circumstances in Rome; (2) that the primary audience in Rome comprises gentile believers; and (3) that Paul's purpose and mission in life is to bring about their obedience of faith by faithfully proclaiming the gospel to them. The question-and-answer is directed toward that purpose.

One does not have to interpret all the questions as posing objections.[98] This creates an adverse situation in which Paul is pictured as arguing against his critics, using the "imaginary interlocutor" model. It does not help to say that the environment was not hostile but academic, that censure and indictments were meant for the purpose of reforming students.[99] Objections focus on opponents and create a tone of tension and argumentation, intended or not. Writing a letter that is governed by answering objections puts Paul on the defensive. Granted, there were probably some critics of Paul in Rome. But is it necessary to assume believers in Rome were all in the critical camp? Were all these questions for self-defense? There is good reason to assume that they were neither limited to, nor primarily committed to, self-defense. On the contrary, the tone of Romans is quite positive. From the outset of the letter, Paul is very careful to write in such a way that he will foster unity in the Christian community in Rome.[100] He addresses them as "beloved of God," "called to be saints," and recognizes that their strong standing in faith is known throughout the world (1:8; 15:14-15;

---

98. Campbell ("Romans III," 258) notes that Paul may be raising a question simply to further his argument or even take up positions held by Roman gentile believers. They frequently serve as headings in new sections of the letter.

99. The terminology used to explain diatribe is not very helpful. Even the term *diatribe* connotes in English a tirade or rant. The terms *censure* and *indictment* are likewise unhelpful. Paul is not trying to "censure" in the sense of blaming or rebuking his listeners. He is not "indicting" people by bringing a formal accusation or charging them with an offense or crime. See Achtemeier, *Romans*, 73–76.

100. Paul is writing an entire letter to those with whom he wants to establish a relationship. He is not trying to pick a fight with or defend himself from supposed Jewish objectors. He is not arguing simply because that is the makeup of his character. He is using protreptic and deliberative discourse for the purpose of exhorting and persuading his audience in Rome of their unity in Christ. He is exhorting them not to judge one another or to view oneself in a more favorable light. This is Paul's way of applying the gospel to Christians who are not fully unified in their relations one to another.

16:19). While he is forthright in stating he was called to be an apostle to the gentiles for their obedience of faith, he is careful to maintain a balance of writing to a Christian community that contains both Jews and gentiles. The gospel is the power of God to the Jew first and also to the Greek. All are under sin and all are of Abraham's seed. God's mercy extends to both Jews and gentiles, and gentiles are to praise God together with the Jews. Actually, the questions raised by Paul along with his answers reflect a Roman Christian community that possessed a rather sophisticated understanding of the gospel. They were not hearing the gospel for the first time. They understood its themes and nuances regarding God's justice and mercy, justification by faith and reconciliation with God, the role of the law of God, and so forth. We may assume they were acquainted with Paul's presentation of the gospel. What seems most likely is that there were both theological and cultural issues dividing the Christian community, and those divisions were occurring largely along ethnic lines.

Paul the Religious Teacher

According to Stowers, one must distinguish between the diatribal style of Romans and the more usual epistolary style. In an epistle, objections respond to real persons. In the diatribe, however, objections rise out of the subject matter.[101] In other words, objections grow out of prior argument within the text and therefore are not directed toward real people or any pressing issues in Rome. Paul's use of objections "does not serve the purpose of advice where a detailed knowledge of the specific situation of the audience comes into the discussion."[102] Rather, he is employing objections as a teacher would using diatribe, directing his speech "toward various types of students, would-be students, auditors and philosophers who characteristically make up his audience and for whom the style has been shaped."[103] Paul is using the style of

---

101. Stowers, *Diatribe*, 178-80. He quotes Günther Bornkamm as saying that the objections "always arise out of the subject, or more accurately out of a misunderstanding of the subject."
102. Ibid., 152.
103. Ibid., 152-53. His specific statement reads: "Rather, his [Paul's] use is didactic, or more specifically diatribal, where in using the methods of indictment and protreptic the teacher employs

indictment and protreptic to present himself to the Roman believers "not as a spiritual father and guide, but as a 'philosophical' or religious-ethical teacher. . . . Clearly the objections and false conclusions in Romans do not reflect the specific positions of the addressees of the letter."[104]

This approach is indeed problematic. First, show us in any of Paul's other letters where he presents himself as a philosophical or religious-ethical teacher. It was not Paul's nature to present himself as a philosopher or teacher detached from the people to whom he was writing. Moreover, one should seriously doubt that Paul was addressing the believers in Rome as teachers would to "various types of students, would-be students, auditors and philosophers." In Romans, he presents himself as a spiritual father and guide by explaining that he prays for them constantly and longs to see them so that he might impart some spiritual gift and obtain some fruit among them. That hardly sounds like a detached philosopher writing to would-be students. The effect of Stowers's approach is to keep Paul at a distance from what is actually happening in the life of the church in Rome and from having real dialogue with his audience. Paul is addressing an imaginary interlocutor rather than an actual audience; objections are framed by diatribe and do not reflect actual concerns in Rome. Neil Elliott says that it poses a "false dilemma between the rhetorical situation's absolute determinacy and the rhetor's absolute creative freedom."[105] Karl Donfried argues that it cannot be demonstrated that diatribe by its very nature cannot be directed toward pressing issues. "The use of such rhetorical patterns was so widespread that one cannot deny that Romans was addressed to a specific situation on the ground that it was influenced by such patterns."[106] For Paul to use the

objections directed toward the various types of students, would-be students, auditors and philosophers who characteristically make up his audience and for whom the style has been shaped. The way Paul writes to the Romans is determined not only or chiefly by the epistolary situation, but also by his previous experience as a teacher of Jews and Gentiles."

104. Ibid., 180.

105. Neil Elliott, *The Rhetoric of Romans: Argumentative Constraint and Strategy and Paul's Dialogue with Judaism*, JSNTSup 45 (Sheffield: JSOT Press, 1990), 127.

106. Donfried, "False Presuppositions," 104–21, esp. 118–19. Donfried reminds us of Minear's intense challenge of views supporting the influence of diatribe on Romans. Minear says Paul is not dealing

rhetorical genre of diatribe framing his response to critics through the means of an imaginary interlocutor (if indeed it can be proved that there was such a rhetorical genre) does not strike me as the way Paul operates. When Paul has something to say to someone, he will say it directly, as he did in his letters to Galatia and Corinth. He wears his thoughts on his sleeve.

By making Paul so dependent on the genre of diatribe that the questions he raises can only be understood as rising from prior argument and not related in any way to the people in Rome, Stowers is essentially treating Romans more as an essay or treatise than as a letter.[107] In prior chapters, I have labored to show by the presence of epistolary formulas and other factors that Romans is a letter. Longenecker writes that any reading must take into consideration that Romans was written to Christians in Rome as a letter.[108] The dialogue is genuine dialogue, written to real people. Romans is not an abstract treatise but a dialogue concerned with applying the gospel to the lives of real people. When Paul raises the question in 3:1, "What advantage has the Jew?" he is raising a question that speaks directly to the situation in Rome. When Paul asserts in 2:1-5 that there are those who judge "the other" (ton heteron), he is directing his exhortation to real people in Rome. While Paul's questions may be at times similar in form to diatribe, they are not locked into a closed genre of diatribe. They should be viewed as leading questions with a specific audience in mind.

In Conclusion

Regarding the above analysis, I am aware that my views of diatribe are outside the mainstream of interpretation. Most commentators agree that Paul is to some extent dependent on Hellenistic diatribe. I would agree that Paul appropriated the Socratic method of question-and-answer and adapted it to his own distinctive style and purposes; but

with some fictitious opponent; he is not setting up mere "straw men" for the sake of argument. He questions the idea of Paul being "face to face with a heckler, who makes interjections and receives replies which sometimes are withering and brusque" (ibid., 106–7).

107. Stowers, *Diatribe*, 181.
108. Longenecker, *Introducing Romans*, 204.

I would not agree that he was dependent on a genre of diatribe. I would not agree that Paul was borrowing the style of philosophers of his day and using it as philosophers would have used it with their students. My disagreement has to do with my perception of Paul and how he communicates by letter. Paul was not writing Romans from the perspective of a religious-ethical teacher delivering indictment-protreptic discourse in a classroom. Rather, Paul was writing as the apostle to the gentiles delivering exhortations in a way reminiscent of his other letters.

Thanks to Stowers, we now have a better picture of diatribe as it was used by philosophers of Paul's day. I have sought to interact with his views to understand the implications of interpreting the question-and-answer in Romans as Hellenistic diatribe. My view is that this approach has hampered studies of Romans. This focus on diatribe has diverted our attention from considering Paul's questions as questions to viewing them as objections being raised by imaginary interlocutors. It has led us to believe that Paul's primary concern was to answer objections rather than to care for the believers in Rome. It has fostered the idea that Paul is primarily engaged in defending himself by answering objections of Jewish opponents (esp. chaps. 1–4 and 9–11). Diatribe has been used to support the notion that Paul is not addressing specific issues in Rome. And it has hampered our approach to Paul by leading us to think that he is being overly argumentative in his discourse. If the diatribe were viewed simply as a form of question-and-answer rhetoric to get a point across, that would be relatively harmless. But when it becomes the centerpiece for objections and false conclusions voiced by an imaginary interlocutor, the nature of the dialogue changes.

At the beginning of my discussion, I raised these questions:

- Are the primary features of Paul's dialogue (1) address to an imaginary interlocutor and (2) objections from that interlocutor?

- Does Paul periodically pause to address an imaginary interlocutor in an indicting tone?

- Is the body of the letter (chaps. 1–11) structured around objections and false conclusions from such interlocutors?

- Is 3:1-9 meant to be understood as a response to a Jewish interlocutor who is objecting to propositions just made in 2:17-29?

- Is Paul relating to his readers in Rome as a "philosopher or religious-ethical teacher" would to his students, seeking to transform them through an "indictment-protreptic" process of teaching?

Stowers would answer all these questions in the affirmative. My response would be that the differences between Paul's style and diatribe are significant. Paul uses inclusive language so that questions may be viewed as internal dialogue with his audience rather than dialogue with an imaginary interlocutor. Paul uses questions to lead his readers and to define the issues he wishes to raise rather than framing them as objections to defend himself. The questions are not objections by an interlocutor, but questions guiding the discourse. In 3:1-9, we do not have to posit an imaginary interlocutor or a series of objections for the questions and answers to make sense. Paul is directing his exhortations to real people with pressing issues rather than to various types of students in a classroom. He is writing as the apostle to the gentiles for their spiritual growth in grace rather than as a philosophical-ethical teacher in a classroom using indicting statements to transform his students.

A Debate with Jews?

We turn, then, to the related issue of whether Paul is really having a debate with Jews, and this involves a tradition of interpretation. F. C. Baur argued in the nineteenth century that chapters 9–11 were written with pressing issues at Rome in mind. His view was that those pressing issues had to do with Paul's debate with Judaism.[109] More recently, Werner G. Kümmel used the term *Doppelcharakter* (double

---

109. F. C. Baur, "Römischen Gemeinde," 59–178, as referenced by Wolfgang Wiefel, "Jewish Community in Ancient Rome and the Origins of Roman Christianity," in Donfried, *Romans Debate*, 85–101 (here 85).

character) to describe Romans: "Romans manifests a double character: it is essentially a debate between the Pauline gospel and Judaism, so that the conclusion seems obvious that the readers were Jewish Christians. Yet the letter contains statements which indicate specifically that the community was Gentile-Christian."[110] In other words, in a letter directed primarily to gentile Christians, Paul is really carrying on a debate with Jews, hence the "double character."

Proceeding from this assumption, many interpreters make the case that Paul was writing with his Jewish opponents in mind. For example, they often interpret 2:1–3:20 as directed primarily to Jews, with Jews doing the judging in 2:1-5. They view 3:1-8 as a response to an assumed hypothetical Jewish objector. They assume the question in 3:9, "Are we better than they," to be Jewish. The catena of Old Testament quotations in 3:10-18 must apply to the Jews. Paul's entire discourse on the righteousness of God apart from the works of the law in 3:19–4:25 is directed toward Jewish self-righteousness. Even the questions in 6:1-3 are viewed as answering Jewish critics rather than dealing with actual antinomianism within the gentile-Christian community.[111] According to Peter Stuhlmacher, the rhetorical questions found throughout the letter—questions such as "Do we then nullify the law through faith?," "Should we sin because we are no longer under law but under Grace?," "Is the law sin?"—reveal the criticisms of Paul's opponents. And who were his opponents? "Jews and Jewish Christians as far as Rome."[112] In other words, we are to read all these rhetorical questions with his Jewish opponents in mind.

Along this same line of reasoning, commentators have labored to show that Romans is essentially Jewish in nature. The issues with

---

110. Werner G. Kümmel, *Introduction to the New Testament*, trans. Howard Clark Kee (Nashville: Abingdon, 1975), 309. Elliott (*Rhetoric of Romans*, 13n2) notes that Paul Feine originally used the term "Doppelcharakter" (*Der Römerbrief* [Gottingen: Vandenhoeck & Ruprecht, 1903]), and then others adopted it.

111. Käsemann's commentary (*Romans*, ix–xi, 33–34, 37, 53, 85, 91) is a good example of this approach. Another more recent example is Byrne, who writes in his commentary (*Romans*, 26) that 1:18–4:25 "sets itself apart from the rest of the letter by reason of having an implied Jewish rather than Gentile Christian 'audience.' To enhance the claims made for the sole saving power of the righteousness based upon Christian faith, Paul conducts a 'dialogue' with a Jewish partner not yet won to faith in Christ in order to exclude the possibility of any rival source of righteousness."

112. Stuhlmacher, *Romans*, 8–10.

which Romans deals are Jewish—for example, the justice of God, the validity of the law, how one becomes righteous before God, the seed of Abraham and then the sin of Adam, the choice of Israel, and the promises of God. The myriad of questions also relate to the Jews and the law. All this is supported by Old Testament Scriptures to convince Jews of Paul's arguments. Then the question is often raised: What relevance would all these arguments have for gentiles (as though God-fearing gentile converts would not need the same Old Testament proof)?[113]

A comparison is also made with Galatians, where Paul is definitely exposing the error of Judaizers who were undermining the faith of converts; and it is obvious that their themes are similar. In both, Paul stresses that justification is by faith alone and not by works. He spends whole chapters on the truth that those who are of faith are children of Abraham. In both letters, he emphasizes that we are to walk in the Spirit, not in the flesh. The themes are even dealt with in the same order.

Galatians		Romans
2–4	Faith, not works	3–5
3	Abraham as illustration	4
3:6	"Abraham believed God . . ."	4:3
3:11	"The righteous shall live . . ."	1:17
3:12	"He who practices . . ."	4:4
3:16, 19	"Seed . . ."	4:13
5–6	Spirit, not flesh	7–8

This similarity of structure and themes suggests a similarity of purpose, namely, a polemic against Judaism. However, is that what we find? Galatians is definitely polemical and confrontational from start to finish—from the initial anathemas to his confrontation with Peter (2:11-14) to his calling the Galatians "foolish" (3:1-5) to saying that if

---

113. Scripture could be used and expanded to show gentiles how Jews held a significant role in the redemptive purposes of God and how the basis of their faith lay in the old covenant. Paul's extensive use of the OT may also reflect Paul's background as much as the reader's.

they receive circumcision they are "severed from Christ" (5:2-4) to the concluding statement, "From now on let no one cause trouble for me." Romans does not share that same spirit. It is conciliatory in tone, a dialogue with both gentile and Jew—All are under sin! All are justified by faith! Abraham is the father of many nations! The commandment is holy and righteous and good! Circumcision is spoken of in a positive light. Whereas Galatians heightens the discontinuity between the law and the previously ratified covenant with Abraham, Romans stresses their continuity; and whereas gentiles appear to be succumbing to Judaizers in Galatians, in Romans gentiles appear to have an attitude of superiority toward the Jews (11:13-25). So the themes common to both letters are directed to different circumstances.

A variation of this double-character approach is held by Walther Schmithals, who views the letter as addressed to gentiles who were Godfearers or perhaps even proselytes, strongly influenced by Judaism and recently separated from the synagogue; hence, the Jewish nature of the letter.[114] He is followed in this view by J. Christiaan Beker, who explains that "Romans must be characterized primarily as a dialogue with Jews . . . [for] the Jewish debate about the law and salvation-history is always in the background."[115] More precisely, it is a dialogue with Jews rather than with Jewish Christians, because Judaism is "the major heritage and source of Jewish Christianity."[116] This dialogue with Jews "was necessary to determine not only the legitimate role of Jewish Christianity but especially that of the law-free Gentile mission."[117] Moreover, it was necessary background information for former gentile "Godfearers" and Jews, for it shows God's faithfulness to his promises to Israel together with their priority as well as the equality of both in the body of Christ. I would agree with Beker that these themes are important for believers in Rome. But assuming that the letter was addressed to gentile Christians, do we need to characterize it as a dialogue with Jews?

114. Walter Schmithals, *Der Römerbrief als historisches Problem* (Gütersloh: Mohn, 1975), 23, 83.
115. Beker, *Paul the Apostle*, 86.
116. Ibid., 89.
117. Ibid., 90–91; or review all of 74–93.

Could it be that Paul was having a dialogue primarily with his gentile-Christian audience? After all, much of Romans is an apology for Jews and the law. He was not dealing with gentiles who were being taught the need to be circumcised, or with an organized "anti-Pauline opposition," as in Galatia. As Elliott notes, "There is no explicit evidence in Romans that Paul addresses Christians enthralled by the synagogue or cowed by the impressive salvation-historical claims of Israel. On the contrary: Paul's warning in ch. 11 . . . presents a very different picture of the Gentile Christianity that Paul would address. Far from being overwhelmed by Jewish claims of privilege, they run the risk, in Paul's estimation, of holding God's mercy in contempt by boasting of having 'replaced' Israel (cf. 11:17-24)."[118] Similarly, Campbell states with respect to Beker's views, "It is not too much Judaism that Paul fears but too little an appreciation of the Jewish roots of the church. If they have left the synagogue already and despise the Jews as chapter 11 suggests, their sin is presumptuous Gentile pride—every bit as serious as that Jewish pride so frequently deplored in interpretations of Romans."[119]

There are those who rightly insist that the entire argument of Romans is directed toward the explicitly identified target audience—the gentiles (1:13-15; 15:14-19). Most are ready to concede that, far from being parenthetic, chapters 9–11 constitute the heart of what Paul is trying to convey to the gentile believers, and that chapters 1–8 lead up to 9–11.[120] Ben Witherington writes that "Paul has finally arrived at what has concerned him the most about the theological misunderstanding in Rome," which, according to Witherington, is the misunderstanding gentile Christians had about their Jewish brothers and sisters.[121] As Campbell explains,

> The dual character of the letter is explained by the fact that it is addressed to a predominantly Gentile Christian community about the role of Israel in salvation history and in relation to the gospel. There was probably debate

---

118. Elliott, *Rhetoric of Romans*, 38.
119. Campbell, "Revisiting Romans," 8.
120. Dahl holds that chaps. 9–11 unfold the theological theme of the letter (*Studies in Paul*, 139–42).
121. Witherington, *Romans*, 17.

among the Romans about the significance of "Jewishness" for the Church; this suggests that there was also a group of Jewish-Christians or Jewish-influenced God-fearers who may have needed Paul's protection against the arrogance of the strong (chs. 14–15).[122]

This does not mean that Paul's letter was not also addressed to the Jews in Rome or that there was no application for them as well. It is my strong opinion that one must seek to imagine how this letter would be received and understood by both Jewish and gentile believers listening together as it is being read. There is no need to import assumed Jewish antagonists into the letter, especially when the letter presses the priority of the Jew and the holiness of the law. There is also no need to assign large portions of the letter to a debate with Jews. As Elliott notes, the letter is addressed to gentile believers and it is inconceivable that they would be listening for long periods of time to discourse actually aimed for the ears of Jews.[123]

Another variation of this dual approach is found in Longenecker's insistence that the Christians in Rome relied heavily on the Jerusalem church. It was not that the gentiles in Rome were pro-Pauline and the Jews were non-Pauline in outlook. Both were dependent on Jerusalem for their understanding of the gospel. Both espoused Mosaic law and Jewish rites and practices, though they were not Judaizers. Hence, the

---

122. Campbell, "Freedom and Faithfulness," 39. Elsewhere Campbell describes the problem as "nascent anti-Judaism among the Roman Gentile Christians" ("The Rule of Faith in Romans 12:1–15:13: The Obligation of Humble Obedience to Christ as the Only Adequate Response to the Mercies of God," in *Pauline Theology*, vol. 3, *Romans*, ed. David M. Hay and E. Elizabeth Johnson [Minneapolis: Fortress Press, 1995], 259–86 [here 260–61]).

123. Neil Elliott, *The Arrogance of Nations: Reading Romans in the Shadow of Empire* (Minneapolis: Fortress Press, 2008), 19, also 177n67. Elliott writes: "Most scholars concede that the letter explicitly addresses its recipients as from 'the nations.' . . . A minority of scholars have insisted, rightly, that the letter's argument must be read as directed to the *explicitly named* audience rather than by importing a supposed Judean opposition into the letter, however congenial such a maneuver may seem to Christian apologetics. The goal of rhetorical-critical interpretation of Romans should be to understand how the argumentation of the whole letter would have functioned to achieve the adherence of the explicitly named non-Judean audience" (ibid., 19 [emphasis original]). Elliott lists a few of those who have rightly insisted that the whole of Romans was directed to the stated audience of gentiles rather than to a supposed Jewish opposition: Johannes Munck, *Paul and the Salvation of Mankind* (Richmond, VA: John Knox, 1959); Lloyd Gaston, *Paul and the Torah* (Vancouver: University of British Columbia Press, 1987); John G. Gager, *The Origins of Antisemitism: Attitudes Toward Judaism in Pagan and Christian Antiquity* (Oxford: Oxford University Press, 1983); Stowers, *Rereading of Romans*, 29–36; and Witherington, *Romans*, 1–8. In this footnote (*Arrogance of Nations*, 177n67), Elliott approves of Stowers's characterization of those who insist that Romans is directed toward a Jewish-Christian minority as an "obsession."

dispute in 14:1–15:13 was not based on ethnicity, with Jewish Christians being the weak in faith and gentile Christians being the strong; for the entire church looked to Jerusalem. Both parties included Jews and gentiles.[124] In passages such as 1:16; 2:16; 3:8; 3:31; 4:1; 6:1, 15; 7:7, 13, 14, we must "mirror read" these statements by Paul. Former commentators viewed these statements as "part of Paul's anti-Judaistic polemic." We must view them as "fervent knee-jerk responses" to criticisms and misrepresentations of his message and person then circulating among the believers in Rome.[125] Of course, this mirror reading requires several assumptions: (1) All gentile Christians in Rome looked to the Jerusalem church; (2) the guidance they received from Jerusalem and James was not Judaistic as it was in Antioch (Gal. 2:11-14) and in Galatia; (3) there was some criticism other than Judaistic coming from these sources; (4) Paul's statements were "knee-jerk responses" to these criticisms; and (5) such criticisms and misrepresentations were circulating in Rome and then being communicated back to Paul. That is how we are to understand the rhetorical questions. The same goes with the final exhortation in 16:17-20, to "watch out for those who cause divisions and put obstacles in your way." This is how Longenecker mirror reads these passages, despite Paul's statement that they, the Christians in Rome, were "good" and "properly founded" (15:14; 16:17).

I am not questioning the possible origin of Roman Christianity from Jews in Jerusalem. (This is an unresolved issue.) Nor am I questioning the general relation of Rome with the mother church in Jerusalem (if indeed it is the mother church). But to the degree that differences arose in Rome and that those differences were along ethnic lines, and given that Jew-gentile relations were becoming increasingly strained throughout the first century CE due to what was occurring throughout the empire with heightened animosity and even pogroms against Jews based on perceived Jewish customs and tenacity, it is reasonable to suppose that these differences could begin to be reflected in the life

---

124. Longenecker, *Introducing Romans*, 143–44.
125. Ibid., 146; also the bottom of 130.

of the church in Rome. To discount ethnic culture and customs and the tenacity of Jewish particularism as issues seems too far reaching an assumption.

Did all of their theological influence come exclusively from Jerusalem? Was there no influence from Paul's camp? Did no one affected by Paul's gentile mission come to Rome and help influence the church there? What about Paul's friends mentioned in chapter 16? If the Roman Christians relied heavily on Jerusalem, would you not expect the criticisms that came Paul's way would come from the same Jewish sources as in the past? As A. J. M. Wedderburn notes, there is "tantalizingly scanty" evidence that this is the case. Romans is not directed against Judaizers advocating some form of legalistic Christianity. Paul's statements about sin and law and righteousness and works of the law do not fit a legalistic narrative.[126] If the Roman Christians were so dependent on Jerusalem, in line with Jewish rites and practices and reverencing the law, why does Paul feel the need to argue that the law is holy, and the commandment holy and righteous and good? Why does he emphasize the priority of the Jew and Jewish advantage? Why does he talk about gentile arrogance and conceitedness toward Jews? Why does he carefully frame the letter from a Jewish perspective? Why is there so much attention devoted to Jew-gentile relations? And why does Paul begin his letter by stressing that his call is to bring about the "obedience of faith among the gentiles" if his real intention is to debate Jews? Even if the majority of Christians in Rome were of Jewish ethnicity, the discourse in the letter does not fit a debate with Jews. In other words, why should Paul be arguing with some Jewish interlocutor when throughout the letter he is trying to uphold the Jews and the law of God? Why should he be arguing with a Jewish interlocutor when his primary target audience was the gentiles whose obedience to the gospel he was seeking to advance?

126. A. J. M. Wedderburn, *The Reasons for Romans* (Edinburgh: T&T Clark, 1988), 54.

6

The Circumstances of Romans

Historical Factors

The idea that Paul is having a "dialogue with Jews" is misguided. Paul is focusing his remarks on Christian gentiles. While Jewish believers were among the recipients of the letter, they were not the primary focus of his remarks. His letter was sent in the midst of an amazing sequence of events, and we learn of these events primarily from secular sources. The first documented reference to Christians in Rome comes from Suetonius, who writes that the emperor Claudius expelled from Rome Jews who were causing disturbances at the instigation of Chrestus (*Iudaeos impulsore Chresto assidue tumultuantes Roma expulit*). Suetonius makes it sound like some local person named Chrestus was the troublemaker.[1] But the most plausible explanation for this account is that it refers to conflicts that developed in Jewish synagogues with Jewish Christians declaring Jesus to be the Christ. This is comparable to what happened in Jerusalem at the Synagogue of the Freedmen with the death of Stephen, and in Pisidian Antioch, Iconium, Lystra, Derbe,

---

1. Suetonius, *Claudius* 25.4.

Thessalonica, Berea, Corinth, and Ephesus (Acts 6–7; 13–19). Christians must have proclaimed the gospel in Roman synagogues resulting in such significant controversy that even the emperor had to take notice. Also, Claudius at some point prohibited Jews from assembling, perhaps in conjunction with the edict.[2] This prohibition would have included Christians as well. According to Orosius, the edict took place in 49 CE.[3] Thus Christians were in Rome at least by that date.

The second documented reference to Christians in Rome comes from the historian Tacitus, who describes the persecution of Christians under Nero in 64 CE.[4] Nero blamed the fire that swept through Rome on the Christians. By that time, Christians both Jew and gentile were being singled out by the emperor and the public as an entity separate from the community of Jews in Rome. Christians suffered terribly in the persecution that followed. This is all the more egregious since they had received no more than seven years prior the letter from Paul exhorting them in 13:1-7 to be in subjection to the governing authorities. We also learn from Tacitus that the Christian community had grown quite significantly by that time. He refers to the number condemned as *multitude ingens* (large numbers).

In between these two secular references, the letter to Rome was written and arrived around the year 57. So the origin of Christianity

---

2. According to Dio Cassius (*Historiae Romanae* 60.6.6; early third century), Claudius revoked the right of Jews to assemble, but he says nothing about the expulsion. Suetonius (early second century) records the expulsion. Acts 18:2 confirms there was an expulsion. Orosius (*Adversus paganos* 7.6.15; early fifth century) says the expulsion occurred in the ninth year of Claudius's reign (49 CE). This would coincide favorably with the chronology of the Acts 18 account. James D. G. Dunn (*Romans 1-8*, WBC 38A [Waco: Word, 1988], xlviii–xlvix) tries to reconcile all the accounts by suggesting there were two actions taken by Claudius, one in 41 (first year of reign) curtailing the assembly of Jews, and the other in 49 banishing Jews from Rome. It seems better to suppose that two actions were taken, but that the action regarding the denial of free assembly took place later in Claudius's reign (perhaps around the time the agitations were taking place) since the Jews appear to have been more in his favor in his initial years. This is essentially the argument of Wolfgang Wiefel ("Jewish Community in Ancient Rome and the Origins of Roman Christianity," in *The Romans Debate*, ed. Karl P. Donfried, rev. and expanded ed. [Peabody, MA: Hendrickson, 1991], 85–101 [here 92–94]) with which I agree.

3. Orosius, *Adversus paganos* 7.6.15. As for the question of the precise date of the expulsion, whether to accept Orosius's date or to view it as occurring earlier in Claudius's reign, see Harry Joshua Leon, *The Jews of Ancient Rome* (Peabody, MA: Hendrickson, 1995), 24–25. For an excellent overview of the issues surrounding the expulsion, see E. Mary Smallwood, *The Jews under Roman Rule* (Leiden: Brill, 1976), 210–16.

4. Tacitus, *Annals* 15.44.

in Rome occurred prior to 49, perhaps in the early to mid-40s; the expulsion of Jewish Christians occurred in 49; the return of Jewish believers occurred presumably following the death of Claudius in 54; the letter to Rome addressing two distinct groups of Christians, Jew and gentile, arrived possibly in the spring of 57;[5] and the execution of many Christians in Rome (as distinct from non-Christian Jews) occurred in 64. These events all happened in a relatively short span of time, affecting believers in a profound way. First they were embedded in the Jewish community; then they were expelled from the Jewish community, with many being expelled from Rome itself; then those remaining had to proceed forward without those who were expelled; then many of those expelled returned to the church they formerly led. It was while exiles were returning that Paul wrote the letter. These were clearly unsettling years in the lives of believers in Rome. One wonders whether references in the letter to hope in the midst of suffering relate to actual or anticipated suffering in Rome.[6]

From these historical references, we may arrive at some reasonable assumptions. First, from Suetonius's account we may surmise that the origin of the church in Rome occurred primarily within the Jewish ranks. Christianity in Rome was initially Jewish. It was begun by Jews meeting in the synagogues of Jews. Wolfgang Wiefel points out that

> the existence of a larger Jewish community in Rome offered the necessary precondition for the creation of a new Christian congregation. . . . The multitude of congregations, their democratic constitutions, and the absence of a central Jewish governing board made it easy for the

---

5. My tentative chronology is as follows: Paul's third missionary journey (Acts 18:23–20:3) was in 53–57; he spent three years in Ephesus (20:31) and three months in Greece (20:3); and then, passing through Macedonia, he sailed from Philippi "after the days of Unleavened Bread," the spring of 57 (20:6). Prior to leaving Greece, he would have sent the letter with Phoebe and others. Paul then went to Jerusalem, where he was incarcerated for two years in Caesarea (24:27). His trip to Rome would have been in 59–60, for they had to spend three months of winter in Malta along the way (27:12; 28:11). This placed him personally in Rome in 60–62.

6. For summaries of the external evidence historically from 49–64 CE, see James C. Walters, *Ethnic Issues in Paul's Letter to the Romans: Changing Self-Definitions in Earliest Roman Christianity* (Valley Forge, PA: Trinity Press International, 1993), chap. 3, "Christians and Jews in Rome between 49 and 64 C.E.," 56–66; A. Andrew Das, *Solving the Romans Debate* (Minneapolis: Fortress Press, 2007), chap. 4, "Claudius' Edict of Expulsion: The External Evidence," 149–202. For a different view of the external evidence, see Mark D. Nanos, *The Mystery of Romans: The Jewish Context of Paul's Letter* (Philadelphia: Fortress Press, 1996), appendix 2, 372–87.

missionaries of the new faith to talk in the synagogues and to win new supporters. Permission for missionaries to remain in the autonomous congregations could only be revoked if the governing body considered exclusion to be necessary and enforceable. However, since Rome had no supervising body which could forbid any form of Christian propaganda in the city, it was possible to missionize in various synagogues concurrently or to go successively from one to the other. It is likely that the existence of newly converted Christians alongside the traditional members of the synagogue may have led to increased factions and even to tumultuous disputes.[7]

Second, from Suetonius's account we may assume that Christians and Jews no longer met with each other following the edict. Mark Nanos contends that Christians in Rome were still meeting in Jewish synagogues when Paul wrote the letter in 57.[8] However, Suetonius described the conflict between them as tumultuous, and the edict was obviously a catalyst for change. According to James C. Walters,

> The Claudian edict did not create the tensions between Christians and non-Christian Jews in Rome; however, it exacerbated them. The edict in effect drove a wedge between them by dramatically communicating— especially to non-Christian Jews—that it would be in their best interests to go their separate ways. By reducing interactions between Christians and non-Christian Jews and by altering the context in which those interactions took place, the edict affected the evolution of Christian self-definition in the capital.[9]

At the time Paul wrote Romans, there is no suggestion in the letter that there was a close relation between the house churches in Rome and Jewish synagogues. In chapters 9–11, the distance between them is

---

7. Wiefel, "Jewish Community," 89–92. Dunn (*Romans 1-8*, xlvi-l) makes a strong case that Christianity in Rome began within the Jewish community.
8. Nanos, *Mystery of Romans*, 372–87. Nanos would have us believe that when Paul wrote Romans, Christians were still entirely located within synagogues in Rome. Christians and nonbelieving Jews had not yet parted ways. Suetonius's mention of "Chrestus" had nothing to do with infighting about Jesus, but rather referred to debates regarding Jewish messianic figures. Also, Roman authorities were unable to distinguish Christians from Jews when Paul wrote Romans. His arguments, however, are not convincing. Nero was quite able to distinguish Christians from Jews only a few years later in 64. If Nero could do so, Claudius was no doubt able to do so when dealing with the conflict about "Chrestus." Moreover, in Romans, there is no mention of nor implication that Christians were meeting with non-Christian Jews in Roman synagogues.
9. James C. Walters, "Romans, Jews, and Christians: The Impact of the Romans on Jewish/Christian Relations in First-Century Rome," in *Judaism and Christianity in First-Century Rome*, edited by Karl P. Donfried and Peter Richardson (Grand Rapids: Eerdmans, 1998), 175–95 (here 178).

painfully clear. Precisely when the divide was a fait accompli is an open issue. But we know for sure that it was accomplished by 64, when the Roman authorities selected only Christians to persecute. Acts 28:17-28 affirms there was no direct relation between them in the year 60 when Paul met with the Jewish leaders in Rome. On that occasion, the Jews spoke of Christians as a sect spoken against everywhere (28:21). This was only three years after Paul wrote Romans, and only a little more than a decade after the edict of expulsion in 49. In his essay, Walters lays out quite cogently the entire rationale for the assumption that the disputes regarding "Chrestus" that brought about the edict of Claudius were instrumental in causing the final split between the two communities in Rome.[10]

Third, from Suetonius's account as well as Paul's letter, we may assume that the edict expelling Jews had to have had an impact on the ratio of Jews to gentiles in the church, perhaps significantly lowering their number in relation to gentile believers. We do not know the number of Jews expelled,[11] but Prisca and Aquila were among their number (Acts 18:2). Could it be that along with some nonbelieving Jews, a major number of believing Jews were expelled including the leadership? If so, that would be a major turning point for the young church.[12] Following Claudius's death in 54, Prisca and Aquila apparently returned along with other Jews to Rome. When they arrived, they found house churches organized independently of the synagogues and under the leadership of gentile believers. The split with the Jewish community together with the prohibition to assemble

---

10. Ibid., 178–83.
11. How many Jews were expelled? It is hard to tell. Acts 18:2 says, "Claudius commanded all the Jews to leave Rome." Was this hyperbole, or a reference to all the Jews involved in the conflict? Estimates of the number of Jews in Rome range from fifteen thousand to fifty thousand. Some were Roman citizens, and would Christians who were Roman citizens have been forced to leave Rome? The numbers are unknown. But the disturbance was significant enough for Claudius to pass an edict of expulsion and for Prisca and Aquila to leave as a result. Probably most of those involved in the disturbances were expelled, and the number was doubtless significant. Walters (*Ethnic Issues*, 58–59) holds that the edict also removed gentile Christians who lived like Jews and were involved in the disturbances. His view is that we should not view the expulsion in strictly ethnic terms but rather in terms of their convictions.
12. Whether only those involved in the dispute or many more were expelled, the result would have been the same, the end of the Christian community as it had originally been composed mainly of Jewish believers.

had forced those who remained in Rome to meet in separate home sites. The warm relationship with the Jewish community was a thing of the past. The relationship with gentiles in house churches was the new reality. All this would have been challenging for the returning exiles.

Wiefel describes it in this way. When the Jews returned, they

> found a "new" Christian congregation completely different in organizational structure and spiritual outlook from the old one which had existed in the synagogue. Now they are only a minority in a congregation which previously they had shaped. From this emerges the possibility of specifying the *Sitz im Leben* of Romans: it was written to assist the Gentile Christian majority, who are the primary addressees of the letter, to live together with the Jewish Christians in one congregation, thereby putting an end to their quarrels about status.[13]

Similarly, Walters contends that the edict would have caused the entire "ethnic and socio-religious composition" of the church to shift, because:

> Christian Jews, and Gentiles who lived like Jews, were expelled (many if not most of them). The Christians who played the chief roles in defining the character of the Christian gatherings after the edict, therefore, would have been those Roman Christians who were least shaped by the Jewish context of earliest Christianity in Rome. . . . [Thus when Jewish Christians] returned to Rome after the edict had lapsed, they encountered Christians whose socialization had changed markedly. Not only were Christians assembling in house churches that were independent of Jewish gatherings, these house churches were populated by persons who—for the most part—no longer observed Sabbath and dietary laws and who were not eager to resume such behaviors, as Romans 14:1–15:13 indicates.[14]

---

13. Wiefel, "Jewish Community," 96. Regarding the remarks by Dio Cassius that Claudius revoked the right of assembly (*Historiae Romanae* 60.6.6), Wiefel says that this encouraged the growth of house churches led primarily by gentile believers. Upon the return of Jewish Christians, the gentiles would have been reticent to come under their leadership. This development of homogeneous churches could then lead to tensions regarding belief and practice.

14. Walters, "Romans, Jews, and Christians," 178. Das (*Paul and the Jews*, 60) writes: "A Christian population that had originally consisted primarily of Jewish believers would now be losing its Jewish character and would be faced with the problem of its Jewish origin. New converts who had never associated with the Jewish religious assemblies would not have had the same appreciation for Judaism as the earlier members of the church. This would have raised new issues for Roman Christianity, not the least of which would have been the role of the Jewish Law and the Jewish heritage. Tensions would have arisen over Jewish customs and identity." Regarding the views of Wiefel, Walters, and Das, I maintain that they are reasonable and reflect in general what was occurring in Rome.

This jeopardized the unity of the church. One of Paul's purposes in writing was to show the common ground that existed between Jewish and gentile Christians and to help the gentiles make room for the Jewishness of their Jewish counterparts.

Ethnic Socioreligious Factors

From other sources, we understand that there was significant ethnic tension between Jews and non-Jews throughout the Roman world. This was due in large part to the very nature of Judaism, for Judaism was at core an ethnic tradition.[15] Jews were united by their ancestry, by their father Abraham and circumcision, by Moses and the law, by their love for the land and the temple. They paid the annual temple tax and observed the Sabbath and dietary laws. They worshiped together in synagogues, and the Law and the Prophets were read every Sabbath. According to Emil Schürer, the nonobservance of the law would not have been tolerated anywhere in the synagogue communities of the Diaspora.[16] They celebrated annual festivals and erected booths at the Feast of Tabernacles. They took pilgrimages to Jerusalem during those festivals. They sought to live together, separate from their non-Jewish neighbors. In Alexandria, they were concentrated in two of five districts, and in Rome in a very large district across the Tiber, which reminds us of the Oracle of Balaam: "Behold, a people who will dwell alone, and will not be reckoned among the nations" (Num. 23:9).

Of course, there were defections to paganism and syncretism. Hellenism exerted a strong influence, and there was a diversity among Diaspora Jews.[17] But as an ethnic group, they were remarkably able

---

15. John M. G. Barclay, *Jews in the Mediterranean Diaspora: From Alexander to Trajan (323 B.C.E.–117 C.E.)* (Edinburgh: T&T Clark, 1996), 407–9.

16. Emil Schürer, *The History of the Jewish People in the Age of Jesus Christ*, rev. and ed. Geza Vermes, Fergus Millar, and Martin Goodman (Edinburgh: T&T Clark, 1986), 3:140.

17. Victor Tcherikover (*Hellenistic Civilization and the Jews* [Philadelphia: Jewish Publication Society of America: Philadelphia, 1959], 354) writes that there were times when the Jews succumbed to the temptation to become like the people around them. "But if instead of the isolated instances of Hellenization, we note the entire trend of Jewish life outside Palestine, and if we take into account the existence of organized Jewish communities for many generations in given localities, and the synagogues scattered over the whole world, we shall easily see that the Diaspora Jews were closely attached to their nationality and that the overwhelming majority of them did not incline to assimilation."

to maintain their identity. Victor Tcherikover attributes this mainly to "the vital strength of the Jewish communities. Just as the civic organization of the Greeks in the Greek cities secured the preservation of Greek culture outside Hellas, so the organization of Jews in independent communities safeguarded Jewish traditions."[18] However, this also served to set them apart from the pagan world. Jewish beliefs and customs were repulsive to the average pagan. Schürer notes they were regarded almost everywhere with ill-will and that they were mocked primarily on three points: (1) their observance of the Sabbath (a means to be lazy); (2) their observance of dietary laws (a profound kindness for pigs); and (3) their view of imageless worship (a form of atheism).[19] We might add that circumcision was a matter of scorn;[20] and their desire to proselytize was especially objectionable.[21] Many authors followed Cicero's lead when in 59 BCE he referred to Judaism as a *barbara superstitio*.[22]

Consequently, repeated efforts were made to hinder Jews from practicing their religion. This occurred in communities scattered around the Mediterranean, from Asia Minor and the Near East all the way to Cyrenaica. So laws were written to settle those disputes and to protect the Jews. They were laws of toleration that allowed Jews to gather for worship and common meals, to observe the Sabbath and dietary laws, to send money to the temple in Jerusalem, and to be absolved from military service. Jews were even allowed to try Jews in their own Jewish courts for breaking Jewish law.[23] Nevertheless,

---

18. Ibid., 356.
19. Schürer, *History of the Jewish People*, 3:152. John M. G. Barclay (*Pauline Churches and Diaspora Jews* [Tübingen: Mohr Siebeck, 2011], 16) lists "circumcision, Sabbath-observance and food-regulations" as "integral to Jewish social identity in the Diaspora."
20. Tacitus (*Histories* 5.5) said that circumcision is a sign of sexual lust.
21. Horace, *Sermones* 1.4.143; 1.9.67–72.
22. Cicero, *Pro Flacco* 28.66–67; Quintilian, *Institutio Oratoria* 3.7; Seneca, in Augustine's *City of God* 6.11; Pliny the Elder, *Natural History* 31.11. Juvenal (*Satires* 2.11, 14.105, 6.541–544) depicts Jews as lazy, beggars, and fortune-tellers. Wiefel ("Jewish Community," 97–99) provides a litany of first-century authors derisive of Jews, and says this rebuke would summarize their perspective: *adversus omnes alios hostile odiom* (hostile hatred against all others); see also M. Stern, "The Jews in Greek and Latin Literature," in *The Jewish People in the First Century: Historical Geography, Political History, Social, Cultural and Religious Life and Institutions*, ed. S. Safrai and M. Stern in co-operation with D. Flusser and W. C. van Unnik, Compendia Rerum Iudaicarum ad Novum Testamentum I-2 (Philadelphia: Fortress Press, 1976), 1101–59, and review his bibliography on 1159.
23. This is in accord with the account of Leon, *Jews in Rome*, 9-10. According to Leonard Victor Rutgers

these special privileges became objects of gentile resentment, even to the point of violent confrontation. Schürer writes: "Hatred against the Jews repeatedly broke out in the cities, and of course especially where the Jews had the most marked communal rights, as in Alexandria, Antioch, many cities in Asia Minor, and even in Caesarea in Palestine where pagans and Jews had received equality of rights from Herod the Great."[24] This is confirmed by what happened in Ephesus in Acts 19. Policies had been established by Octavian (largely through Marcus Agrippa) that were favorable to Judaism. They specifically granted the Jews permission to keep the Sabbath and observe the customs of their ancestors, to celebrate their holidays, and to send the temple tax to Jerusalem.[25] There were no pogroms or riots to speak of. Yet when Alexander, a Jew, entered the amphitheater, what happened can only be viewed as a spontaneous racial riot that began when the people gathered in the amphitheater recognized that he was a Jew.

I would add that prejudice against Jews appears to have been increasing during the first century up to and beyond the first Jewish War in 66–70. This is seen in the increase of violent confrontations during that time. During the reign of Gaius, a riot occurred in Alexandria in which many Jews were expelled from their homes and robbed, and multitudes were murdered. This was the first major anti-Jewish riot recorded in Roman territory. Again during the reign of Gaius, rioting occurred in Syrian Antioch, resulting in many Jews being

("Roman Policy toward the Jews: Expulsions from the City of Rome during the First Century C.E.," in *Judaism and Christianity in First-Century Rome*, ed. Karl P. Donfried and Peter Richardson [Grand Rapids: Eerdmans, 1998], 93–116) there never was a uniform policy for the Jews. Policies were made in response to specific situations; and the earlier decrees during the triumvirate and reign of Octavian served as legal precedents for later disputes. But policies were subject to change. They were written to maintain law and order. And as long as there were no disturbances by the Jews, the Jews had nothing to fear. From a policy perspective, the Jews faired quite well politically. I would also note that a policy of toleration was practiced by the Medo-Persians as well as Greeks preceding Roman dominance. There were times such as recorded in Esther and Maccabees when Jews were persecuted with attempted pogroms. But overall, toleration was practiced throughout those centuries. Due to the Jews' support of Julius Caesar in his war against Pompey, they were rewarded with edicts guaranteeing their freedom to worship and pursue their traditions (Josephus, *Antiquities of the Jews* 14.10). These edicts were renewed by Octavian and the emperors that followed. Even after the first Jewish War in 66–70, the policy of toleration still stood (see Leon, *Jews of Rome*, 28).

24. Schürer, *History of the Jewish People*, 3:132.
25. M. Stern, "The Jewish Diaspora," in Safari et al., *Jewish People in the First Century*, 146; There was also an earlier policy of toleration enforced by Marcus Brutus in 42 BCE (see ibid., 144).

killed and synagogues burned. Rioting of a significant kind would have happened in Judea had Gaius succeeded in his quest to erect a statue of himself in the temple. Then at the arrival of the first Jewish War, pogroms broke out all over the Roman world, in Alexandria, Cyrenaica, Syria, and Asia Minor. There was at that time a tremendous amount of hostility that erupted against Jews throughout the Roman Empire.[26]

In Rome itself, historians tell us that in the past authorities were set on curbing foreign cults and ideas that could undermine Roman values. For this reason, they had already expelled the Jews (and others) twice from Rome. In 139 BCE, Jews were expelled for proselyting activities and their places of worship were destroyed. More recently in 19 CE, they were expelled by Tiberius. Both Tacitus and Suetonius record that this was part of a wider attempt to suppress foreign cults.[27] Dio Cassius says the expulsion was due to the Jews' proselyting activities.[28] Philo blamed it on Sejanus, who was left in charge of affairs in Rome when Tiberius was gone and who wanted to destroy the Jews.[29] Josephus alone records that the Jews were expelled in part due to four Jewish con men who swindled a Roman noblewoman named Fulvia, wife of a Roman senator and proselyte to Judaism, on the pretext of collecting funds for the temple in Jerusalem.[30] Perhaps it was a combination of the above.[31] It is

---

26. Schürer (*History of the Jewish People*, 3:132n22) summarizes some of the conflicts:

> In Alexandria Jews and pagans lived from the foundation of the city onwards in continual disharmony, *B. J.* ii 18, 7 (487–93); at the time of Caligula it was the pagan mob there who above all persecuted the Jews, even before the emperor himself proceeded against them (Philo, *In Flaccum*). In the reign of Vespasian the Alexandrians addressed the emperor with the request that the Jews there should be deprived of their rights, *Ant.* xii 3, 1 (121). In Antioch in the time of Vespasian it came to bloodshed, *B. J.* vii 3, 3 (43–53); Titus received a request that the Jews should all be driven from the city, and when Titus did not grant this, that at least they should be deprived of their rights, *B. J.* vii 5, 2 (100–11); *Ant.* xii 3, 1 (121). In Asia Minor the city communes continually renewed their efforts to hinder the Jews in the practice of their religion, and thus necessitated the Roman edicts of toleration, *Ant.* xii 3, 2 (125–7); xvi 2, 3–5 (27–65), and above all the edicts in *Ant.* xiv 10 (186–267) and xvi 6 (160–78). The same happened in Cyrene, *Ant.* xvi 6, 1 and 5 (160–1, 169–70). In Caesarea pagans and Jews were repeatedly involved in bloody conflict, *Ant.* xx 8, 7, 9 (173–8, 182–4); *B. J.* ii 13, 7 (266–70); 14, 4–5 (284–92); 18, 1 (457). Even in cities where there is no evidence that the Jews enjoyed established rights, the hatred of the pagan mob broke out against them from time to time, in particular at the outbreak of the Jewish war in Ascalon, Ptolemais, Tyre, Hippos, Gadara, *B. J.* ii 18, 5 (477–8) and Damascus, *B. J.* ii 20, 2 (559–61). Of the Ascalonites Philo says that they bore implacable hostility towards Jews, *Leg.* 30 (205). Of the Phoenicians, the Tyrians were, according to Josephus, especially hostile in their attitude to Jews, *C. Ap.* i 13 (70).

27. Tacitus, *Annals* 2.85.4; Suetonius, *Tiberius* 36.
28. Dio Cassius, *Historiae Romanae* 57.18.5.
29. Philo, *Legatio ad Gaium* 159–60.

also possible that the robbery mentioned by Josephus might have been the catalyst for the expulsion, and along with the expulsion placed a stigma on Jews, as referenced in Rom. 2:22b: "You who abhor idols, do you rob temples?" The passage goes on to quote Isaiah, "The name of God is blasphemed among the gentiles because of you."[32] The numbers affected by the expulsion must have been considerable since Josephus tells us that in a punitive measure, the Roman authorities not only conscripted four thousand Jews for military service and sent them off to the island of Sardinia, but also punished a greater number of them who were unwilling to become soldiers due to their keeping the laws of their forefathers.[33] This expulsion occurred only thirty years prior to the expulsion under Claudius.

Accordingly, I assume that Rome itself could hardly have been immune to the presence of antisemitism. The Jews practiced the same customs that drew resentment throughout the Roman world. They kept the Sabbath and dietary laws and sent the temple tax to Jerusalem. They lived in their own Jewish neighborhoods and worshiped in their own synagogues.[34] They were known for proselytizing, which was not appreciated by authorities.[35] At the same time, they were protected

30. Josephus, *Antiquities of the Jews* 18.3. It is not always easy to discern how far to trust what Josephus records, though in this instance the expulsion is attested by other Roman historians.

31. Smallwood (*Jews under Roman Rule*, 201–10) argues the decree was the result of a broader range of proselytizing activities.

32. Most interpret 2:22b as robbing objects in heathen temples. Thus John Murray (*The Epistle to the Romans*, NICNT [Grand Rapids: Eerdmans, 1965], 1:84) argues that there is "no good reason for departing from the literal rendering and import" of the text. But it seems highly unlikely that those who abhor idols would be robbing pagan temples, especially to the extent that this would be listed among the causes of blasphemy by gentiles (2:21-24). It is uncertain why Jews would be near pagan temples, let alone plundering them. On the other hand, the cause for being expelled from Rome would be something to be remembered. To swindle a noblewoman and wife of a senator and thereby be partly to blame for the expulsion of Jews from Rome would bring disgrace on Jews as a race and fulfill the words of Isaiah. Dunn (*Romans 1-8*, 114–15) is one of the few who even mention the potential relation of 2:22b to the scandal, though he is still inclined to think it refers to the actual plunder of pagan temples.

33. Josephus, *Antiquities of the Jews* 18.3.

34. Cf. Schürer, *History of the Jewish People*, 3:150–51; Leon, *Jews of Rome*, 250–56.

35. There is a difference of opinion as to the extent of Jewish proselytizing. Schürer (*History of the Jewish People*, 3:159–76) and Leon (*Jews of Rome*, 15) hold that the Jews were aggressive in securing converts. There is evidence that they had some success in these endeavors, many gentiles observing the Sabbath and food laws and attending synagogue services. The missionary journeys in Acts bear witness to this fact. There are even accounts of Godfearers sending donations to the temple in Jerusalem. Others hold the opposite view. Scot McKnight (*A Light among the Gentiles: Jewish Missionary Activity in the Second Temple Period* [Minneapolis: Fortress Press, 1991], 74) contends that Judaism was not a missionary religion; cf. Martin Goodman, "Jewish

by policies of toleration. In fact, those policies remained unchanged throughout the expulsion under Tiberius, the irresponsible rule of Gaius, the expulsion under Claudius, and even during and after the first Jewish War during the reign of Nero. For this reason, Harry Leon maintains that the years under the tyranny of Nero were tranquil for the Jewish people in Rome.[36] But a policy of toleration does not eliminate antisemitism. According to Tcherikover in his *Hellenistic Civilization and the Jews*, when a historian begins to investigate antisemitism in a given epoch, the main danger is for the enquiry to confuse

> the inner quality of anti-Semitism, which is always and everywhere the same, and its various manifestations, which alter according to place and circumstance. The inner quality of anti-Semitism arises from the very existence of the Jewish people as an alien body among the nations. The alien character of the Jews is the central cause of the origin of anti-Semitism, and this alien character has two aspects: The Jews are alien to other peoples because they are foreigners derived from another land, and they are alien because of their foreign customs which are strange and outlandish in the eyes of the local inhabitants.[37]

Moreover, Wiefel has provided a great service by demonstrating the presence of anti-Jewish sentiment in Rome not only in earlier years but also at the very time Paul was writing. The remarks of authors who either came to Rome or grew up there in the first century CE betray this prejudice. Wiefel summarizes, "They are characterized by the disdain with which one often looks at things foreign and by a grotesque ignorance toward everything Jewish: origins, history, and lifestyle."[38]

Proselytizing in the First Century," in *The Jews among Pagans and Christians in the Roman Empire*, ed. Judith Lieu, John North, and Tessa Rajak (London: Routledge, 1992), 53–78. It is interesting to note that all three expulsions of Jews from Rome (139 BCE, 19 CE, and 49 CE) may have resulted from the government's response to Jewish proselyting in some form. Jesus' statement in Matthew 23 is also interesting in this regard: "You travel about on sea and land to make one proselyte; and when he becomes one, you make him twice as much a son of hell as yourselves."

36. Leon (*Jews of Rome*, 28–29) says it is "completely unknown" how the Jews fared in Rome during the years following Nero's violent end and the beginning of Vespasian's reign, when Titus entered Rome with Jewish captives of war in chains behind him, etc.

37. Tcherikover, *Hellenistic Civilization and the Jews*, 358.

38. Wiefel, "Jewish Community," 98.

But was this prejudice against things Jewish present in the church? Did it in any way influence what was taking place as Jewish exiles were returning to Rome? The contemporary writers alert us to that possibility, but only the text of Romans can provide the answer.

The Circumstances in Rome:
Related to Ethnic Socioreligious Factors

Assuming as I have that Paul is addressing circumstances in Rome (see chap. 1), we can appreciate the multiple ways the text reflects the historical and ethnic socioreligious factors affecting those circumstances. But what were those circumstances, and how does Paul address them? First, could there have been an element of antisemitism at play in Rome? There is one glaring example of what can only be described as prejudice against Jews. It comes in the major block of discourse where Paul is revealing his deep concern for Israel. Addressing his gentile readership directly, he insists, "stop being 'arrogant' of the branches [Jews]. And if you are arrogant [a simple fact condition implying that they are]. . . ." Then he adds, "Stop being conceited,"[39] and finally, "I do not want you to be ignorant lest you are wise in your own estimation" (11:18-25). These are strong admonitions to be included in the very heart of the letter (chaps. 9-11). Was this arrogance directed only toward nonbelieving ethnic Israel as a whole? Or was it directed toward Jews as an ethnic group not limited to non-believing Jews? One can appreciate (though not condone) how gentiles felt toward nonbelieving Jews after being expelled from their synagogues and watching them distance themselves before the Roman imperium. But did this prejudice carry over into their relations with believing Jews?

There are subtle and not so subtle indicators that this was the case. The strong exhortation to accept the one who is weak in faith without judging his or her opinions (14:1-15:6) falls into the category of the not so subtle. What makes them weak in faith? They are holding to

---

39. In both 11:18 and 20, *mē* plus the present imperative is used, which should be translated "Stop doing what you are presently doing," a strong prohibition.

certain practices they consider essential to their faith, matters having to do with what they eat and drink and days they observe. The eating revolves around the Levitical laws of unclean foods (14:14, 20b); the "days" bring to mind Jewish observances of the Sabbath and feast days. Some question whether the weak and the strong are to be distinguished mainly along ethnic lines. Why did he not use the terms Jew and gentile? However, 15:7-9 provides clear evidence that this was a Jew-gentile issue, for the exhortation to accept one another is in the context of the oppositional pairings, circumcision versus gentiles. Therefore it is quite natural to view the entire passage as referring to discord between Jewish and gentile Christians.[40] That is not to say the strong and the weak were split strictly along ethnic lines, for it is quite conceivable that there were godly gentiles (Godfearers) who may have been convicted to keep food regulations, and there may have been Jewish believers such as Prisca and Aquila who could have been considered "strong in faith." However, it is highly probable that the majority of each was split along ethnic lines, and that the gentiles, the strong, were being called on to accept the weak in faith and to bear their weaknesses (14:1; 15:1). Paul, by the way, identifies himself with the strong (15:1).

The reason why this passage (14:1–15:6) is not subtle about their prejudices is that almost every verse expresses in some way the discord between them. In the first four verses, Paul tells the strong not to take issue with the opinions of the weak and not to despise the weak. He tells the weak not to judge the strong; and he tells both not to judge the servant of another (i.e., the Lord). In 14:5-12, he points out that we are the Lord's, and everything we do is to the Lord; then he asks, why do you judge your brother and why do you despise your brother? In

---

40. Francis Watson ("The Two Roman Congregations: Romans 14:1–15:13," in Donfried, *Romans Debate*, 203–15 [here 205]) points out: "15:7-13 speaks unambiguously of the duty of Jews and Gentiles to welcome one another as Christ has welcomed them. There is no break between 14:1–15:6 and this passage, and it is therefore natural to conclude that the whole passage concerns the relationship between Jewish and Gentile Christians. Indeed, this final point puts this identification virtually beyond doubt." The strong inferential particle *dio* introduces 15:7, thereby indicating that what follows is the clear inference of what precedes.

14:13–15:6, Paul focuses on how the strong should respond to the weak. He writes:[41]

14:13: Do not put an obstacle or stumbling block in a brother's way.

15: Do not destroy with food that one for whom Christ died.

16: Do not let that which is good be blasphemed (spoken evil of).

19: Pursue the things that make for peace and the edification of one another.

20: Do not tear down the work of God for the sake of food.

21: Do not eat meat or drink wine or do anything by which your brother stumbles.

15:1: We who are strong ought to bear the weaknesses of those without strength.

2: Let each of us please our neighbor for his good to his edification.

The entire passage reveals major disharmony within the body. It could hardly have been stated more strongly. The weight of responsibility is clearly on the strong, though both parties were at fault. The Jews "judged" the gentiles, while the gentiles "despised" the Jews. The term "despised" (*exoutheneō*) is the stronger term, meaning to treat with contempt, to look down on or count as nothing. It fits with the attitude of arrogance in 11:18. But while the strong were despising the weak, the weak in return were judging the strong, probably from their Jewish perspective that the law of God prescribed these observances. So the judging went both ways. Nevertheless, the impact was more difficult

---

41. Some commentators interpret the passage as focused primarily on the judging being done by the weak; but this is clearly not the case. Not only does this entire section of the letter open and close by focusing specifically on the strong (14:1; 15:1), but also, after the neutral injunctions applying to both parties in 14:3-12, virtually all the exhortations in 14:13–15:6 focus on how the strong are to treat the weak in faith. Following the initial exhortation to stop judging one another (14:15: *mēketi* present subjunctive), Paul enjoins the strong not to set up stumbling blocks for the weak. In 14:15, 16, and 20, he uses *mē* present imperative to press home that the recipients of the letter are to "stop doing what they are presently doing": 14:15: "Stop destroying with your food the one for whom Christ died"; 14:16: "Stop letting that which is a good thing be blasphemed"; 14:20: "Stop destroying the work of God for the sake of food." These are strong exhortations directed to the "strong in faith" at the time they were engaged in such responses.

for the weak in faith. These were customs that defined the Jew as a Jew, and they were being instructed in the letter that these practices were no longer essential to their faith as Christians. The gentiles, on the other hand, are to regard the customs as permissible and not incompatible with the faith. That is not as difficult a requirement. But gentile prejudice was difficult to overcome. They are not to "despise" the Jews for these practices as was the case in the Roman world around them. "The kingdom of God is not eating and drinking, but righteousness and peace and joy in the Holy Spirit" (14:17). John Barclay points out that Paul's policy with regard to the observance of both days and foods is "socially indecisive." Paul left it up to a matter of "faith" and not putting an obstacle in a brother's way (14:13-15, 21-23).[42] One wonders whether this was a surface issue that betrayed a deeper problem of antisemitism. Was it limited to these two issues, or were they illustrative of faith and culture issues that accompanied Jew-gentile relations in general?

Add to this the caveat that sandwiched in between chapters 9–11 and 14–15 are the exhortations in 12:3-16. These exhortations are focused almost entirely on the unity of the body of Christ—"we who are many are one body in Christ" (12:5); "let each exercise his or her gifts accordingly" (12:6); "let love be without hypocrisy" (12:9); "be devoted to one another" (12:10). And hidden except to Greek students is the fact that the entire discussion is framed by two verses calling on believers not to be "high-minded" (proud, arrogant) but to be of the same mind (from the stem *phron-*):

12:3: For through the grace given to me, I say to everyone among you not to think more highly [*mē hyperphronein*] than you ought to think [*dei phronein*], but to think [*phronein*] so as to think sensibly [*eis to sōphronein*].

12:16: Be of the same mind [*to auto . . . phronountes*] toward one another; do not be high-minded [*mē ta hypsēla phronountes*], but associate with the lowly. Do not be wise in your own estimation [*phronimoi par' heautois*].

This is the same stem used of the gentiles' attitude toward Jews in

42. Barclay, *Pauline Churches and Diaspora Jews*, 16–17.

11:20, "Stop being high-minded" (*mē hypsēla phronei*), as well as Paul's final exhortation to the strong and weak in 15:5, "Be of the same mind with one another" (*to auto phronein en allēlois*). Its prominent use throughout the latter chapters, especially with reference to the attitudes of gentiles and the strong, suggests that their arrogance was directed toward believing Jews as well.[43] All these exhortations—not to be arrogant, not to be high-minded (conceited), not to judge, and not to despise—betray serious sins that were causing division. There is every reason to believe that Paul was addressing circumstances in Rome when he was making these exhortations.

What we have observed thus far is this. There was major discord among believers in Rome. This discord was along ethnic lines. We can speculate as to why it was there. The judging and despising of each other is one reason. The question about foods would have affected their fellowship and perhaps their partaking of the Lord's Supper together. The arrogance and high-mindedness of the gentiles is another factor. Paul directs his strongest admonitions to the gentiles and the "strong." They were at fault. Their prejudice toward the returning Jewish exiles was an issue. They needed to "accept the one who is weak in faith." Paul also had to deal with the judgmental attitude of the Jews. Both needed to hear the words "Accept one another just as Christ has accepted us to the glory of God" (15:7). There was an additional factor about which there is little information. Paul closes the letter with a warning, more like a command, to watch out for those who cause disputes and arouse opposition to the gospel.[44] The tone of this warning

---

43. Cf. 2 Cor. 13:11; Phil. 2:2; and 4:2, where Paul uses the phrase *to auto phronein* (to think the same thing) to encourage the unity of the body of Christ.

44. The warning comes somewhat as a surprise following a series of greetings. The term *parakaleō* that introduces the warning should probably be translated "I adjure you." The Greek terms for division (*dichostasias poein*) means "to cause dissensions"; *dichazō* means literally to divide in two or to separate. The idea is "to cause to separate" (William F. Arndt and F. Wilbur Gingrich, *A Greek Lexicon of the New Testament* (Chicago: University of Chicago Press, 1957), 199). The term that I have translated "arouse opposition" is *skandalon*, a noun having to do with that which causes offense or is an enticement to sin (ibid., 760). Ernst Käsemann (*Commentary on Romans*, trans. Geoffrey W. Bromiley [Grand Rapids: Eerdmans, 1980], 417) writes that the terms *dichostasiai* and *skandala* are referring to "more than group conflicts about suitable conduct or divergent theological opinions. They denote the rending of the community on the basis of seduction into heresy." One may question whether Käsemann is correct regarding seduction into heresy, but the terms definitely denote the rending of a community.

appears to go beyond the tone of exhortations in the letter. It suggests that there were troublemakers in Rome of which Paul was aware who were behind the scenes causing division. He does not identify them, only characterizes them as divisive. To summarize the circumstances noted thus far: there were relational problems that affected the unity of the body. They were a community divided largely along ethnic lines. The gentiles were primarily at fault, though the Jews were not completely innocent. Not all were divided, but a number were, and some were deliberately divisive.

On the more subtle side of things, Paul does not address believers in Rome as one congregation. In fact, he consistently refers to his readers as two separate ethnic groups, Jews and non-Jews, in one form or another: Jew/Greek, in law/without law, circumcision/uncircumcision, Israel/gentiles, weak/strong (1:16; 2:9-10, 12-13, 14-16/17-24, 25-27; 3:1, 9, 29-30; 4:9-10; 9:24, 30-31; 10:12; 11:7/11-13, 25; 14:1–15:6; 15:8-12). These oppositional pairings extend throughout the letter. They stand over against each other. Paul does not attempt to erase these separate pairings, for that was the reality of the situation. For Paul and the believers in Rome, there were Jews and there were non-Jews; and this was the issue Paul was addressing in his letter, the relation between them.[45]

This oppositional pairing is further accented by Paul's references to Jewish ancestry and marks of ethnic identity.

> 2:17-20: But if you bear the name Jew, and rest on the law, and boast in God, . . . being instructed out of the law, and are confident that you yourself are a guide to the blind. . . .

> 9:4-5: Who are the Israelites, to whom belongs the adoption as sons and the glory and the covenants and the giving of the law and the [temple] service and the promises, whose are the fathers, and from whom is the Christ according to the flesh. . . .

---

45. Hans-Werner Bartsch, "The Historical Situation in Rome," trans. Wallace Gray, *Encounter* 33 (1972): 329-39, esp. 333. Bartsch notes that these pairings in various forms occur more often in Romans than in all the other Pauline letters. They often mark the beginning or end of a train of thought. Thus they confirm that Paul is writing to circumstances in Rome.

11:1: For I too am an Israelite, a descendant of Abraham, of the tribe of Benjamin.

Numerous times he refers to Abraham (4:1, 2, 3, 9, 12, 13, 16; 9:7; 11:1), Isaac and Jacob (9:7-13), the fathers (9:5; 11:28; 15:8), David (1:3; 4:6; 11:9; 15:12), and Moses (5:14; 9:15; 10:5, 19). He passionately refers to "my kinsmen according to the flesh" (9:3; 16:7, 11, 21) and once refers to them simply as "my flesh" (11:14). One block of material in Romans is set aside to deal with the role of the law of God in the life of believers (chaps. 6-8). One block of material is set aside to deal with the place of Israel in redemptive history (chaps. 9-11). One section of exhortations is set aside to deal with the socioreligious issues of days (Sabbath, feast days) and foods (dietary laws) (14:1-15:13). While closing the letter Paul mentions that he is making a pilgrimage to Jerusalem to deliver the collection for the poor (Jewish believers). Jewish identity was rooted in these customs and in their ancestry. None of the terms for non-Jews—gentiles, Greeks, uncircumcision, without law—come with such modification. "Gentiles" is a label applied by Jews to non-Jews. "Greeks" is a designation of non-Jews influenced by Hellenism. To classify Jews and non-Jews as "the circumcision" and "the uncircumcision" seems to be unique to Paul among Jewish authors;[46] but to call non-Jews "the uncircumcision" is clearly for the purpose of setting them apart from the Jews and conveys nothing with reference to their ancestry (an idea to be pursued below).

Nevertheless, Paul's purpose in the letter is to bring Jew and gentile believers together. In his introduction, 1:13-18, Paul details his longing to come to Rome and specifies to whom he is writing and why he is writing. He wants to bear some fruit

among you
as also among the rest of the gentiles.

He says he is under obligation

---

46. Caroline Johnson Hodge, *If Sons, Then Heirs: A Study of Kinship and Ethnicity in the Letters of Paul* (Oxford: Oxford University Press, 2007), 60–62.

both to Greeks and to barbarians,
both to the wise and to the foolish.

Thus he is eager to proclaim the gospel

to you who are in Rome.

This is his primary audience, and it corresponds with his calling and mission in life, "to bring about the obedience of faith among all the gentiles for his name's sake" (1:5). Then in 1:16-17, he says that the gospel is the power of God

to everyone who believes,
to the Jew first and also to the Greek.

For in the gospel, the righteousness of God is revealed

from faith to faith.

Hans-Werner Bartsch has sought to persuade us of something very important. He suggests that the much-disputed phrase "from faith to faith" is to be explained in its relation to the prior phrase, "to the Jew first and also to the Greek."[47]

to the Jew first	and also to the Greek
from faith	to faith

That makes a lot of sense, the last pair parallel to the former. It is consistent with his use of parallel phrases throughout 1:13-18, the latter either modifying or building on the former. He notes that this is the theme developed in chapter 4, where "Abraham believed God and it was reckoned to him as righteousness" (4:3). The faith that was originally exercised by Abraham and his seed is the faith offered to

---

47. Bartsch, "Historical Situation in Rome," 331-33. Actually, Bartsch also says that "from faith to faith" is to be understood in relation to the phrases in 1:14, "both to Greeks and to barbarians, both to the wise and to the foolish." He contends that the word "barbarians" includes "the Jews and the Jewish Christians who had been exiled by the edict" (ibid., 331). I hold that in 1:14 Paul is saying that he is under obligation to all gentile humanity. See above, chap. 1, n47.

the gentiles for the taking. The goal is "the unity of the believing Jews and Gentiles."[48] This, then, begins the conversation of gentile indebtedness to their Jewish brothers and sisters. As Bartsch explains, Paul's purpose is to eliminate the devaluation of Jews in Rome. When Paul says that the gospel is "to all who believe," that is not only a theological statement but also an antidiscriminatory statement. By its very nature, it serves to unify all believers and make irrelevant oppositional designations. I would add that this is also the intent of passages that emphasize that all are under sin, all are justified by faith ("for there is no distinction, for all have sinned" [3:22-23]), all are children of Abraham, all those justified are also reconciled to God, and all must view their lineage from Adam or from Christ (chaps. 3–5). These are not simply theological statements; they are inclusive statements meant to support the unity of the body of Christ. So while repeatedly recognizing the opposing designations of Jew and non-Jew in chapters 1–4 (and 5), Paul is purposely fostering their merger.

To Bartsch's invaluable insight I would add that when Paul says the gospel is "to the Jew first and also to the Greek," that is a priority statement that stands alongside the antidiscriminatory statement. By its very nature, it serves to accentuate the advantage of the Jew.[49] This combination of antidiscriminatory (unifying, inclusive) and priority (advantage) statements standing alongside each other for the purpose of assimilating gentiles into the orbit of the Jews is the tale of the letter. On the one hand, the gentiles needed to understand their equality with the Jews before God. On the other hand, they needed to recognize their belonging with the Jews before God. So Paul tackles the question of gentile equality and Jewish priority directly, and thoughtfully, and does so progressively through the body of the letter. There are three,

48. Ibid., 332.
49. Bartsch (ibid., 331) does not agree with this view. He says that "the emphasis on faith [i.e., to everyone who believes] is directed against that division or discrimination which was persisting in Roman Christendom. Hence the addition of 'first' (v.16) which seems to give precedence to the Jews has only a problematic or relative importance. The word is considered original, particularly since its deletion, in some manuscripts, is understood as a Marcionite 'correction.'" I would suggest that the priority statement is purposely and significantly stated by Paul not only to accentuate the advantage of the Jew but also in the process to eliminate further any devaluation of the Jew.

actually four, major passages that are pivotal for pulling gentiles into the orbit of ethnic Israel. They are, sequentially, 2:25-29; 4:1-25; 11:11-32; and 15:7-13.

First, in the context of the premise of the letter (1:19–2:29), which stresses the impartiality of God toward all humankind (anti-discriminatory rhetoric), 2:25-29 concludes that apart from an internal reality, the name Jew and mark of "circumcision" do not matter as regards the keeping of God's law.

2:25: For indeed circumcision profits if you practice the law; but if you are a transgressor of the law, your circumcision has become uncircumcision.

2:26: If therefore the uncircumcision keeps the righteous ordinances of the law, will not his uncircumcision be reckoned as circumcision?

2:27: And will not the one who is uncircumcised by nature, if he fulfills the law, judge you who, through the letter (of the law) and circumcision, are the transgressor of the law?

2:28: For a Jew is not one who is external, and circumcision is not that which is external in the flesh.

2:29: But a Jew is one who is internal, and circumcision is of the heart, in spirit, not in letter, whose praise is not from men but from God.[50]

The name and the mark are no doubt the most distinctive external signs of Jewish ethnicity separating Jews from non-Jews. But here, Paul is saying that they are not to be regarded as necessary for Christian identity. Paul is not saying circumcision is wrong, but he is reminding his readers of the true nature of circumcision. It is meant to point to an internal reality. He ranks "circumcision of the heart" above "circumcision in the flesh." Indeed, if the internal reality is present in "the uncircumcised," they will be viewed by God as "circumcised";

---

50. Paul is alluding to the meaning of the name Jew (praise/praiseworthy, Gen. 29:35; 49:8), and to the OT statements that circumcision is of the heart (Deut. 10:16; 30:6; Jer. 4:4; 9:25-26; Ezek. 44:7). The initial purpose of circumcision as the sign of the covenant was that the person so marked was obligated to keep the stipulations of the covenant (Gen. 17:9-14). Thus, when Paul says that "circumcision profits if you practice the law," he does so in the context of covenant obligations. John Calvin (*Commentaries on the Epistle of Paul the Apostle to the Romans* [Grand Rapids: Eerdmans, 1947], 111) points out that Paul calls the outward rite if accompanied without piety the "letter"; and the spiritual design of this rite the "spirit."

and the one who is "by nature" uncircumcised may judge the one who is physically circumcised yet breaks the law. It shifts the focus from external marks to internal matters of the heart and eliminates the necessity of these external signs for gentiles. This in effect opens the door for the uncircumcised to live alongside the circumcised without constantly being reminded of that mark that serves to separate them. This is of immense social significance. On this basis, one cannot discriminate between them. The ethnic identities of Jew and non-Jew are not eliminated, but they are diminished in significance. All this is antidiscriminatory discourse that affirms the equality of gentile and Jew before God and in turn serves as a uniting factor. But it stands alongside and ushers in the question that becomes the predominant question for gentile enquiry: "What then is the advantage of the Jew? And what profit is circumcision?" (a priority question). Judeans have failed to believe. They now present themselves as the enemy of the gospel (11:29). God has shown mercy on us gentiles. If these distinctive marks are not necessary and we are on an equal footing with Jews in the body of Christ, what is their advantage? Paul's immediate answer is, "much in every way"; and then he devotes three chapters (9–11) to explaining their advantage.

Second, in 4:1-25, Paul goes one step further. Not only does he eliminate the necessity of the external sign of circumcision (4:9-12), but he also now joins Jew and gentile believers in a common lineage going back to Abraham. It is not that the gentiles retain their heritage and the Jews are now no longer Jews; rather, it is the Jews who retain their ethnic identity with the gentile believers now numbered among them. One assumes when Paul asks, "What then shall we say that Abraham our forefather according to the flesh has found?" (4:1), that the pronoun "our" refers to those physically descended; and the assumption is no doubt correct. Paul is speaking as one physically born a Jew.[51] However, one cannot help but think that the pronoun was meant to have a more inclusive nuance; for the overriding point of

51. Notice the similar use of *sarka* to refer specifically to Jews in 9:1 (my kinsmen according to the flesh, *tōn syngenōn mou kata sarka*) and 11:14 (my flesh, *mou tēn sarka*).

the entire chapter is to take the readers from Abraham "our father according to the flesh" to Abraham "the father of nations" (4:17-18). "He is the father of all who believe" (4:11), "the heir of the world" (4:13), "the father to all the seed . . . the father of us all" (4:16). Romans 4:23-25 says that what was reckoned to Abraham was also reckoned to us who believe in him who raised Jesus from the dead. That is, gentiles are part of that lineage that goes beyond external name and mark by virtue of their faith in Christ. Paul is ushering gentiles into the lineage of the Jews; gentiles are part of the Jewish family tree and are to consider themselves as heirs of Abraham. There is a priority of the Jew here. Jews retain their ethnic identity, whereas the gentiles lose whatever they had and are united to theirs. Gentiles are effectively made children of Abraham. At the same time, this becomes inclusive rhetoric as well, for the gentiles are now one with the Jews by lineage. This is true of "everyone who believes" (4:24). It serves to unite gentile with Jew.[52]

Third, in the metaphor of the olive tree in chapter 11, Paul goes another step further. He is saying to his gentile audience that they are wild olive branches that have now been grafted into a cultivated olive tree. They have become partakers of the rich root of the olive, which in effect means they are united organically to Israel. They are not just affiliated, but fused together with the olive tree that is Israel. The metaphor is meant to convey the deep relation and union the gentiles have with the Jews. One might object that the construction of ethnicity through metaphor is not the same as through physical kinship. That is true, but one cannot deny that the metaphor is meant to convey a profound spiritual reality nonetheless. In other passages such as Eph. 2:11-22, Paul explains how in Christ Jesus Jews and gentiles are made into "one new man," a new entity; the two are made one

---

52. Barclay (*Pauline Churches and Diaspora Jews*, 13) writes: "In establishing communities consisting of both Jews and non-Jews, he [Paul] sometimes appears to cancel out the previous ethnicity of non-Jewish believers (1 Cor 12.2) and to graft them into a Jewish lineage: as 'children of Abraham' (Gal 3.6-9; Rom 4.10-12), they are encouraged to look to biblical history as the story of 'our fathers' (1 Cor 10.1; cf. Rom 2.29). . . . The context in which Paul's Gentile converts undergo resocialization 'in Christ' is not the Jewish community, whose ethnicity is practiced within kinship-households and through shared ancestral customs, but the house-assemblies, whose strong social ties cross over (without erasing) ethnic differentials."

(2:11-22). But here Paul grafts the gentiles into the olive tree that is "Israel." Again, it is not that the Jews are grafted into the wild olive tree, but that the gentiles are cut off from the wild olive and joined to Israel. The Jews retain their ethnic identity, while the gentiles are now one of them. This speaks to the real issue at hand, for the gentiles were apparently viewing themselves as having priority, hence their arrogance and high-mindedness. But Paul pictures two different trees, one definitely better than the other; and the gentiles are identified with the wild tree and wild branches who by the mercy of God are grafted into the good olive tree alongside the natural branches of Israel. This speaks to a hierarchical relationship between gentiles and Jews with the Jews having the priority ("to the Jews first and also to the Greeks"). This priority is not limited to a chronological or historical priority, but includes an ethnic priority. The gentile believers are assimilated into Israel.

Fourth, in the closing exhortation of 15:7-13, the text both concludes and confirms the broader intention of the letter as a whole, truths that Paul desires his gentile audience to understand: (1) "that Christ has become a servant of the circumcision on behalf of the truth of God in order to confirm the promises of the fathers; and [2] that the gentiles are to glorify God for his mercy" (15:8-9). A litany of Old Testament Scriptures then follows which confirms that the gentiles are to praise God with his people (Israel). Again, the Scriptures do not call on the Jews to join the gentiles in praising the Lord. The gentiles are to join the Jews. Historically, in 54–57 CE, the returning Jews were seeking to join the gentiles in worship and fellowship. Paul is reminding the gentiles that they are being called on to join the Jews in praising God. Just as gentile proselytes were made to resocialize in order to fit in with the Jews, so gentile believers are called on to deny their past heritage to join God's people. Everything flows in the direction of Israel. Moreover, the text says that Christ has become a servant of the circumcision, and it does not continue by saying that he is also the servant of the uncircumcision. It only says that the gentiles are to glorify God for his mercy.[53] This properly places the priority on the

Jews, while the gentiles should correctly view themselves as privileged for being recipients of God's mercy and included with God's people.

What are these four passages communicating to the gentile majority? They are saying there is no place for gentile arrogance or conceit. Gentiles need to reverse course and accept the Jews, even as they have been accepted by God. They are not to judge "the other" (ton heteron). This is no time for raising the question, "Are we better than they?" Rather, they need to realize that they are one with Jewish believers and that they have left their ethnic identity behind (whatever that was) to be joined with ethnic Israel. They are part of the true Jewish family tree, and have been grafted into the good olive tree. Their high-mindedness should be replaced with humility that they have received mercy and are able to participate with their Jewish brothers and sisters in Christ. The priority belongs to Israel. The Jews retain their ethnic identity, with the gentiles swallowed up in theirs. Rather than being at odds with their Jewish brothers and sisters, they should realize that they are actually one with them.[54]

---

53. One may try to find a way exegetically that 15:8-9 could be saying that Christ had become a servant both to the circumcision and to the gentiles. But a careful analysis of the text will not allow it. In fact this text confirms the broader intention of the letter, for properly translated it reads:

> [8]For I say that Christ has become a servant of the circumcision on behalf of the truth of God, in order to confirm the promises of the fathers. [9]And [I say] that the gentiles are to glorify God on behalf of his mercy, as it is written. . . .

> [8]legō gar Christon diakonon gegenēsthai peritomēs hyper alētheias theou, eis to bebaiōsai tas epangelias tōn paterōn, [9]ta de ethnē hyper eleous doxasai ton theon. kathōs gegraptai. . . .

Christ is the subject of the subclause in 15:8, and gentiles is the subject of the subclause in 15:9. Notice my change of punctuation in the translation and my insertion of an implied "I say" in 15:9.

54. C. J. Hodge (If Sons, Then Heirs, 140–41) explains it this way: "Paul never says . . . that the Ioudaioi have to give up any portion of their ethnic and religious identity. Their God, their practices, their scriptures are all intact. The gentiles, by contrast must give up goods that are central to their identity: their gods, religious practices, myths of origin, epic stories of their ancestors and origins. To receive the same judgment and mercy as the Ioudaioi, the gentiles must adopt the God of Israel and Jewish narratives of origin and ancestry. Although Ioudaioi and Greeks receive equally impartial treatment from God, these two peoples arrive at this position with different ethnic identities and ethnic histories. The Ioudaioi are marked by ethnic continuity and the Greeks by ethnic disruption and rearranging." There are antidiscriminatory passages in Paul that stress that we are all one in Christ—Jew and Greek, slave and free, male and female, circumcision and uncircumcision, barbarian and Scythian (1 Cor. 12:13; Gal. 3:27-28; Col. 3:11). These passages emphasize that having been baptized into Christ, we are all one in Christ. This can be said without abandoning obvious identities. Male and female are obvious sexual identities. Jew and gentile are obvious ethnic identities. These antidiscriminatory passages state the truth that both are "one in Christ." But in Romans, Paul is stating something more, that gentiles are to understand as

We return then to the question, was there antisemitism in the church in Rome? From the above evidence from Scripture, it seems evident that for some gentile believers, that was the case. Cultural identities and attitudes often influence the church and become a source of tension. A number of scholars agree with this assessment. Bartsch says that the real problem was not the infiltration of Judaizers, but gentiles guilty of antisemitism.[55] Nanos finds that Paul was countering "gentilizing," not "Judaizing" tendencies. He was addressing gentile behavior detrimental for their relation with Jews.[56] William Campbell maintains that gentiles were resisting fellowship with Jewish believers.

> A division had apparently arisen because the liberal-minded gentile Christian majority (the strong in faith) were unwilling to have fellowship with the conservative Jewish Christian minority (the weak in faith). In the letter which is primarily addressed to the former since they were chiefly to blame for the dispute (cf. 15:1), Paul undertakes an exposition of the righteous purpose of God for Jew and gentile as fulfilled in Jesus Christ and revealed in the Gospel.[57]

All of this is true, yet we should not neglect to mention that the Jews were not without fault. Their response was a judgmental one, as appears in 14:10 and may be implied in earlier references to Jews boasting in the law.[58] But the weight of responsibility clearly lies with the gentile majority.

---

believers that they are now joined to the family of Abraham. They have left their ethnic identity behind to be joined with ethnic Israel.

55. Bartsch, "Historical Situation in Rome," 330–31; see also Bartsch "The Concept of Faith in Paul's Letter to the Romans," *BR* 13 (1968): 41–53.

56. Nanos, *The Mystery of Romans*, 38; cf. 33n20.

57. William S. Campbell, "Why Did Paul Write Romans?" *ExpTim* 85 (1974): 264–69.

58. In Romans, there are multiple uses of the root *kauch-* (2:17, 23; 3:27; 4:2; 5:2, 3, 11; 11:18, 18; 15:17). Paul says boasting is legitimate if you are boasting in God or what God is accomplishing through you (2:17; 5:2, 3, 11; 15:17). Boasting is illegitimate if you are boasting in your own accomplishments (e.g., "Where then is boasting? It is excluded. By what kind of law? Of works? No, but by a law of faith" [3:27]; "If Abraham was justified by works he has something to boast about but not before God" [4:2]). Moreover, you cannot boast in the law if you are trespassing the law (2:23). It is interesting to note that the compound *katakauchaomai* is used to convey the gentile's arrogance in 11:18. It is a stronger form of *kauchaomai* and means "to boast against" or "to despise."

The Circumstances in Rome: Related to Historical Factors

This matter of church unity was important for another reason. The Roman believers were about to enter a time in which there would be active hostility from outsiders. Returning to the historical factors behind the writing of the letter, Paul understood the implications well. There was the edict of expulsion in 49, the return of the Jewish exiles following Claudius's death in 54, the writing of the letter in 57, the presence of Paul in Rome in 60–62, and the persecution of Christians by Nero in 64 (all dates relative). Within this timeline, Roman authorities arrived at the point of being able to distinguish between nonbelieving Jews and Christian Jews and gentiles. It is unclear how they were able to do so; however, they did, and they chose to persecute the one rather than the other. Christians were tortured and killed as scapegoats for the burning of Rome, but nonbelieving Jews were left untouched. The view that the Jews were behind the targeting was stated by early Christian apologists.[59] Many scholars today refute that notion.[60] But the idea that the Jews found it in their best interests to separate themselves from Christians and to do so in such a way that the imperium understood the difference is no doubt part of the equation. Separation kept the Jews from being persecuted as well. Moreover, Christians were outspoken in their faith in Christ. Paul writes in the time frame of 61–62 CE that his bonds were well known "throughout the whole praetorian guard and to everyone else' and that most of the believers had courage to speak the Word of God without fear" (Phil. 1:12-14).[61] This proclamation was no doubt viewed adversely by authorities who did not like the presence of foreign cults. All these factors probably contributed to their persecution. According to Walters:

Without the shelter of Judaism, the Christians were in danger of Roman

---

59. W. H. C. Frend, *Martyrdom and Persecution in the Early Church* (Oxford: Oxford University Press, 1965), 161–71, esp. 164.
60. E.g., Leon, *Jews of Rome*, 28; Stern, "The Jewish Diaspora," 165.
61. This statement aligns with the Acts 28:30-31 account that Paul was proclaiming the Lord Jesus Christ "with all openness, unhindered."

censorship as a superstitious, non-national foreign cult of recent origin with riotous tendencies. The Jewish communities in all likelihood, consciously lobbied Roman administrators in order to distinguish themselves from the Christians. The Jews had nothing to lose and everything to gain by making their autonomy clear. . . . The fact that in the persecution of 64 C.E. the Romans had no difficulty distinguishing Christians from Jews indicates both the attainment of the Jews' objective and its disastrous consequences for the Roman Christian communities.[62]

With these historical factors in mind, one is reminded of those passages in Romans referring to hope in the midst of tribulation and suffering. Traditionally, those passages have been interpreted as referring to normal suffering that occurs in the lives of believers—sickness, bereavement, death, and so forth. Few have related them to circumstances in Rome. Rather, they are made applicable in a general way to any audience. But the passages seem to address a more intense form of suffering that comes from persecution. Once one is aware of the historical factors behind the letter, it becomes more likely that these passages were in fact speaking directly to potential and/or actual persecution in Rome.[63] There are three passages in particular that should be read from that perspective: 5:1-11; 8:18-39; and 12:17–13:14. In each of these passages, nestled within the theological truths they convey, are strong references to hope in the midst of suffering. In each case, the message is that present suffering must be viewed from the perspective of hope in the glory of God, for the latter far outweighs the suffering they are experiencing in the present age.

Beginning with 8:18-39, we can maintain with some certainty that the sufferings to which Paul refers are primarily external in nature, not internal distress (though such external suffering will inevitably lead to internal distress). We know this from the entire passage and the strong terms that are used.[64] First, Paul transitions into this section

---

62. Walters, *Ethnic Issues*, 62; see also, Walters, "Romans, Jews, and Christians," 179–83. Das, *Paul and the Jews*, 60; Das, *Solving the Romans Debate*, 197–201.
63. It may be that actual persecution was occurring even at the time Paul was writing. For it is improbable that no persecution was taking place until the massive persecution in 64.
64. The structure of 8:18-39 may be viewed in two parts, 8:18-30 and 8:31-39; 8:17 is transitional. Romans 8:18-30 proceeds logically according to the statements: "For I reckon" (8:18-21); "For we know" (8:22-27); "But we know" (8:28-30). Romans 8:31 then introduces the seven questions that dominate the second part of the section.

with the theology of the cross (8:17): "since indeed we suffer together [*sympaschomen*] *with him*, in order that we may also be glorified together [*syndoxasthōmen*] *with him*."[65] That is, the one who presently suffers with Christ will participate in his glory (cf. Mark 8:34-38; 2 Cor. 1:5, 7; Phil. 3:10-11; 2 Tim. 2:11-12). Second, he then says that the sufferings of "the now time" (*tou nyn kairou*) are not worthy to be compared to the glory "about to be revealed" (*mellousan . . . apokalyphthēnai*), suggesting both the imminence of the revelation as well as the heightened comparison of the glory to follow (cf. 2 Cor. 4:17). The world in its corrupt state "eagerly longs" (*apokaradokia*) and "expectantly awaits" (*apekdechetai*) the revelation (*apokalypsin*) of the sons of God.[66] All of the above are carefully crafted statements that correspond eschatologically with the hope of glory to which Paul is pointing.[67] Third, Paul acknowledges that while we "wait expectantly" for the deliverance to come, our "hope" is held with "endurance" as well as the help of the Spirit, who "intercedes with inexpressible groanings" on our behalf. In other words, while we do hope, it is a struggle while experiencing present suffering (8:22-27). Then Paul assures them that all things work together for good for those who love God, for those who are called according to his purpose. For our calling, even our glorification, are already ours (the "already now")[68] (8:28-30).

---

65. Robert Jewett, *Romans*, Hermeneia (Minneapolis: Fortress Press, 2007), 502–3; C. E. B. Cranfield, *A Critical and Exegetical Commentary on the Epistle to the Romans*, ICC (Edinburgh: T&T Clark, 1975), 1:407. The introductory particle *eiper* may be interpreted either as introducing a condition, "if indeed," or stating a fact, 'since indeed." The latter sense is to be preferred for several reasons. First, it is used in this sense previously in 8:9; second, the verb "suffer together" (*sympaschomen*) is in the present tense; third, it is immediately followed in 8:18 by reference to "the sufferings of the present time' (*tou nyn kairon*). Notice the parallelism between present sufferings and future glory in 8:17 and 18.

66. By contrasting the world and its corruption with the eagerly awaited and anticipated glory to come, Paul is painting a picture of two opposite worlds, a creation that is fallen and corrupt (reminiscent of the fall and of Rom. 1:19-32), and a new order and revelation of the sons of God (8:19-21). It is interesting that in 8:16-17 the Spirit bears witness with our spirit that we are children of God. Then in 8:18-21, the revelation to come is of the sons of God.

67. Paul uses the term *apokaradokia* (eager longing, 8:19) once, *apekdechomai* (wait expectantly) three times, and *elpizo/elpis* (hope) six times in 8:18-27.

68. Herman Ridderbos, *Paul: An Outline of His Theology*, trans. John R. DeWitt (Grand Rapids: Eerdmans, 1979), 52–53. Ridderbos distinguishes between "the 'already now' of the time of salvation that has been entered upon as well as of the 'even now' of the world time that still continues" (ibid., 52). However, he cautions that "Paul himself gives no explanation of this tension between the 'even now' and the 'already now' in the categories of an eschatological system. For he was not a 'theologian who thought in terms of the aeons,' but a preacher of Jesus Christ, who has come

The second part of the section begins with the questions, "What shall we say to these things? If God is for us, who is against us?"[69] The final question is, "Who will separate us from the love of Christ? Shall tribulation, distress, persecution, famine, nakedness, danger, or the sword?" This list depicts various forms of intense suffering: "tribulation" (*thlipsis*) can be translated oppression or affliction, and is often associated with the end times (Matt. 24:9, 21; Col. 1:24; Rev. 7:14); Käsemann defines "distress" (*stenochōria*) as "hemmed in with no way out," and in this setting as a "blocked exit";[70] "persecution" (*diōgmos*) refers to religious persecution;[71] "famine" and "nakedness" (*limos* and *gymnotēs*) are descriptive of human deprivation; "danger" (*kindynos*) can be translated as "peril" (cf. 2 Cor. 11:26, where it is used eight times of perilous circumstances); and "sword" (*machaira*) no doubt refers to execution or violent death.[72] The scriptural support that immediately follows (Ps. 44:22; LXX 43:23) was commonly used by rabbis to refer to martyrdom.

> For your sake we are being put to death all day long;
> we are considered as sheep to be slaughtered.

This pretty much says it all. In the words of Käsemann, this is "a call for suffering and death."[73] Then Paul responds,

> In all these things we overwhelmingly conquer (*hypernikōmen*) through the one who loved us. For I am persuaded that neither death nor life nor angels nor authorities nor things present nor things to come nor powers nor height nor depth nor any other created thing will be able to separate us from the love of God which is in Christ Jesus our Lord.

and is yet to come." These distinctions are helpful for interpreting this passage, the "even now," the "already now," as well as the "not yet" of the future kingship of God. Note that the aorists in 8:29-30 denote simple action and suggest that these actions—foreknew, pre-encircled, called, justified, and glorified—are part of the "already now."

69. There are seven questions in a row (8:31-35). Q1 begins with *Ti oun* and serves to introduce the rest. Q2 and Q4 and Q6 may be the primary series of questions, with Q3 and Q5 and Q7 answering the immediately preceding ones. Together they arrive at a crescendo with Q6 and Q7, the quote from Ps. 44:22, and the statements in 8:37-39 concluding with "in Christ Jesus our Lord."
70. Käsemann, *Romans*, 60, 249. Dunn (*Romans 1-8*, 505) agrees.
71. Arndt and Gingrich, *Lexicon*, 200.
72. For a much deeper analysis of each of these terms, see Jewett, *Romans*, 543-48.
73. Käsemann, *Romans*, 250.

This, of course, is a profound statement of assurance and trust and hope in God. The "love of God," the "love of Christ," and "the one who loved us" are all interchangeable and enable us overwhelmingly to conquer these circumstances. One can hardly read this passage and not conclude that it was addressing harsh circumstances in Rome. The entire section is based on the theology of the cross and is written to uphold and encourage the believers' "hope" in the Lord.

In light of 8:18-39, we should consider 5:1-11 from the same perspective. It is a carefully conceived discourse drawing attention to the marvelous truth that Christ died for sinners and that the justified person is thereby reconciled to God. But nestled very early in this discourse are the following words:

> And we boast in hope of the glory of God. And not only, but also, we boast in tribulations, knowing that tribulation produces endurance, and endurance proven character, and proven character hope, and hope does not disappoint because the love of God has been poured out in our hearts through the Holy Spirit. (5:2-5)

These are the same themes accented in 8:18-39—hope of the glory of God in the midst of tribulation, based on the love of God. Robert Jewett holds that "in the (our) tribulations" (*en tais thlipsin*) designates the ground of boasting in the same way "in my weaknesses" (*en tais astheneiais* [*mou*]) serves in 2 Cor. 12:5 (also 11:30; 12:9). Paul's weaknesses included "insults, distresses, persecutions, and calamities for Christ's sake" (12:10) and is expanded in the discourse of 2 Cor. 11:16-30, which details his extensive persecution as an apostle. Jewett contends that Paul had specific hardships in mind that the believers in Rome knew of, hardships inflicted beginning in the year 49 and continuing to the present.[74] Moo notes that while some confine these tribulations to sufferings caused by religious persecution, to do so is questionable since all sufferings are part of this present evil age.[75] This may be true, and its application may extend in this way. But why does Paul bring up the subject in the first place? What was the historical

---

74. Jewett, *Romans*, 353.
75. Douglas J. Moo, *The Epistle to the Romans*, NICNT (Grand Rapids: Eerdmans, 1996), 302–3.

context? The danger is that when we extend the application in this way, we are treating Romans more as an essay directed to an audience at large rather than as a letter addressing circumstances in Rome. What were the circumstances he was addressing? I think it is safe to say that those circumstances included present and/or potential persecution for the sake of Christ.

The final passage is 12:17–13:14. It is part of the larger block of paraenesis in 12:1–15:13, which consists basically of two sections, 12:1–13:14 and 14:1–15:6. Within 12:1–13:14, the exhortations in 12:3-16 apply to life within the body of Christ, and 12:17–13:14 apply to relationships outside the body.[76] This latter section should not be regarded as "standard *paraenesis*" with no direct application to the circumstances in Rome.[77] I have already shown how 12:3-16 addresses the need for unity within the body, and 14:1–15:6 addresses fellowship issues within the body. Romans 12:17–13:14 also addresses their circumstances. Paul was aware of the hostile environment (12:17-21) as well as the obvious fact that they were living in the capital of Rome itself under the watchful eye of the government (13:1-7). His response is to remind them to live according to the divine commandment, "to love your neighbor as yourself" (13:8-10), knowing that the day of deliverance is near (13:11-14). The flow of these ideas is quite natural.

First, in response to the hostile environment and those who would do them harm (12:17-21),[78] Paul exhorts them in multiple ways:

76. It is not agreed exactly as to where the boundary line is between the two. Some place it before 12:12; first exhortations end and the second begin. Some place it before 12:14, which appeals, "bless those who persecute you." Others think it should be placed before 12:16b, which begins, "Do not be haughty, but associate with the lowly." I have argued above in this chapter that 12:3 and 16 bracket the first section. But this matter is not of major significance. We must remember that this is a letter and that Paul was more concerned about communicating the subject matter at hand as he was dictating it to Tertius.

77. Martin Dibelius (*From Tradition to Gospel*, trans. Bertram Lee Woolf [New York: Charles Scribner's Sons, 1971], 238–40) held that the hortatory sections of Paul's letters are to be viewed as traditional paraenesis. They "lack an immediate relation with the circumstances of the letter. The rules and directions are not formulated for special churches and concrete cases, but for the general requirements of earliest Christendom" (ibid., 238). Victor P. Furnish (*Theology and Ethics in Paul* [Nashville: Abingdon, 1968]) challenged this view, but the question is still to what degree the exhortations are focused on specific circumstances facing the Roman Christian community. I would argue that all of them, from 12:1 to 15:13, are directly addressing circumstances in Rome. Cf. Robert J. Karris, "The Occasion of Romans," in Donfried, *Romans Debate*, 81–84; James D. G. Dunn, *Romans 9-16*, WBC 38B (Waco: Word, 1989), 705.

78. I view 12:17-21 as a smaller paragraph within the larger segment of 12:17–13:14. Note that 12:21

> Do not return evil for evil. . . . Do good before all men. . . . Do not take your own revenge. . . . Care for "your enemy." . . . Overcome evil with good.

In these five verses, Paul includes five supporting Old Testament references (sequentially, Prov. 3:4; Ps. 34:14 [LXX 33:15]; Lev. 19:18a; Deut. 32:35; Prov. 25:21-22a). This heavy concentration of scriptural references demonstrates the importance of these appeals. He also exhorts them to live peaceably with all people (13:18). But he does so with a double qualification:

> If possible, as far as it depends on you, live peaceably with all men.

In the words of James Dunn: "Paul clearly recognizes that such harmonious living with neighbors might not be possible nor lie within their own power: hostility and persecution was too familiar a rule for any such assumption to be made."[79] Dunn also makes the astute observation that the believers in Rome "were an endangered species, vulnerable to further imperial rulings against Jews and societies. He therefore urges a policy of living quietly, and of nonresponse to provocation."[80] It is a form of social passivism. Whether these provocations were coming from Jews or pagans is not stated, but they were present nonetheless.

Second, the question of pagan hostility leads naturally into consideration of the political reality of living in Rome itself.[81] Historically, this passage (13:1-7) has served as the locus classicus for

---

takes up and concludes the subject matter of 12:17, a form of *inclusio*, or ring composition. I recognize that 12:14 already brings up the issue of blessing those who persecute you; but I believe that it is best to view all of 12:14-16 as part of 12:3-16, which, as I have shown above in this chapter, has a ring composition of its own, the use of the root *phron-* in 12:3 and 16. Some commentators also point out that the exhortations shift from participles to imperatives in 12:14; but I would point out that Paul is constantly shifting from participles to imperatives to infinitives back to participles to imperatives to participles to imperatives all the way through 12:21 to express his exhortations.

79. Cf. Dunn, *Romans 9-16*, 748.

80. Ibid., 738. Note that this is the one place in the letter where Paul addresses the recipients in the vocative as "Beloved" (*agapētoi*), to encourage them. This personal address is additional evidence that Paul was addressing circumstances in Rome.

81. Paul enters the paragraph somewhat abruptly. The abruptness is marked by the lack of an introductory conjunction (asyndeton) together with his switch to the third person. It simply begins, "every soul" (*pasa psychē*). Nevertheless, we should not view this section, 13:1-7, as an independent insertion unrelated to the surrounding context.

the doctrine of the state, and the words "Let every soul be subject to the governing authorities" have been viewed as binding even in times when Peter's pronouncement to the Sanhedrin would have served better: "We ought to obey God rather than men."[82] Commentators have mostly focused on the doctrine and not on how this passage relates to circumstances in Rome. Nevertheless, a few point out that the letter was written in the early years of Nero's reign, when he was influenced by Seneca and times seemed to be quite stable. Ben Witherington suggests that this allowed Paul to encourage Christians to be subject to the government and to pay their taxes.[83] Willi Marxsen on the other hand suggests that "what we have here is not a dogmatic treatise on government and the State, but a demand for loyal conduct in order to avoid a fresh edict."[84] Dunn says Paul's purpose was to protect the believers in Rome, to help them avoid drawing the attention of the Roman government. The harsh political realities of the imperium demanded a cautious and submissive response. Paul was advising a form of political quietism.[85] There is some truth to this. Paul describes the government as being "an avenger of wrath" and "not bearing the sword in vain." He mentions the "fear" factor several times and notes that believers would have nothing to fear if they do good. It appears that Paul was advising Christians from both a biblical and practical perspective. Biblically, we know that God ordains the powers that be (e.g., Prov. 8:15-16; 24:21). From a practical perspective, we know that

---

82. An obvious example would be the Christian community's response to the Third Reich and the genocide of Jews and other innocents. Käsemann (*Romans*, 351) points out that 13:1 aligns with the apostolic understanding of authority and order as established by God. But due to worldwide abuse of power, many have taken offense at the wording "be subject." However, it may also be noted that the present abuse of power may be analogous to the Rome of Paul's day. While I believe that God has ordained all authority, that belief does not come without qualification. We need to use the analogy of Scripture.

83. Ben Witherington III, *Paul's Letter to the Romans: A Socio-rhetorical Commentary* (Grand Rapids: Eerdmans, 2004), 306.

84. Willi Marxsen, *Introduction to the New Testament: An Approach to Its Problems* (Philadelphia: Fortress Press, 1980), 100 (brought to my attention by Dunn, *Romans 9-16*, 768).

85. Dunn, *Romans 1-8*, 772-73. Dunn writes (ibid., 773): "Paul does not idealize the situation he is addressing. He does not pretend the authorities of whom he speaks are models of the good ruler. His advice does not particularly arise out of his own experience of Roman protection and the *pax Romana*. He and his Jewish readers in Rome knew well enough the arbitrary power of Rome.... Paul would have no illusions that a quiet subservience would be sufficient to guarantee peace. But his advice is not conditional on Roman benevolence. It is simply a restatement of the long established Jewish recognition of the reality and character of political power."

Christians living in Rome had good reason to fear the power of Rome. They had already experienced the state's crackdown on their evangelistic activities (49 CE). Now nonbelieving Jews were distancing themselves from Christians and the Roman government was able to distinguish between them. They were truly in a vulnerable and defenseless position. Danger was on the horizon, and Paul was advising them how to respond. He was not advising them to deny their faith; but he was advising them to live within the realities of the present age.

This admonition to obey authorities includes an admonition to pay taxes (13:6-7).[86] At first glance, it seems a bit strange that Paul would include advice about paying taxes in his letter. But these two verses are important in this respect. In the mid-50s, there was widespread dissatisfaction among Roman citizens toward Nero's taxation policies. Both Suetonius and Tacitus document a citizens' revolt against his policies.[87] All this unrest was taking place at the time Paul was writing the letter. For Paul to include this advice betrays the fact that he was aware of what was going on in Rome.[88] It supports the view that Paul knew of their circumstances.

Third, the final two paragraphs serve to remind believers of what underlies their response to pagans and the Roman government. The trifold emphasis on loving one's neighbor (13:8, 9, 10) effectively governs their response to their hostile environment. The command to love their "neighbor" is not restricted to "believers only," but in the context is to be applied especially to nonbelievers. The imminence of their salvation is the other motivating factor (13:11-14). "Do this, knowing the time," clearly referring to the time of Christ's return and the believer's final redemption.[89] The imagery is strongly temporal: "The hour is already come . . . now is our salvation nearer . . . the night is far advanced and the day is at hand. There is also an urgency conveyed in the imagery: "Awaken from sleep, put off deeds of

---

86. Structurally, it appears that 13:6-7 are part of 13:1-5, for 13:7 offers a summary for all of 13:1-7 and the entire paragraph is an admonition to submit to government authorities.
87. Suetonius, *Nero* 44; Tacitus, *Annals* 13.
88. Cf. Dunn, *Romans 9-16*, 772.
89. Cf. Moo, *Romans*, 820–21.

darkness and put on the armor of light, walk decently as in the day, and put on the Lord Jesus Christ" (13:11-12). The night is not yet over and the day has not yet come, but it is *at hand!* They are to love their pagan neighbors and live in the light of Christ's coming. How much more direct could Paul be with regard to the circumstances of the believers in Rome? These appeals are directly relevant to their circumstances. The hostility they faced, the imperious government, the principle of responding according to the great commandment of love, and the appeal to live in the light of the imminent return of Christ—were all germane to what was happening in Rome. The exhortations to "repay no one evil for evil . . . but overcome evil with good" (12:17, 21) or "do good and you will have praise" from the authorities (13:3) are written in the context of Rome itself. They are not general paraenesis to be applied to Christians everywhere. They are appeals by Paul to believers in a hostile environment under an authoritarian pagan government. It is only with this initial understanding that one can then begin to apply these passages to Christians everywhere.

Concluding Observations

There is ample evidence in the body of the letter to demonstrate that Paul was writing to circumstances in Rome. Those circumstances included both internal problems of discord that existed primarily along ethnic lines, and external pressures from society at large. They were a community involved in advancing the gospel while at the same time experiencing uncertainty as to their security. This was especially challenging for the returning Jewish believers who found themselves without a comfortable home among the gentiles. In their arrogance, the gentiles were not accommodating in this regard, and Paul had to address them directly. The unity of the body was all important. The assurance of hope for the body in the face of persecution was all important. The need for applying the gospel to believers living in Rome in that social and historical context was all important. These were the circumstances to which Paul was writing. He was writing as he himself stated in the introduction of his letter, "to bring about the obedience of faith among all the gentiles for his name's sake," and "to proclaim the gospel" to those in Rome.

7

———

The Coherence of Romans

We have found that the entirety of Romans should be viewed as a letter, not a letter-essay. As a letter, it was written to address circumstances in Rome. Those circumstances included the division of believers primarily along ethnic lines and the prospect of suffering from outside sources. Paul is addressing both of those concerns in the body of the letter. He is not carrying on a debate with Jews, for the letter has nothing to do with such a debate. He is boldly dealing with judgmental attitudes, especially those of gentile believers toward their Jewish counterparts. The rhetoric and grammar of the letter are quite interactive. Paul's extensive use of questions plays a major role in that interaction. The flow of thought in chapters 3–11 is guided by those questions with relevant exhortations following in chapters 12–15. Thus we arrive at the "surface structure" of the letter.

1:1-18: Opening of the Letter
1:19–2:29: Premise of the Letter
3:1–15:13: Heart of the Letter
   3:1-9a: Main Questions Raised
     3:9b–5:21: Extended Answer to 3:9a
     6:1–8:39: Extended Answer to 3:7-8
     9:1–11:36: Extended Answer to 3:1-6

12:1–15:13: Exhortations That Apply
15:14–16:27: Closing of the Letter

More specifically, regarding the main questions in the heart of the letter, I have maintained that Paul is raising questions in 3:1-9a that he intends to answer in reverse order in 3:9b–11:36.

3:1-2: brief question-and-answer introducing the group of questions
  A. 3:3-4: brief question-and-answer
    B. 3:5-6: brief question-and-answer
      C. 3:7-8: brief question-and-answer
        D. 3:9a: brief question-and-answer with extended A: 3:9b–5:21
      C. 6:1, 15: extended question-and-answer: 6:1–8:39
    B. 9:14: extended question-and-answer: 9:14-32
  A. 11:1, 11: extended question-and-answer: 11:1-36, with context of 9:30–10:21

This is a thoroughly Hebraic way of structuring the discourse of the letter. To think that Paul could not or would not structure the letter in this way is to underestimate the thought processes of Paul. When Paul wrote Romans, he was probably around sixty years old with years of learning going back to his education as a strict Pharisee under the tutelage of Rabbi Gamaliel (Acts 22:3). He had the acumen to think deliberately and precisely in a repertoire of discourse that was fine-tuned through years of extensive debates in synagogues and preaching among the gentiles. He was also able to think relationally, with skill. He had to, for he did not have our modern technical aids to help him correct himself were he to misspeak (as may have happened in 1:11-12). He did have an amanuensis (scribe) who recorded word for word, sentence after sentence, what Paul dictated to him. In 16:22, we read, "I, Tertius, the one who wrote this letter in the Lord, greet you." The process of dictation was slow and time-consuming. On Tertius's part, it would have demanded an ability to write legibly and accurately on a papyrus scroll. It took years of training to learn how to do this, and it must have taken the two of them weeks or even months to compose Romans. No doubt much of Paul's time in Corinth during his third missionary journey was consumed with this task (Acts 20:2-3).[1] On

166

Paul's part, this would have demanded careful planning of the overall structure of the letter. The slow pace would have allowed Paul time to contemplate even the small details of his discourse. How would he keep their attention? How would he lead them step by step through the entire letter? The extensive use of questions and epistolary formulas within groups of questions helped to guide them, but especially the question-and-answer in 3:1-9a. That question-and-answer was an oral map for the audience and a mental outline for the apostle to follow.

Without that oral map, there could be no coherence in the letter. But with that oral map, the content of the body of the letter flows smoothly from one section to the next. The parts of the letter contribute to the whole, and the content of the parts speaks to the circumstances of the recipients. The extended answers in chapters 3–11 address (1) the unity of both Jew and gentile before God (3:9b–5:21), (2) the moral imperative for the gentiles in light of both the grace of God and the law of God (6:1–8:39), and (3) the priority of the Jews in the plan of God (9:1–11:36). These are core issues for the believers in Rome. The exhortations in chapters 12–15 address (1) the unity of the body (12:3-16), (2) how to respond to adversity from outside the body (12:17–13:14), and (3) the need to accept one another within the body (14:1–15:13). The letter deals with unity issues, ethnic issues, customs issues, moral issues, and underlying antisemitic issues. The return of Jewish believers to Rome was not seamless. How would the gentiles view their role in the body, the importance of the law, and their Jewish customs and identity? The surface structure of the body of the letter guided the readers through this labyrinth of issues. What is left for us to consider is how the

---

1. Robert Jewett (*Romans*, Hermeneia [Minneapolis: Fortress Press, 2007], 22–23, 979–80) makes the case that Tertius must have been a highly skilled scribe and available to Paul on a full-time basis, that Phoebe may have borne the expense of the scribe, and that Tertius may have even accompanied the letter to Rome for the purpose of reading the letter to the believers there. (I doubt this latter point since Tertius writes that he sends his greeting.) Ben Witherington suggests it may have been Phoebe who did the reading (*Paul's Letter to the Romans: A Socio-rhetorical Commentary* [Grand Rapids: Eerdmans, 2004], 23). Cf. E. Randolph Richards, *The Secretary in the Letters of Paul*, WUNT 2/42 (Tübingen: J. C. B. Mohr [Paul Siebeck], 1991), 15–67; Richard Longenecker, "Ancient Amanuenses and the Pauline Epistles," in *New Dimensions in New Testament Study*, ed. Richard N. Longenecker and Merrill C. Tenney (Grand Rapids: Zondervan, 1974), 281–97; Leon Morris, *The Epistle of Paul to the Romans* (Grand Rapids: Eerdmans, 1988), 543.

opening of the letter (1:1-18) and the premise of the letter (1:19–2:29) contribute to the letter as a whole.

Prescript, 1:1-7

Romans opens with a long prescript, the longest of Paul's letters, with ninety-three words. In his other letters, they are less than half that length, with the exception of 1 Corinthians, which has fifty-five words.[2] Paul's prescripts always include three elements: the sender, the recipients, and a greeting in the form of a benediction.[3] Romans is no different if we limit our attention to 1:1 and 1:7:

> [1a]Paul, a bond servant of Christ Jesus, called an apostle [the sender] . . . [7]to all who are in Rome, beloved of God, called to be saints [the recipients], grace to you and peace from God our Father and Lord Jesus Christ [the greeting].

This is typically Pauline, containing all three elements with only twenty-seven words in the original.[4] What is exceptional is the material bracketed between 1:1 and 1:7, an additional sixty-six words in which Paul highlights two matters. First, he defines the gospel for which he had been "set apart."[5] It was "promised beforehand through his prophets in the holy Scriptures, concerning his Son."

---

2. For example: 2 Corinthians with forty-one; Galatians with forty-two; Ephesians with thirty (with *en Ephesō*); Philippians with thirty-two; Colossians with twenty-eight (or thirty-two with variant reading); or 1 Thessalonians with nineteen; 2 Thessalonians with twenty-seven.

3. This threefold introduction was typical of letters in the first century. See David E. Aune, "Epistolography," in *The Westminster Dictionary of New Testament and Early Christian Literature and Rhetoric* (Louisville: Westminster John Knox, 2003), 162–68, esp. 166; also 428–32.

4. Aside from the obvious that a Pauline prescript does not display normal sentence structure, lacking verbs and jumping from sender to addressee with a short benediction at the end, this prescript does retain normal grammatical connectives between clauses, and all the clauses, appositives, and prepositional phrases are typical of Paul's style.

5. *Aphōrismenos* is a perfect passive participle used substantivally in apposition to *Paulos*, along with the nouns *doulos* and *klētos*. C. E. B. Cranfield observes that "set apart" refers not to Paul's separation from Judaism, nor to his separation from his brothers in Christ in Acts 13:2, but to his being set apart and consecrated for the gospel of God. Jeremiah (Jer. 1:5) and Isaiah (Isa. 49:1) were set apart by God for a special mission; so also Paul that of taking "the gospel of God" to the gentiles (see Gal. 1:15). See C. E. B. Cranfield, *A Critical and Exegetical Commentary on the Epistle to the Romans*, ICC (Edinburgh: T&T Clark, 1975), 1:53.

Who was born	[*ek*] of the seed of David	A
	[*kata*] according to the flesh,	B
Who was appointed Son of God with power		
	[*kata*] according to the Spirit of holiness	B
	[*ex*] by the resurrection of the dead,	A
Jesus Christ our Lord.		

James Dunn calls this a "Jewish gospel for Gentiles."[6] He notes that "each assertion [throughout the prescript] is carefully formulated in characteristic Jewish terms"[7]—bond servant of Christ Jesus,[8] called an apostle,[9] set apart for the gospel of God, promised beforehand through his prophets in the holy Scriptures,[10] concerning his Son, born of the seed of David, and so forth. Why would Paul frame the gospel in this way? Because it serves to introduce a major theme in the letter, the priority of Israel. Even the gospel the gentiles profess is a Jewish gospel! When they proclaim, "Jesus Christ is Lord," they are declaring their allegiance to the God of Israel. Paul is writing to gentile believers who may have some question about the significance of the Jews and the Old Testament story to their present Christian profession. He is already in the process of answering that question. The gospel the gentiles believe is rooted in Israel and the Old Testament. Their identity as believers is profoundly related to Israel. Every clause in the prescript serves to underscore that theme.[11] This sets the tone of the letter.

6. James D. G. Dunn, *Romans 1-8*, WBC 38A (Waco: Word, 1988), 5–6. The present writer attributes this statement of the gospel totally to Paul. He was not relying on an early Christian confession. The structure is consistent with Paul's use of the Greek. The content fits perfectly the purpose and themes of the letter (see note 11 below). And Paul was perfectly capable of writing this definition of the gospel. Note also its abbreviated use in 2 Tim. 2:8.

7. Dunn, *Romans 1-8*, 5.

8. Designation given to Moses, Joshua, David, prophets (Josh. 14:7; 24:29; Judg. 2:8; 2 Kgs. 17:23; Ps. 89:3); here meant to express total allegiance and submission to the Lord; equivalent to the OT *'ebed YHWH*.

9. Reminiscent of God's calling of Israel in the OT (Isa. 42:6; 48:15; 49:1; 51:2); *klētos* and cognates are found thirteen times in Romans, five times in Romans 9.

10. Ties the gospel to the covenant promises made by OT prophets.

11. It is important also to note that the terms in the prescript foreshadow major themes in the letter—OT Scriptures, calling, seed of David (Abraham, David, Jews, Israel), flesh, Spirit, obedience of faith, etc. Paul is choosing his words carefully.

Second, Paul makes clear the object of his mission. He says, "We have received grace and apostleship[12] for the obedience of faith among all the gentiles . . . among whom you also are the called of Jesus Christ."[13] (I deal with this reference more extensively in chapter 1.) While Christian Jews were among the recipients of the letter, Paul's focus was on his gentile readers and their obedience of faith. Nevertheless, the letter is addressed in 1:7 "to all who are in Rome, beloved by God, called as saints." Paul is including both Jewish and gentile believers in his greeting in a positive and unifying way.[14] In the words of Dunn, we are witnessing "Jewish heritage and Gentile outreach already beginning to emerge as a strong theme of the letter itself."[15]

Thanksgiving and Occasion/Purpose, 1:8-18

It is fascinating to witness how quickly Paul moves from thanking God for them (1:8), to praying for them (1:9), to praying to come see them (1:10), to stating why he wants to come see them, to impart some spiritual gift (1:11), to encourage them (1:12), and to preach the gospel to them (1:15). It seems a bit unusual for Paul to say in the same breath that he prays for them and that he prays to come to see them (1:9b-10). But this was a major concern of his. He wanted them to know of his great desire to be with them. Here is how Paul develops his line of thought in 1:8-18:

---

12. Though 1:5 is translated "grace and apostleship," the nouns are a hendiadys (one through two), namely that his apostleship is a gift of God's grace that he has received. See Paul's use of the word "grace" in Rom. 12:3; 15:15. This view is favored by Cranfield, *Romans*, 1:65–66; William Hendriksen, *Romans* (Grand Rapids: Baker, 1981), 44.
13. Cranfield argues that the clause "among whom also you are called" could be referring simply to the church living in the midst of the Gentile world (*Romans*, 1:68). True, it could be taken in the geographic sense "in the midst of whom." But this is highly unlikely due to other references throughout Romans, especially 15:15-19, which defines how we ought to understand gentiles in this context (also 1:13-15; 11:13). Interestingly, *ethnos* occurs twenty-nine times in Romans, nine in OT quotations.
14. It is noted that Paul does not say, as he does in some of his letters, *tē ekklēsia tē en Rhomē*; rather, *pasin tois ousin en Rhomē*. Many commentators suggest that the absence of the phrase "to the church in Rome" is due to the existence of multiple house churches. This may be reading too much into its absence. Most everyone accepts that there were multiple house churches in Rome, a significant point in understanding the background and diverse audience of the letter. But even when the apostle addresses the Corinthians and uses the singular *tē ekklēsia* (1 Cor. 1:2; 2 Cor. 1:1), are we to suppose that there was necessarily only one congregation in that large city, especially when there were such sharp divisions within the church (1:10-16)?
15. Dunn, *Romans 1–8*, 26.

[8a]But "first of all" I thank my God for all of you . . . [thanksgiving formula]
[9a]For God is my witness how . . . [oath formula]
[11a]For I long to see you in order that . . . [heartfelt expression]
[13a]But I want you to know, brothers, that . . . [disclosure formula]
[16a]For I am not ashamed of the gospel.
[16b]For it is the power of God to everyone . . . Jew first and Greek
[17]For the righteousness of God is revealed from faith to faith . . .
[18]For the wrath of God is revealed against . . .

There are two major paragraphs in 1:8-18 introduced by two leading statements. The first is the thanksgiving formula introduced by *prōton men* ("But first of all"). This should not be translated "first," as if it was the first of a series.[16] The two terms together can also mean "above all else," "first of all," "to begin with," or "foremost." This is how they are used here and should be translated "first of all" or "foremost."[17] What is *foremost* for Paul is his thankfulness for them together with his intense desire to come see them. He swears with an oath "how unceasingly" he prays for them, "always," "if perhaps now at last" he will be "favored by God's will" to come to them. This piling up of adverbs and particles shows how seriously Paul intends for his readers to capture his longing and love for them.

Then comes his disclosure statement, "But I do not want you to be ignorant, brothers, that . . ." (1:13). This rhetorical formula, *de ou thelō hymas agnoein, adelphoi, hoti*, is often used by Paul to introduce concerns of special importance.[18] He uses it only twice in Romans, in 1:13 and in 11:25. Both passages are extremely important for what he wants to communicate. In 1:13, the formula serves to highlight the main purpose for which he is writing the letter. In 11:25, it serves to conclude what may be considered the main point of the letter. In 1:13-15, he writes,[19]

---

16. One could conceivably argue that the *men* in 1:8 is complemented by the *de* in 1:13, thus creating a *men . . . de* contrast, "on the one hand . . . on the other hand." But the two paragraphs are not meant to contrast with each other; the latter flows naturally from the former.

17. Parallel usage may be found in Rom. 3:2 and 1 Cor. 11:18, both of which are without further enumeration and may be translated in any of these alternative meanings.

18. Cf. Rom. 11:25; 1 Cor. 10:1; 12:1; 2 Cor. 1:8; 1 Thess. 4:13. In every instance, the vocative "brothers" is included as a personal form of address.

19. This is a literal translation seeking to preserve the word order of the original, indenting subclauses, and showing the chiastic arrangement of the clauses.

[13]But I want you [pl.] to know, brothers and sisters,

that many times I planned to come to you [pl.],[20]   A

(and I was hindered until now),

in order that some fruit I might have even among you [pl.]

    as also among the rest of the gentiles [pl.].   B

    [14]Both to the Greeks and to the barbarians,   B

    both to the wise and to the foolish [pl.]

    I am a debtor.

[15]Thus I am eager also to you [pl.] who are in Rome   A

    to proclaim the gospel.

This is a literal translation using the word order in the Nestle-Aland text (with a couple minor exceptions). Paul uses a simple chiasm to get across his main point. At the center of the chiasm is his prominent vision of reaching the gentiles. This is made obvious by the emphatic position of the datives in 1:14 as well as his use of asyndeton. It also serves to heighten the object of his mission, the gentiles. He uses the terms "Greeks and barbarians," "wise and foolish."[21] Commentators naturally ask whether these pairings refer to the whole of humankind, or the whole of the gentile world. According to James Dunn, with whom I agree, they refer generally to all races and classes within the gentile world.[22] Paul is using these designations to include "all" without distinction. It does not matter your background or giftedness. Paul is indebted to reach them all with the gospel, including the gentiles in Rome.[23]

On the outer edges of the chiasm, Paul clearly states what he wants

---

20. This clause, "and was hindered until now," is parenthetic, with the *hina* clause following the *hoti* clause. His being hindered is also mentioned in 15:22. Clearly, Paul wanted those in Rome to know that there were reasons why he had not yet come. We are not told what hindered him, though it surely had to do with his responsibilities in Macedonia and Achaia and his obligation to gather and take the offering to Jerusalem. It is also unnecessary to speculate on the character of these hindrances—circumstances over which he had no control; however, he trusted it would be the "will of God" for him now to come to Rome.

21. *Hellēn* can be understood as Greek, or non-Jew, gentile, pagan. *Barbaros* can means "foreigner" or "native," as in Acts 28:2, 4.

22. Dunn, *Romans 1-8*, 33.

23. Compare with my prior analysis of 1:13-15 in chap. 1.

to do when he arrives at Rome, to have some fruit among them (1:13a), that is, to proclaim the gospel to them (1:15). It is his "eager"[24] desire to proclaim the gospel to them. That is precisely what he wants to do. It aligns with his mission statement "to bring about the obedience of faith among the gentiles," as well as his former reference "to impart some spiritual gift."[25] The way all this is stated argues against the view that Paul wrote Romans simply to advance his Spanish mission or to prepare for his debates in Jerusalem, or any number of other reasons. Rather, as the apostle to the gentiles, he desires to proclaim the gospel to them. This is the overriding reason for his intense desire to come to Rome (and it does not conflict with his statement in 15:20 that he does not aspire to preach the gospel where Christ was already named[26]).

But his rationale does not end there, for Paul proceeds in 1:16-18 to explain what the gospel involves. The practice of commentators has been to set apart 1:16-17 as the theme(s) or thesis (or *propositio*) of the letter. C. E. B. Cranfield limits the thesis to 1:16b-17,[27] Dunn to 1:16-17.[28] Nils Dahl includes 1:18.[29] Neil Elliott objects to identifying 1:16-17 as the theme of the letter in defiance of syntactical features of those verses, often with no more appeal than that it is a "consensus"

24. The Greek may be understood either as an articular prepositional phrase (*to kat' eme* serving as the subject and *prothymon* as a predicate adjective), or as an adjective used substantivally (with *to prothymon* as the subject and *kat' eme* in between the article and the adjective). In either case, 1:15 may be translated, "Thus, on my part, I am eager to preach the gospel to you also who are in Rome."

25. "Some spiritual gift" does not have to do with the *charismata* of Rom. 12:6 or 1 Corinthians 12. The phrase is worded vaguely enough that we must understand it as a further enlargement on "the obedience of faith" in 1:5, and leading on to the "proclaiming of the gospel" in 1:15. Notably, Richard Longenecker views this statement, "some spiritual gift," as that which characterizes what Paul writes in the letter (*Introducing Romans: Critical Issues in Paul's Most Famous Letter* [Grand Rapids: Eerdmans, 2011], 353).

26. Much has been made of Paul's noninterference statement in 15:20 that he does not aspire to preach the gospel where it has already been proclaimed lest he build on another man's foundation (see also 2 Cor. 10:13-15). Is Paul discrediting this principle by what he states in 1:5, 13-15; and 15:15-16? Günter Klein ("Paul's Purpose in Writing the Epistle to the Romans," in *The Romans Debate*, ed. Karl P. Donfried, rev. and expanded ed. [Peabody, MA: Hendrickson, 1991], 29–43, esp. 39) contends that Paul did not view Rome as having an apostolic foundation and was therefore able to preach the gospel to them. Klein may have a legitimate point. But I doubt Paul inserted 15:20 for the distinct purpose of contradicting what he had already written in 1:15 about ministering the gospel to them. No matter the origin of the church in Rome, it would have been both appropriate and natural for Paul to apply the gospel to believers in Rome.

27. Cranfield, *Romans*, 1:86–87.

28. Dunn, *Romans 1–8*, 37.

29. See Nils A. Dahl, *Studies in Paul: Theology for the Early Christian Mission* (Minneapolis: Augsburg, 1977), 78–79.

among interpreters.[30] Many make 1:18 the beginning of the body of the letter. Commentators are undecided whether 1:16-17/18 goes with the opening of the letter, stands by itself, or introduces the body of the letter. We may resolve such differences by remembering that the text was read aloud and the transition from one unit of thought to another was through grammatical devices. The author would guide his audience by his choice of connectives. We need to be paying more attention to Paul's use of connectives, especially his use of certain inferential and causal conjunctions and phrases.

It is my contention that the text is quite specific syntactically about how Paul wanted to advance his thoughts about the gospel. He writes, "I am eager to preach the gospel to you who are in Rome"

16a: *For* I am not ashamed of the gospel.

16b: *For* it is the power of God unto salvation to all who believe, both to the Jew first and to the Greek.

17: *For* by it the righteousness of God is being revealed from faith to faith, as it is written, "But the righteous shall live by faith."

18: *For* the wrath of God is being revealed from heaven against all ungodliness and unrighteousness of men who suppress the truth in unrighteousness.

Paul tells them why he is eager to preach the gospel to them in four explanatory clauses that serve as stepping stones (*gar . . . gar . . . gar . . . gar . . .*). Grammarian William Douglas Chamberlain explains Paul's use of *gar* in this passage: "In Rom. 1:16-17, it occurs three times: the first instance introduces the reason for Paul's eagerness to preach the gospel in Rome; the second, his reason for not being ashamed of the gospel; the third, the reason for the dynamic of the gospel."[31]

---

30. Neil Elliott, *The Arrogance of Nations: Reading Romans in the Shadow of Empire* (Minneapolis: Fortress Press, 2008), 17, 175n53.

31. William D. Chamberlain, *An Exegetical Grammar of the Greek New Testament* (New York: Macmillan, 1952), 154. Dahl (*Studies in Paul*, 79) agrees: "The four sentences in Rom. 1:15-18 are all logically connected with one another by means of a *gar* ('for'). The thematic statements all serve as a warrant for the preceding one. The question of whether a sentence belongs to the preceding or to the following paragraph is anachronistic since the text was to be read aloud and the original handwriting did not set the paragraphs off from one another."

Chamberlain should have added 1:18, "the fourth, the reason for the revelation of the righteousness of God."[32] *Gar* is providing in each instance an explanation or reason for what has just been stated. This use of *gar* for successive explanations occurs regularly throughout Romans. Then Paul introduces 1:19 with the much stronger *dioti*.[33] The audience will view this strong connective as introducing a separate line of thought. So in 1:16-18, Paul is explaining why he is eager to proclaim the gospel to them. As we look ahead in the letter, we find that Paul's explanations are actually themes expanded especially in chapters 1–5 in reverse order. The wrath of God against all unrighteousness is expanded in 1:19–2:29 (with a summary in 3:9b-20 and underlying 5:1-21 and the discourse on sin and the law in chaps. 6–8). The righteousness of God is expanded in 3:21–5:21 (and in chaps. 6–8; 9–11, esp. 9:30–10:13). The gospel's power unto salvation for all who believe, to the Jew first and also to the Greek, is expanded throughout chapters 1–5 (and especially in chaps. 9–11). The deliberate way Paul moves from these themes to their expansion in the body of the letter demonstrates that the body cannot be separated from the bookends of the letter. Neither can his purpose for writing, therefore, be limited to the bookends of the letter.

Returning to the use of *gar* in 1:18, we should observe that attempts have been made to diminish or alter its meaning. This is due to a desire either to limit the themes of Romans to 1:16-17 or to exclude 1:18 from being viewed as a vital part of the gospel message. William Sanday and Arthur Headlam do not comment on the connective; they just separate 1:18 from 1:17.[34] Hans Lietzmann views *gar* simply as a transitional

---

32. The close relation between 1:17 and 1:18 due to the parallelism between the righteousness of God revealed and the wrath of God revealed appears to present two sides of the same coin, the gospel. That Paul's gospel included the judgment of God, note 2:16.

33. *Gar* is often used to give further explanations. The inferential *dio* in 2:1 is immediately followed by two explanatory *gar* clauses. The statement regarding the impartiality of God's future judgment in 2:6-11 is followed by four explanatory *gar* clauses. Etc. Similarly, Paul's statement in 1:15 of eagerly desiring to proclaim the gospel to the gentiles in Rome is immediately followed by four explanatory *gar* clauses in 1:16-18. *Dioti* is a much stronger causal conjunction (a compound of *dia* and *hoti*) and begins a new sentence in 1:19. Therefore it is clearly a mistake to translate 1:18-19 as though they were one sentence with a comma ending 1:18.

34. William Sanday and Arthur C. Headlam, *The Epistle to the Romans* (New York: Charles Scribner's Sons, 1897), 40–41. Sanday's lack of commenting on *gar* in 1:18 is surprising since he is so precise about every detail of the letter.

particle.[35] Dunn suggests that it may be used to contrast with 1:17.[36] C. H. Dodd writes, "The adversative conjunction but in 1:18 shows that the revelation of God's *anger* is contrasted, and not identified, with the revelation of His righteousness."[37] He refers to *gar* as an "adversative" and translates it "but." There is no justification for that. It should be given its normal meaning. Robert Jewett affirms that Paul's use of *gar* "indicates that the discussion of wrath directly supports the thesis about the gospel in 1:16-17 rather than expressing its antithesis."[38] Others bring up the addition of the phrase *en autō* ("by it") in 1:17 and reason that the righteousness of God was revealed "by the gospel" whereas the wrath of God was revealed "from heaven." Hence 1:18 is not part of the gospel. However, it is equally possible that the phrase *en autō* serves both 1:17 and 18. The parallelism of the two verses would seem to confirm as much:

> 1:17: The righteousness of God is being revealed [*ek*] from faith to faith.
> 1:18: The wrath of God is being revealed [*ap'*] from heaven.

Both are being revealed in the present time by the gospel (*en autō*). Günther Bornkamm says that both must be viewed eschatologically. The world must be addressed on the basis of its lostness and the judgment of God together with the dawning of the revelation of God's righteousness in Christ Jesus. The *gar* in 1:18 "is not a 'simple transition particle' but explicitly establishes what is said in 1:16f. about salvation."[39] C. K. Barrett acknowledges

> the fact that with the new subject (wrath) Paul uses the same verb, in the same tense, as with the subject (righteousness) in v. 17. Paul does not say that the wrath of God *was* revealed in the old time before the promulgation of the Gospel, or that it will be revealed at the last day. He says that God's **wrath is being revealed from heaven** now; and this is exactly what he has said of God's righteousness. We are therefore

35. Hans Lietzmann, *An die Römer* (Tübingen: J. C. B. Mohr, 1933. Reprint 1971), 31.
36. Dunn, *Romans 1-8*, 54.
37. C. H. Dodd, *The Epistle of Paul to the Romans* (London: Fontana, 1970), 45 (boldface type changed to italic). Moffatt's translation (ibid., 45) is "but."
38. Jewett, *Romans*, 151.
39. Günther Bornkamm, *Early Christian Experience* (New York: Harper & Row, 1969), 62-63.

encouraged to see a close positive relation between vv. 17 and 18; and this is confirmed by detailed exegesis."[40]

If this analysis is correct, then we need to refine the way we think about 1:16-18. All three are part of the "opening of the letter" and explain the gospel Paul wants to proclaim to them. All three (and we may include 1:13-18) serve as the *propositio* (or thesis) of the letter.[41] The iceberg analogy is appropriate here. Romans is an exposition and application of the gospel of God (*euangelion*). Though the noun and verb forms are not used that often, their placement is important. The terms are prominent in both the opening and closing of the letter (1:1, 9, 15, 16; 15:16, 19, 20; 16:25). A definitive statement of the gospel is included in the prescript of the letter (1:3-4). Paul considers himself to be "set apart unto the gospel" (1:1), "eager to proclaim the gospel" (1:15), "not ashamed of the gospel" (1:16),[42] "ministering as a priest the gospel" (15:16), "fulfilling the gospel" (15:19), and "aspiring to preach the gospel" (15:20). In chapter 10, he notes that Israel "did not obey the gospel" (10:15-16). They heard it but did not believe "the word of Christ" (10:17). While his overriding mission is for the obedience of the gentiles, his longing desire is for the salvation of Israel (9:1-5; 10:1; 11:13-16). Returning to 1:16-18, it is informative to note that the gospel is the power of God unto salvation "to everyone who believes," "to the Jew first and also to the Greek." This is the focus of his concerns, the inclusive and antidiscriminatory nature of the gospel as well as the priority of Israel. Paul is introducing the most important concerns of his letter.[43]

---

40. C. K. Barrett, *A Commentary on the Epistle to the Romans* (London: Black, 1957), 33 (emphasis original).
41. We must remind ourselves that the four *gar* clauses in 1:16-18 are further explanations of the disclosure (purpose) statement in 1:13-15.
42. For Paul, as for Jesus, shame is associated with denying Christ (cf. Mark 8:38; Phil. 1:19-20; 2 Tim. 1:8). But Paul is "not ashamed of the gospel" as it is "the power of God" unto salvation. One may surmise that this statement serves to support Christians in a hostile Roman environment.
43. The idea that Romans is an exposition of the gospel Paul desired to proclaim to them fits favorably with the view of Gordon Fee, brought to my attention by Longenecker (*Introducing Romans*, 353–54). Fee observes that a letter in antiquity served as "a second-best substitute for a personal visit." Hence Romans was written to fulfill at the present time what Paul desired to do when he visited Rome, namely, to share "some spiritual gift." Fee writes (*God's Empowering Presence: The Holy Spirit in the Letters of Paul* [Peabody, MA: Hendrickson, 1994], 488): "In its present context, and especially in light of the letter as a whole, the 'Spirit gift' that he most likely wishes to share with them is his understanding of the gospel that in Christ Jesus God has created from among Jews and

Premise of the Letter, 1:19–2:29

When Paul says in 3:9b, "I have already charged that both Jews and Greeks are all under sin," he is referring back to 1:19–2:29.[44] Indeed, the entire section does come across as a "charge" from the initial assertion that humankind fell into idolatry so they are "without excuse," to the charge of judging one another (2:1-5), to the warning of God's impartial judgment on both Jew and gentile (2:6-11), to the fact that both those "without law" and those "in law" will be judged by that law (2:12-13), and finally to the indictments listed in 2:21-23 and 25-29. Paul is writing "boldly" (15:15) to the believers in Rome. This charge serves as the premise of the letter, for it "sets forth" the basis on which the ensuing reasoning proceeds; and it leads into the question-and-answer in 3:1-9a, which anticipates the extended answers in 3:9b-11.[45]

Gentiles one people for himself, apart from Torah. This is the way they are to be 'strengthened' by Paul's coming, and this surely is the 'fruit' he wants to have among them when he comes (v. 13). If so, then in effect our present letter functions as his 'Spirit gifting' for them." Fee is surely correct in his analysis. This is affirmed when Paul admits in the conclusion of the letter that he has written very boldly to them on some points, to remind them that he is "ministering as a priest the gospel of God" (15:15-16).

44. Some commentators question where Paul has made this case. E. P. Sanders (*Paul, the Law, and the Jewish People* [Philadelphia: Fortress, 1979], 125) goes so far as to say that Paul's case for the universal sinfulness of humankind in 1:18–2:29 is "not convincing: it is internally inconsistent and it rests on gross exaggeration." In response, Douglas J. Moo (*The Epistle to the Romans*, NICNT [Grand Rapids: Eerdmans, 1996], 201n18) points out that "Paul characterizes his argument not as a proof of guilt but as an accusation of guilt." Hence Sanders's criticism is wide of the mark. We need to look at the term Paul uses. He does not use *katēgoreō* or *enkaleō*, which carry the sense of making an accusation against someone. He uses *proētiasametha*, which carries the sense of an accusation or charge that assumes the guilt of a party. (Cf. S. Lewis Johnson Jr., "Studies in Romans, Part IX: The Universality of Sin," *Bibliotheca Sacra* 131 [1974]: 163–72 [here 167].) According to Friedrich Thiele ("Guilt, Cause, Convict, Blame," in *The New International Dictionary of New Testament Theology*, ed. Colin Brown [Grand Rapids: Zondervan, 1975], 2:137–39 [here 139]): "The words in this [*aitia*] group are used in the OT and NT to indicate the responsibility of a man for his action, together with the resultant consequences. The same applies to *anapologētos* which occurs twice in Paul's letter to the Romans [1:20, 2:1] and means the state of being without excuse in a legal sense." Thiele goes on to point out that no one, Jew or gentile, is able to make an excuse to God (2:1). Our works are inadequate; everyone is "deservingly subject to death." Hence "man is totally dependent on God's free grace and goodness in Jesus Christ. He took our sentence of death on himself and by this means has truly 'excused' us." This reflects of course the discourse of the first few chapters of Romans.

45. I am aware of the multiple questions surrounding this section of the letter. Is 1:18-32 limited to gentile idolatry and immorality? Is 2:1-5 limited to Jewish judgmentalism? Is 2:17-24 a true description of Jewish behavior? Is Paul borrowing material from contemporary sources? Are there internal inconsistencies within the section? Does this section truly represent Pauline theology? Is he really suggesting that some can be saved by works of the law? Etc. To answer them requires a commentary. My present purpose is to provide a guideline as to how we view the progression of thought of the premise (1:19-2:29) and how it leads to the question-and-answer in 3:1-9a.

The charge that all are "under sin" is accomplished in relatively short order in 1:19-32. That passage includes all humankind and describes not only their idolatry in turning away from God but also their depraved passions and minds—"filled with all unrighteousness, wickedness, greed, evil; full of envy, murder, strife, deceit, malice, gossips, slanderers, haters of God, insolent, arrogant, boastful, contrivers of evil, disobedient to parents, without understanding, untrustworthy, unloving, unmerciful" (1:29-30). That is quite a list of internal sins. Therefore, when he goes on to "charge" in very strong terms that no one is in a position to judge others, he is already applying the premise to believers in Rome. Romans 2:1-5 is inclusive and not limited to charging only the Jews.

However, what I have just stated is at variance with the majority opinion that 1:18-32 depicts gentile idolatry and immorality while 2:1–3:20 addresses Jewish judgmentalism and boasting.[46] From the majority perspective, the depiction of idolatry and immorality in 1:18-32 fits the description of the gentile world as perceived by Jews. Paul was borrowing from Jewish lists of pagan practices. The passage has been compared with the Alexandrian Book of Wisdom, with some scholars holding that Paul was directly dependent on it.[47] Therefore, 1:18-32 is directed toward gentiles. Then in chapter 2, Paul turns his attention to Jews. First, he uses diatribal rhetoric to address Jewish judgmentalism (2:1-5). After inserting the fact of God's impartial judgment on both Jews and gentiles and including a few verses pertaining to gentiles (2:6-16), he again uses diatribe to address Jewish hypocrisy (2:17-29). The diatribe continues in his question-and-answer with a Jewish interlocutor in 3:1-9a. After that brief digression, Paul concludes that no one is justified by works of the law (3:9b-20). This, or a similar progression, is accepted by many. Again, we are dealing

---

46. For a representation of those who hold that 2:1-5 is addressed primarily to Jews: John Murray, *The Epistle to the Romans*, NICNT (Grand Rapids: Eerdmans, 1965), 1:55; Charles Hodge, *A Commentary on the Epistle to the Romans* (1886; repr., Grand Rapids: Eerdmans, 1950), 71; Matthew Black, *Romans*, NCB (London: Marshall, Morgan & Scott, 1973), 54; Paul S. Minear, *The Obedience of Faith: The Purposes of Paul in the Epistle to the Romans*, SBT 2/19 (London SCM, 1971), 46-48; Moo, *Romans*, 125-27. Also see Cranfield's seven-point defense of this position, *Romans*, 1:137-9.

47. See Sanday and Headlam, *Romans*, 51-52; Bornkamm, *Early Christian Experience*, 53-59.

with whether Paul is in a debate with Jews and whether he is using Hellenistic diatribal rhetoric. These issues have been analyzed above in chapter 6. But it is evident that one's view of 1:19–3:20 greatly influences one's view of all of Romans. Were I to agree with the majority opinion, I would need to revise my thinking about whom Paul is addressing, why he was writing this letter, and the structure of the letter. So I will add a few more thoughts to the discussion.

First, the text in 1:18-32 does not appear to be limited in any way to gentiles. It is preceded by inclusive rhetoric in 1:16-18: "to everyone who believes, to the Jew first and also to the Greek . . . for the wrath of God is revealed from heaven against all ungodliness and unrighteousness of men." What follows in 1:19-32 is dominated by third-person-plural pronouns and verb endings.[48] The rhetoric is universal and reminiscent of the creation/fall narrative in Genesis 1–3.[49] The word "gentile" (*ethnē*) is never used in that narrative. In 2:1-5, the connective *dio*[50] (therefore) is followed by the generic "you are without excuse, O man, everyone who judges." If Paul wanted to identify a particular group such as Jews, he would have been more specific. *Ō anthrōpe* is vocative, and *pas ho krinōn* is an appositive to *ō anthrōpe*, the same terms repeated in the same way in 2:3. Why does he use these generic attributes rather than referring specifically to Jews? Then notice the flow of thought in 2:1-11. The "you" who is identified only as "O man, the one who judges those who practice such things and does them" is the "you" who is treasuring up wrath in the day of wrath and righteous judgment of God, who will render to each one (generic) according to his or her works; and "each one" is shown to include "the Jew first and also . . . the Greek" in 2:9-10. In other words, up to this point in the section, Paul is including both Jews and Greeks. It is at this point in the discourse, and only at this point, that Paul

---

48. In 1:19-32, the third-person-plural pronoun (*autos*) is used thirteen times, and the third-person verb ending is used thirteen times. Paul is referring to all of humankind.

49. In the words of Dunn (*Romans 1–8*, 53): "It was Adam who above all perverted his knowledge of God and sought to escape the status of creature, but who believed a lie and became a fool and thus set the pattern (Adam = man) for a mankind which worshiped the idol rather than the Creator."

50. As a strong inferential, *dio* connects what follows closely to what precedes. Multiple word chains do the same. Because what follows refers generically to "O man," it affirms the view that neither 1:19-32 nor 2:1-5 is limited to depicting either gentiles or Jews.

separates gentile from Jew and deals with them separately. He does so initially in 2:12-13 by distinguishing between "as many as sinned without law" and "as many as sinned in law." Then he applies the standards stated in 2:12-13 first to gentiles in 2:14-16, and then to Jews in 2:17-24. The section ends in 2:25-29 raising the issue of the standing of the Jew while leading up to the question in 3:1, "What advantage has the Jew?" Herein lies the important decision for the majority of commentators. Will they continue to view 1:18–3:20 as a unit with the question-and-answer in 3:1-9a as a digression or parenthesis? Or will they view 1:19–2:29 as a unit leading up to the question-and-answer in 3:1-9a with 3:9b-20 beginning the response to that question-and-answer?

Second, regarding Paul's dependence on the Alexandrian Book of Wisdom, Sanday and Headlam insist that Paul was quite dependent on this work. They place the text of 1:18-32 alongside passages from Wisdom (primarily chaps. 12–14). They then conclude that while there can be no question of direct quotation, the resemblances are so strong that Paul must have devoted a considerable amount of time to studying the Book of Wisdom. However, Sanday and Headlam also acknowledge that the parallelism is "not quite exact. St. Paul says, 'They did know but relinquished their knowledge,' Wisd. 'They ought to have known but did not.'"[51] That is a notable difference! Likewise, Günther Bornkamm argues for the dependence of Paul on Wisdom and Hellenistic-Jewish literature. But he too shows how Paul differs conceptually from that literature.[52] W. D. Davies suggests that what Paul writes is within the rabbinic tradition. "However much Paul may

---

51. Sanday and Headlam, *Romans*, 51–52.

52. Bornkamm, *Early Christian Experience*, 54–56 and 67n38; consider carefully 50–59. Bornkamm writes that 1:18–3:20 "is not an apology but an accusation. In this direction it differs terminologically and conceptually from the parallel [Hellenistic] literature." This is especially true with regard to how one attains knowledge of God. Paul does not understand it "as an open possibility closed to no one, but as the reality under which the whole world in fact stands." After enlarging on that difference, Bornkamm then shows how Paul's progression of thought runs very differently from the parallel Hellenistic literature. He offers that "Paul frees the concepts and arguments that he takes from contemporary non-Christian philosophy and theology from the presuppositions of Greek thought, and the sense in which he uses them becomes entirely different." Then in ibid., 67n38, Bornkamm shows influences from the OT. After reading Bornkamm, one could argue that while Paul had knowledge of Hellenistic-Jewish literature such as Wisdom, he was anything but dependent on that literature.

have been indebted to Alexandrian ideas in the thought of Romans 1, he was still moving strictly within the realm of Rabbinic ideas."[53] Due to Paul's extensive background in rabbinic Judaism, it is more likely that Paul was dependent on a common rabbinic tradition than that he was copying out of the Alexandrian Book of Wisdom. He uses similar words and thoughts but is much more precise and careful in his presentation. In addition, we should look at the context of 1:19-32 to determine about whom he is writing; and we have just seen that the rhetoric is universal. Therefore, the view that 1:19-32 must be limited to the gentile world is not a given.

Third, some insist that 2:1-5 must be addressing Jews. An initial reading might suggest as much if you agree with the majority opinion. First, it is argued, you have a listing of gentile sins in 1:18-32. Then you have others in 2:1-5 who are judging them. Not only were Jews known for judging others; but their hardness of heart together with the kindness and patience of God historically is what comes to mind in 2:4-5. Cranfield argues, "An attitude of moral superiority toward the Gentiles was so characteristic of the Jews (as vv.18ff themselves indicate), that, in the absence of any indication to the contrary, it is natural to assume that Paul is apostrophizing the typical Jew in 2:1ff."[54] What Cranfield is saying is that in 2:1-5, Paul is interrupting his discourse regarding gentile immorality to dialogue with an imaginary Jewish person who is prone to judge gentiles. He uses the second-person singular pronoun (sy) to do this. It is an element of diatribe to help Paul get his point across. (Recall the analysis of diatribe in chapter 6.)[55] In this way, Paul is not accusing Jews directly of anything. This

---

53. W. D. Davies, *Paul and Rabbinic Judaism* (London: SPCK, 1970), 27–31, cf. 30.

54. Cranfield, *Romans*, 138. Minear holds (*Obedience*, 48) that Paul's intention was to present first a "colourful appraisal of the Gentile world." It was a portrait with which the Jews would readily agree. But then, "once they had marched into the trap, he would close the exits." They were without excuse since they were guilty of doing the same things! So, for Minear, Paul was being "brutally sharp" in chap. 2 in his charge against "the weak in faith." Brendan Byrne, SJ (*Romans*, SP [Collegeville, MN: Liturgical Press, 1996], 70, 79–80) agrees that 2:1-5 was a rhetorical trap for the Jew who is not explicitly identified until 2:17.

55. Also in chap. 6, we specifically show variances of form in 2:1-5 with Hellenistic diatribe. These variances demonstrate that one does not have to posit an imaginary interlocutor in this passage for it to make sense.

would require the second-person plural. Rather, he is "apostrophizing the typical Jew."[56]

All of that reasoning may make sense if 1:18-32 can be limited to a description of gentile immorality. But if 1:18-32 is referring universally to all humankind, which it is, then limiting the judging in 2:1-5 to Jews does not make any sense. Moreover, the context of the entire letter suggests that both Jews and gentiles were judging each other. One does not have to posit an encounter with an imaginary Jew for 2:1-5 to make sense. Whenever Paul uses the pronoun *sy* in Romans, he is driving home a point to his readers.[57] Putting aside the use of pronouns in quotations from Scripture, there are (1) passages where the second-person singular dominates, and (2) isolated passages where the second-person singular appears briefly. Both serve to inform how Paul uses the second-person singular. Passages where the second-person-singular pronoun and verb endings dominate are 2:1-5; 2:17-27; 11:17-24; and 14:4, 10-22. Isolated passages include 8:2 ("for the law of the Spirit of life in Christ Jesus has freed *you*"); 9:19-20 ("Who are *you*, O man, who answers back to God?"); 10:9 ("if *you* confess with *your* mouth the Lord Jesus and believe in *your* heart"); 12:20-21 ("Do not [*you*] be overcome with evil, but [*you*] overcome evil with good"); 13:4 ("Do *you* want to have no fear of authority? Do what is good and *you* will have praise from the same. For it is a minister of God to *you* for good"). In all these isolated texts, Paul reverts to the second-person singular to apply his point to every individual recipient of his letter. None of these passages (except 9:19-20) are viewed as diatribal. This is also how he uses the second-person singular in passages where it dominates. In 11:17-24, he is directing his exhortation specifically and strongly to gentile believers, and there is no need in that context to project an imaginary gentile interlocutor.[58] Paul is simply making a very strong

56. Those who hold this view note the similarities between 2:1-5 and 2:17-29. Both 2:3 and 2:17 use the second-person-singular pronoun *sy* (you) with 2:17 referring specifically to Jews. In 2:1, "you" judge "the other"; in 2:21, Jews teach the "other" (*ton heteron*). Paul uses rhetorical questions in both 2:3-4 and 2:20-22, 26-27. Moreover, the issue of not practicing the law (2:1-3) is brought up again in 2:25. These similarities suggest to many that the two passages are addressing the same group, the Jews. However, this view overlooks the progression of thought of 1:19–2:29.
57. In Romans, the total number of second-person-singular pronouns is forty-seven, and the total number of second-person-singular verb endings is sixty-seven.

point to his gentile hearers and he does this using the second-person singular. In 14:4, 10, 15, 20-22, he is directing his exhortation to both the strong and the weak, though mostly to the strong (14:15, 20); and there is no need in that context to project an imaginary person.[59] He is simply using the second-person singular to drive home his point. We are left, then, with the two passages in chapter 2. In 2:17-27, he is addressing at some length a Jew, while in 2:1-5 he is driving home the point that no one should judge the other (*ton heteron*). In both cases, he is not mincing words, for he goes on to warn that the righteous judgment of God will render to each person according to his or her works (2:6-11). We should also note that a number of the scriptural quotes in Romans use the second-person singular in the same way. One does not have to revert to Hellenistic diatribe to interpret those passages.

But why the extended address to the Jew at the end of the premise of the letter?[60] Paul begins by listing their privileges (2:17-18) and then their claims (2:19-20). Their privileges include their name, resting in the law, and knowing God. Their claims are that the privileges place them in a position superior to those around them. These are the factors that served to set Jews apart from gentiles. As noted previously,[61] Jewish identity is rooted in these privileges and claims. The description in 2:17-20 is a perfect summary. These are the identity markers of the Jew (together with circumcision), markers that served historically to separate Jew from gentile. Paul is highlighting these privileges and claims, and then proceeds to reveal the hypocrisy of these claims.[62] The Jews are transgressors of the law. Hence, the strong rebuke from

---

58. Contra Stanley K. Stowers, *The Diatribe and Paul's Letter to the Romans*, SBLDS 57 (Chico, CA: Scholars Press, 1981), 80.

59. Contra ibid., 81, 117.

60. Paul is not addressing any particular Jew or group of Jews, but is using the second-person singular to drive home his point concerning Jews as an ethnic group. In 2:12-14, he "explains" how the gentiles who do not have the law will be judged by the law. In 2:17-24, he "charges" the one who bears the name "Jew," who has the law and rests in the law and teaches the law with trespassing that law.

61. See chap. 6.

62. Murray (*Romans*, 1:81): "The impressive catalogue of advantages is the preface to the exposure of Jewish hypocrisy in verses 21, 22.... The more enhanced the privilege the more heinous become the sins exposed."

Scripture: "The name of God is blasphemed among the gentiles because of you" (2:24). Paul is not describing something untrue. He is drawing on well-known traditions of rebuke and exhortation. One can find similar charges in the Prophets, rabbinics, and on the lips of Jesus.[63] In the words of Dunn,

> Paul's target is not any or all Jews as individuals, but Jewish assurance of standing in a position of ethical privilege by virtue of the law. . . . For Paul the fact that there are Jews who do what their law clearly forbids should be enough to undermine the confidence that the Jew *per se* stands in a position of superiority or advantage over the non-Jew by virtue of being a member of the people of the law.[64]

This is precisely Paul's point in 2:25-29. If Jews who have the law fail to keep the law, why should they be regarded in any way as special before God? Why does their name matter, or the mark of circumcision? The name and mark are only as legitimate as the reality to which they point. This places both Jew and gentile on equal footing before God. It settles any question concerning the impartiality of God (the underlying theme of the premise). "All who have sinned under the law will be judged by the law" (2:12), so Jews are not exempt. Also, gentiles are not at a disadvantage. It is "antidiscriminatory rhetoric" that effectively leads to the question, "What then is the advantage of the Jew? Or what is the profit is circumcision?" This is where the premise was headed all along. Paul was leading his gentile audience to the question of Jewish priority and their place in the body of Christ. This is the issue that needed to be addressed in the letter. Paul does not want to undersell to the gentiles his description of the Jew. He purposely draws out his portrait in a way that every distinctive mark of Jewry would be acknowledged, and then dispensed, for the purpose of leading to this very question. Indeed, it leads not only to this one question, but to

---

63. The following are references listed by Dunn, *Romans 1-8*, 113. In the OT, Isa. 3:14-15; Jer. 7:8-11; Ezek. 22:6-12; Mal. 3:5 (add Ps. 50:16-21); in rabbinic literature, see Str-B 3:105–11; and in the Gospels, Luke 11:39-52//Matthew 23.
64. Dunn, *Romans 1-8*, 114. Dunn writes (ibid., 113), Paul is not "exaggerating or generalizing from a few isolated cases or disqualifying the whole for the crimes of a few . . . or condemning the Jewish nation *in toto*."

all the questions in 3:1-9a which in turn anticipate the discourse that follows.

In Conclusion

I have maintained in this study that Romans is a letter, not an essay. In the past, the tendency has been to call it a letter, then treat it as an essay. When we outline Romans simply on the level of ideas, the flow of Paul's dialogue is obscured. The flow of Paul's dialogue is captured in his rhetoric, especially his extensive use of questions in chapters 3–11. His use of questions was not meant as diatribe to transform his students or to answer his Jewish critics. His use of questions served to guide the narrative and to point to the issues that were driving the narrative. The issues that drove the narrative were the circumstances in Rome. Paul was addressing those circumstances and doing so in an interactive way. Thus any outline we impose should conform to that interaction. For Romans is a letter that was heard orally by the believers in Rome. That interactive rhetoric would be guiding them through the letter. That interactive rhetoric is the key to the organization of the letter. The rhetoric flows in this way: the opening prescript, thanksgiving, and *propositio* are followed by the premise of the letter that leads into the main questions that anticipate the extended answers that follow through chapter 11. Then come the exhortations that apply, followed by his closing comments and greetings.

1:1-18: Opening of the Letter
1:19–2:29: Premise of the Letter
3:1–15:13: Heart of the Letter
  3:1-9a: Main Questions Raised
    3:9b–5:21: Extended Answer to 3:9a
    6:1–8:39: Extended Answer to 3:7-8
    9:1–11:36: Extended Answer to 3:1-6
  12:1–15:13: Exhortations That Apply
15:14–16:27: Closing of the Letter

The flow of the letter is coherent. The parts of the letter relate to the whole. The bookends are vitally related to the body of the letter. We can see why Paul included every part of the letter. The main question is, "What advantage has the Jew?" If one really wants to know the answer to that question, then read Romans!

Appendix I: Epistolary Formulas within the Body of the Letter

Vocative of Direct Address

- Nine times: 2:1, 3; 7:1, 4; 8:12; 9:20; 10:1; 11:25; 12:1
- Seven times with appositives serving as vocatives: 2:1 (×2), 3, 21 (×2), 22 (×2)

Personal Expressions of Joy, Grief, Astonishment

- 7:22: "For I joyfully concur with the law of God"
- 7:24: "Wretched man that I am! Who will set me free from the body of this death?"
- 9:2-3: "I have great sorrow and unceasing grief in my heart."
- 10:1: "Brethren, my hearts desire and prayer to God for them is . . ."

Request Formulas Using The Verb Παρακαλέω (I Exhort)

- 12:1: "I urge you, brothers"

Disclosure Formulas, Reflecting Shared Knowledge

- 2:2: "And we know that . . ."

- 3:19: "Now we know that . . ."
- 6:3: "Do you not know that . . ."
- 6:16: "Do you not know that . . ."
- 7:1: "Do you not know . . ."
- 7:14: "For we know that . . ."
- 7:18: "for I know that . . ."
- 8:22: "For we know that . . ."
- 8:26: "for we do not know how to pray as we should"
- 8:28: "And we know that . . ."
- 11:2: "or do you not know"
- 11:25: "I do not want you to be uninformed [ignorant], brothers"
- 13:11: "And do this, knowing the time"

Confidence Formulas (Some Overlapping with Disclosure Formulas)

- 2:3: "Or do you reckon . . ."
- 2:4: "Or do you think lightly . . . not know that . . ."
- 3:28: "For we reckon that"
- 8:18: "For I consider that the sufferings of this present time . . ."
- 8:38: "For I am persuaded that . . ."
- 14:14: "I know and am convinced in the Lord Jesus that . . ."

Attestation Formulas, "God Is My Witness" or "I Am Speaking the Truth"

- 3:5: "I am speaking in human terms"
- 3:9b: "For we have previously charged"
- 6:19: "I am speaking in human terms"

- 9:1: "I am speaking the truth, I am not lying"
- 10:2: "For I bear them witness"

Thanksgiving Formulas, "I Thank My God ..."

- 6:17: "But thanks be to God that ..."
- 7:25: "Thanks be to God through Jesus Christ our Lord"

Responsibility Statements, Showing Obligation

- 9:1: "I could wish that ..."
- 11:13-14: "Inasmuch then as I am an apostle of gentiles, I magnify my ministry, if somehow I might move to jealousy my fellow countrymen and save some of them."
- 12:3: "For through the grace given to me ..."

Verbs of Saying

- 2:22: "you who say that"
- 3:3: "What then [shall we say]?" (similar to 6:15)
- 3:5: "What shall we say?"
- 3:8: "And why not say ..."
- 3:9: "What then [shall we say]?" (similar to 6:15)
- 3:27: "Where then is boasting?" (similar kind of question)
- 4:1: "What then shall we say?"
- 4:9: "For we say ..."
- 6:1: "What then shall we say?"
- 6:15: "What then [shall we say]?"
- 7:1: "for I am speaking to those who know the law"
- 7:7: "What then shall we say?"

- 8:31: "What then shall we say in response to these things?"
- 9:14: "What then shall we say?"
- 9:19: "You will say to me then"
- 9:30: "What then shall we say?"
- 10:18: "But I say"
- 10:19: "But I say"
- 11:1: "I say then"
- 11:11: "I say then"
- 11:13: "Now, I am speaking to you who are gentiles"
- 11:19: "You will say then"
- 12:3: "for I say . . . to every one of you"
- 15:8: "For I say that"

Appendix II: Rhetorical Devices in Romans

How Rhetoric Is Heard (Orality)

- *Anaphora* (repetition of words/phrases at beginning of sentences):

  - 1:24, 26, 28 (God gave them over); 1:31 (repetition of alpha-negatives); 3:10-18 (sixfold repetition of *ouk estin* ["there is not"]); 8:33-39 (fourfold repetition of *tis* [what?]); 12:6-8 (sevenfold construction of "if" (*eite*) and "in" (*en*); repetition of *ti oun* {*eroumen*} introducing questions found in 3:1; 3:5; 3:9; 4:1; 6:1; 6:15; 7:7; 8:31; 9:14; 9:19; 9:30; 11:7.

- *Homoioptoton* (repetition of same case endings): 1:23; 1:29-31; 7:15-16a

- *Homoioteleuton* (similar sounding endings): 1:29; 5:16; 12:15

- *Assonance* (repetition of vowel sounds/syllables):

  - 1:23, 25, 27, 28, 29, 31 (*aphthartou // phthartou, ktisei // ktisanta, arsenes // arsesin, edokimasan // adokimon, phthonou // phonou, asynetous // asynthetous*)

- *Paronomasia* (play on words that sound alike): 5:12-21 (-*ma* endings); 12:3 (*hyperphronein, phronein, phronein, sōphronein*)

How Rhetoric Is Structured—in Concert with Grammar

- *Parallelism* (synonymous, synthetic, antithetical, structural):

  - Synonymous parallelism (same thought): 1:21; 3:1; 7:7b; 9:2

  - Synthetic parallelism (building on thought): 4:25; 10:10; 11:30-32

  - Antithetical parallelism (contrasting thoughts): 2:7-10; 5:15-19; 8:5-6, 10, 13, 15

  - Structural parallelism (a parallel structuring of sentences): a frequent occurrence

- *Chiasm* (an inverted parallelism of words, phrases, sentences and paragraphs):

  - Words and phrases arranged chiastically: 1:3-4; 2:1b, 25-27; 3:10-18, 19; 6:3; 10:2-3, 19; 11:3, 10, 22; 15:9b

  - Sentences and larger concepts arranged chiastically: 2:7-10; 5:1-11 (and 5:6-8); 6:8-10; 10:9-10; 14:7-9

- *Inclusio/Ring Composition* (similar phrases or clauses at beginning and end of a text):

  - 5:1-11 (some view 5:1 and 8:39 as *inclusio*)

- *Anacoluthon* (sentence has no ending): 2:17-24; 3:21-26.

- *Asyndeton* (sentence is not bound to a prior sentence by a connective): 1:14; 2:9; 7:24; 9:1

- *Word Chains* (the repetition of words and introduction of new words): e.g., 1:18–3:20

- *Enumeration* (numerical sequences in series): 10's, 7's, 5's, 4's, 3's[1]

---

1. See Robert Jewett, *Romans*, Hermeneia (Minneapolis: Fortress Press, 2007), 32–39.

Rhetorical Modes of Persuasion

- *Rhetorical Questions/Diatribe* (question-and-answer discourse):

  ○ 2:1-5, 17-24; 3:1-9, 27-31; 4:1, 9; 6:1, 15; 7:7, 13; 9:14, 19-21; 11:1, 13-24; 14:4, 10-11

- *Apostrophe* (interruption of discourse to address a person or personified idea; viewed as an element of diatribe):

  ○ 2:1-5; 2:17-27; 9:19-20; 11:17-24; 14:4, 10, 15, 20-22

- *Speech-in-character* (writer creates a character who speaks in his own voice as an actor):

  ○ 7:7-25: "I" is every person who tries to keep the law and finds a war going on in his or her heart; 11:17-21: a gentile Christian interlocutor who brags about displacing the original Jewish branches of the olive tree

- *Prosopopoeia* (allowing a person/thing to speak for itself):

  ○ 2:1-5, 17-29; 3:1-9; 3:27–4:2 reflect this style

- *Analogy* (inference by comparison): 4:4; 5:7; 6:1-14, 15-23; 7:1-6; 9:20-24; 11:16-24

- *Metaphor* (direct comparison): 11:17-24

- *Synkrisis* (comparative juxtaposition of people or things): 5:12-21

- *Paradeigma* (example): 1:26b-27: same-sex relations; 4:1-23: Abraham; 11:13-14: Paul himself; 12:4-5: body; 15:2-3: Christ is example

- *Syllogism* (a fully developed logical argument):

  ○ 7:1-4; 10:14-21; 14:7-9

  ○ The *a minore ad maius* argument: 5:9, 10, 15, 17; 11:12, 15, 24

- *Enthymeme* (an abbreviated syllogism):

  o 4:14-15; 5:15; 6:5-7, 8-10; 11:6; 11:12-15; 11:16-21; 11:28-32

- *Midrashim* (a Jewish argumentative form normally consisting of a main text interpreted by other texts): chapter 4

Supporting Formulations and Citations

- *Creedal Formulations* (faith citations shared by all):

  o 1:3-4 (introduces letter with supposed creedal formulation); 1:4 (brief formulas or clichés); 3:30 (God is one); 4:24 (who raised Jesus from the dead); 5:6; 5:8 (Christ died on our behalf); 7:4, 8:32, 34 (the one raised from the dead, delivered up for us all, raised, at the right hand of God); 9:5b (from whom is the Christ according to the flesh, who is over all, God blest forever. Amen); 10:14 ("call on him"; appears in Acts); 14:8-9 (we belong to the Lord; Lord over both the dead and the living). Shorter formulas: 3:25-26a; 4:25 (who was handed over for our transgressions; based on Isaiah 53?); 10:9-10 (if you confess with your mouth the Lord Jesus and believe in your heart that God has raised him from the dead . . . [chiastic arrangement])

- *Liturgical Formulations* (benedictions and doxological citations shared by all):

  o 1:25 (who is blessed forever! Amen!); 6:17 (thanks be to God); 8:38-39 (Paul creates a hymn); 11:33-36 (doxology with 11:36: to him be glory forever! Amen!); 13:11-12 (an agape hymn); 15:5-6 and 15:13 (two benedictions).

- *Scripture Citations* (OT quotations and allusions):

  o Eighty-four OT quotations: "28 citations from Isaiah, 20 from the Psalms, 15 each from Deuteronomy and Genesis, 6 from Exodus,

4 each from Leviticus and Hosea, 3 from Proverbs, 2 each from Habakkuk, 1 Kings, and Job, and one each from Malachi and Joel."[2]

○ Catenae of OT quotations: 3:10-18; 9:25-29; 11:8-10, 33b-35; 15:9-12

○ Multiple allusions to OT: 2:25-29 (circumcision); 4:1-22 (Abraham and David), 9:20-24 (potter and clay), 11:17-24 (olive tree)

---

2. Quote is from Jewett (*Romans*, 25), who references the research of Dietrich-Alex Koch (*Schrift*, 33).

Appendix III: The Question-and-Answer of Romans 3:27-31

First Set of Questions

Q1: ^{27}Ποῦ οὖν ἡ καύχησις; A: ἐξεκλείσθη.
 Q2: διὰ ποίου νόμου; Q3: τῶν ἔργων;

A: οὐχί, ἀλλὰ διὰ νόμου πίστεως.
 ^{28}λογιζόμεθα γὰρ δικαιοῦσθαι πίστει ἄνθρωπον χωρὶς ἔργων νόμου.

Therefore, where is boasting? It is excluded.
 By what kind of law? Of works?

No, but by a law of faith.
 For we reckon that a man is justified by faith apart from works of Law.

Second Set of Questions

Q1: ^{29}ἢ Ἰουδαίων ὁ θεὸς μόνον; Q2: οὐχὶ καὶ ἐθνῶν;

A: ναὶ καὶ ἐθνῶν, ^{30}εἴπερ εἷς ὁ θεός,
 ὃς δικαιώσει περιτομὴν ἐκ πίστεως καὶ ἀκροβυστίαν διὰ τῆς πίστεως.

Or, is God the God of Jews only? Not also of Gentiles?

Yes also of Gentiles, if indeed God is one
who will justify the circumcision by faith and the uncircumcision
through faith.

Final Question

Q1: ³¹νόμον οὖν καταργοῦμεν διὰ τῆς πίστεως;

A: μὴ γένοιτο, ἀλλὰ νόμον ἱστάνομεν.

Therefore, do we nullify the law through faith?

May it not be, but we establish the law.

Appendix IV: The Question-and-Answer of Romans 3:1-9

Section 1[1]

Q: ¹Τί οὖν {ἔστιν} τὸ περισσὸν τοῦ Ἰουδαίου,
ἢ τίς ἡ ὠφέλεια τῆς περιτομῆς;
What then is the advantage of the Jew?
Or what is the benefit of circumcision?

A: ²πολὺ κατὰ πάντα τρόπον.
πρῶτον μὲν [γὰρ]² ὅτι ἐπιστεύθησαν τὰ λόγια τοῦ θεοῦ.
Much in every way.
Foremost, that they were entrusted with the words of God.

Section 2

Q: ³τί γάρ εἰ ἠπίστησάν τινες;³
μὴ ἡ ἀπιστία αὐτῶν τὴν πίστιν τοῦ θεοῦ καταργήσει;
For what if some did not believe?

---

1. The introductory particles in the Greek text as well as the brief responses are highlighted in bold type. This is done to help clarify the structure of the question-and-answer. For further explanation, see the discussion above on pages 62–63.
2. It is difficult from the variant readings to determine whether *gar* is authentic.
3. Some view the first question as consisting simply of the *ti gar* (e.g., the Nestle-Aland text). I choose to place the question mark after *tines*, with *mē* serving to introduce the second question (as it does in 3:5). However, in either case, the second question builds on the first and the content of the two questions remains the same.

Their unbelief will not nullify the faithfulness of God, will it?

A: [4]μὴ γένοιτο.
γινέσθω δὲ ὁ θεὸς ἀληθής,
πᾶς δὲ ἄνθρωπος ψεύστης,
καθὼς γέγραπται,
ὅπως ἂν δικαιωθῇς ἐν τοῖς λόγοις σου
καὶ νικήσεις ἐν τῷ κρίνεσθαί σε.
May it never be!
But may God be true,
and every man a liar,
as it is written,
"That you may be justified in your words
and vindicated while you are being judged."

Section 3

Q: [5]εἰ δὲ ἡ ἀδικία ἡμῶν θεοῦ δικαιοσύνην συνίστησιν, τί ἐροῦμεν;
μὴ ἄδικος ὁ θεὸς ὁ ἐπιφέρων τὴν ὀργήν;
(κατὰ ἄνθρωπον λέγω)[4]
But if our unrighteousness commends the righteousness of God,
what shall we say?
The God who inflicts wrath is not unjust, is he?
(I am speaking according to man.)

A: [6]μὴ γένοιτο.
ἐπεὶ πῶς κρινεῖ ὁ θεὸς τὸν κόσμον;
May it never be!
Otherwise how will God judge the world?

Section 4

Q: [7]εἰ γὰρ ἡ ἀλήθεια τοῦ θεοῦ ἐν τῷ ἐμῷ ψεύσματι ἐπερίσσευσεν εἰς τὴν
δόξαν αὐτοῦ, τί ἔτι κἀγὼ ὡς ἁμαρτωλὸς κρίνομαι;

---

4. Parentheses are added for clarification.

^{8}καὶ μὴ [τι λέγωμεν] (καθὼς βλασφημούμεθα καὶ καθώς φασίν τινες ἡμᾶς λέγειν)^{5} ὅτι ποιήσωμεν τὰ κακά, ἵνα ἔλθῃ τὰ ἀγαθά;

For if the truth of God by my lie abounded to his glory, why am I also still being judged as a sinner?

And why not [say], (as we have been slandered and as some say that we say), "Let us do evil that good may come"?

A: ὧν τὸ κρίμα ἔνδικόν ἐστιν.

Whose judgment is just!

Section 5

Q: ^{9}Τί οὖν; προεχόμεθα;

What then? Are we better than they?

A: ^{9}boὐ πάντως· προῃτιασάμεθα γὰρ Ἰουδαίους τε καὶ Ἕλληνας πάντας ὑφ' ἁμαρτίαν εἶναι.

Not at all, for we have already charged that both Jew and Greek are all under sin.

---

5. Both the bracketed words and the parentheses have been added for clarification; the *ti* in 3:7 serves both questions with the connective *kai* beginning 3:8; and the *legomen* in 3:8 is understood.

Bibliography

Achtemeier, Paul J. *"Omne Verbum Sonat*: The New Testament and the Oral Environment of Late Western Antiquity." *JBL* 109 (1990): 3–27.

———. *Romans*. IBC. Atlanta: John Knox, 1985.

Anderson, R. Dean, Jr., *Ancient Rhetorical Theory and Paul*. Leuven: Peeters, 1999.

Arndt, William F., and F. Wilbur Gingrich. *A Greek Lexicon of the New Testament*. Chicago: University of Chicago Press, 1957.

Aune, David E. "Epistolography." In *The Westminster Dictionary of New Testament and Early Christian Literature and Rhetoric*, 162–68. Louisville: Westminster John Knox, 2003.

Barrett, C. K. *A Commentary on the Epistle to the Romans*. London: Black, 1957.

Barclay, John M. G. *Jews in the Mediterranean Diaspora: From Alexander to Trajan (323 B.C.E.–117 C.E.)*. Edinburgh: T&T Clark, 1996.

———. *Pauline Churches and Diaspora Jews*. Tübingen: Mohr Siebeck, 2011.

Bartsch, Hans-Werner. "The Concept of Faith in Paul's Letter to the Romans." *BR* 13 (1968): 41–53.

———. "The Historical Situation in Rome." Translated by Wallace Gray. *Encounter* 33 (1972): 329–39.

Beker, J. Christiaan. *Paul the Apostle: The Triumph of God in Life and Thought*. Philadelphia: Fortress Press, 1984.

Black, Matthew. *Romans*. NCB. London: Marshall, Morgan & Scott, 1973.

Bornkamm, Günther. *Early Christian Experience*. New York: Harper & Row, 1969.

———. "The Letter to the Romans as Paul's Last Will and Testament." In *The*

Romans Debate, edited by Karl P. Donfried, 16–28. Rev. and expanded ed. Peabody, MA: Hendrickson, 1991.

Bruce, F. F. *The Epistle to the Romans*. TNTC. Nottingham: Inter-Varsity Press, 1985.

Byrne, Brendan, SJ. *Romans*. SP. Collegeville, MN: Liturgical Press, 1996.

Calvin, John. *Commentaries on the Epistle of Paul the Apostle to the Romans*. Grand Rapids: Eerdmans, 1947.

Campbell, William S. "The Freedom and Faithfulness of God in Relation to Israel." *JSNT* 13 (1981): 43–59.

____. "Revisiting Romans." *ScrB* 12 (1981–1982): 2–10.

____. "Romans III as a Key to the Structure and Thought of the Letter." In *The Romans Debate*, edited by Karl P. Donfried, 251–64. Rev. and expanded ed. Peabody, MA: Hendrickson, 1991. Originally in *NovT* 23 (1981): 22–40.

____. "The Romans Debate." *JSNT* 10 (1981): 19–28.

____. "The Rule of Faith in Romans 12:1–15:13: The Obligation of Humble Obedience to Christ as the Only Adequate Response to the Mercies of God." In *Pauline Theology*. Vol. 3, *Romans*, edited by David M. Hay and E. Elizabeth Johnson, 259–86. Minneapolis: Fortress Press, 1995.

____. "Why Did Paul Write Romans?" *ExpTim* 85 (1974): 264–69.

Chamberlain, William D. *An Exegetical Grammar of the Greek New Testament*. New York: Macmillan, 1952.

Cosgrove, Charles H. "What If Some Have Not Believed? The Occasion and Thrust of Romans 3:1–8." *ZNW* 78 (1987): 90–105.

Cranfield, C. E. B. *A Critical and Exegetical Commentary on the Epistle to the Romans*. 2 vols. ICC. Edinburgh: T&T Clark, 1975.

Dahl, Nils A. *Studies in Paul: Theology for the Early Christian Mission*. Minneapolis: Augsburg, 1977.

____. "Two Notes on Romans 5." *ST* 5 (1951): 37–48.

Dana, H. E. and Julius R. Mantey. *A Manual Grammar of the Greek New Testament*. New York: Macmillan, 1927.

Das, A. Andrew. *Paul and the Jews*. Library of Pauline Studies. Peabody, MA: Hendrickson, 2003.

____. *Solving the Romans Debate*. Minneapolis: Fortress Press, 2007.

Davies, W. D. *Paul and Rabbinic Judaism*. London: SPCK, 1970.

Deissmann, Adolf. *Light from the Ancient East: The New Testament Illustrated by Recently Discovered Texts of the Graeco-Roman World.* Translated by Lionel R. M. Strachan. London: Hodder & Stoughton, 1927.

Dibelius, Martin. *From Tradition to Gospel.* Translated by Bertram Lee Woolf. New York: Charles Scribner's Sons, 1971.

Dodd, C. H. *The Epistle of Paul to the Romans.* London: Fontana, 1970.

Doeve, J. W. "Some Notes with Reference to τὰ λόγια τοῦ θεοῦ in Romans III, 2." In *Studia Paulina in honorem Johannis de Zwaan septuagenarii.* Haarlem: Bohr, 1953.

Donfried, Karl P. "False Presuppositions in the Study of Romans." In *The Romans Debate,* edited by Karl P. Donfried, 102–24. Revised and expanded ed. Peabody, MA: Hendrickson, 1991.

———. "A Short Note on Romans 16," In *The Romans Debate,* edited by Karl P. Donfried, 44–52. Rev. and expanded ed. Peabody, MA: Hendrickson, 1991.

Dunn, James D. G. *Romans 1–8.* WBC 38A. Waco: Word, 1988.

———. *Romans 9–16.* WBC 38B. Waco: Word, 1989.

Elliott, Neil. *The Arrogance of Nations: Reading Romans in the Shadow of Empire.* Minneapolis: Fortress Press, 2008.

———. *The Rhetoric of Romans: Argumentative Constraint and Strategy and Paul's Dialogue with Judaism.* JSNTSup 45. Sheffield: JSOT Press, 1990.

Fee, Gordon D. *God's Empowering Presence: The Holy Spirit in the Letters of Paul.* Peabody, MA: Hendrickson, 1994.

Fitzmyer, Joseph A. *Romans: A New Translation with Introduction and Commentary.* AB 33. New York: Doubleday, 1992.

Frend, W. H. C. *Martyrdom and Persecution in the Early Church.* Oxford: Oxford University Press, 1965.

Furnish, Victor P. *Theology and Ethics in Paul.* Nashville: Abingdon, 1968.

Gamble, Harry. "The Redaction of the Pauline Letters and the Formation of the Pauline Corpus." *JBL* 94 (1975): 403–18.

———. *The Textual History of the Letter to the Romans.* SD 42. Grand Rapids: Eerdmans, 1977.

Garvey, A. E. *Romans.* NCB. New York: Oxford University Press, n.d.

Godet, Frédéric Louis. *Commentary on St. Paul's Epistle to the Romans.* Translated by A. Cusin. Edinburgh: Funk & Wagnalls, 1883.

Goodman, Martin. "Jewish Proselytizing in the First Century." In *The Jews among Pagans and Christians in the Roman Empire*, edited by Judith Lieu, John North, and Tessa Rajak, 53–78. London: Routledge, 1992.

Hall, David R. "Romans 3:1-8 Reconsidered." *NTS* 29 (1983): 183–97.

Hendriksen, William. *Romans*. Grand Rapids: Baker, 1981.

Hodge, Caroline Johnson. *If Sons, Then Heirs: A Study of Kinship and Ethnicity in the Letters of Paul*. Oxford: Oxford University Press, 2007.

Hodge, Charles. *A Commentary on the Epistle to the Romans*. 1886. Reprint, Grand Rapids: Eerdmans, 1950.

Hooker, Morna D. "Adam in Romans 1." *NTS* 6 (1960): 297–306.

———. "A Further Note on Romans 1." *NTS* 13 (1966): 181–83.

Jervell, Jacob. "The Letter to Jerusalem." In *The Romans Debate*, edited by Karl P. Donfried, 53–64. Rev. and expanded ed. Peabody, MA: Hendrickson, 1991.

Jewett, Robert. "Following the Argument of Romans." In *The Romans Debate*, edited by Karl P. Donfried, 265–77. Rev. and expanded ed. Peabody, MA: Hendrickson, 1991.

———. *Romans*. Hermeneia. Minneapolis: Fortress Press, 2007.

———. "Romans as an Ambassadorial Letter." *Int* 36 (1982): 5–20.

Johnson, S. Lewis, Jr. "Studies in Romans, Part VII: The Jews and the Oracles of God." *Bibliotheca Sacra* 130 (1973): 235–49.

———. "Studies in Romans, Part IX: The Universality of Sin." *Bibliotheca Sacra* 131 (1974): 163–72.

Karris, Robert J. "Romans 14:1–15:13 and the Occasion of Romans," In *The Romans Debate*, edited by Karl P. Donfried, 65–84. Rev. and expanded ed. Peabody, MA: Hendrickson, 1991.

Käsemann, Ernst. *Commentary on Romans*. Translated by Geoffrey W. Bromiley. Grand Rapids: Eerdmans, 1980.

Kaye, Bruce Norman. *The Thought Structure of Romans with Special Reference to Chapter 6*. Austin: Schola Press, 1979.

Kennedy, George A. *New Testament Interpretation through Rhetorical Criticism*. Chapel Hill: University of North Carolina Press, 1984.

Günter, Klein. "Paul's Purpose in Writing the Epistle to the Romans." In *The Romans Debate*, edited by Karl P. Donfried, 29–43. Rev. and expanded ed. Peabody, MA: Hendrickson, 1991.

Kruse, Colin G. *Paul's Letter to the Romans*. PiNTC. Grand Rapids: Eerdmans, 2012.

Kümmel, Werner Georg. *Introduction to the New Testament*. Translated by Howard Clark Kee. Nashville: Abingdon, 1975.

Ladd, George Eldon. *A Theology of the New Testament*. Grand Rapids: Eerdmans, 1993.

Lampe, Peter. "The Roman Christians of Romans 16." In *The Romans Debate*, edited by Karl P. Donfried, 216–30. Rev. and expanded ed. Peabody, MA: Hendrickson, 1991.

Leenhardt, Franz J. *The Epistle to the Romans: A Commentary*. London: Lutterworth, 1961.

Leon, Harry Joshua. *The Jews of Ancient Rome*. Peabody, MA: Hendrickson, 1995.

Lietzmann, Hans. *An die R?mer*. Tübingen: J. C. B. Mohr, 1933. Reprint 1971.

Lightfoot, J. B. *Biblical Essays*. London: Macmillan, 1893.

____. *Saint Paul's Epistle to the Galatians*. London: Macmillan, 1865.

Longenecker, Richard N. "Ancient Amanuenses and the Pauline Epistles." In *New Dimensions in New Testament Study*, edited by Richard N. Longenecker and Merrill C. Tenney, 281–97. Grand Rapids: Zondervan, 1974.

____. "The Focus of Romans: The Central Role of 5.1–8.39 in the Argument of the Letter." In *Romans and the People of God*, edited by Sven K. Soderlund and N. T. Wright, 49–69. Grand Rapids: Eerdmans, 1999.

____. *Introducing Romans: Critical Issues in Paul's Most Famous Letter*. Grand Rapids: Eerdmans, 2011.

Malherbe, Abraham J. *Ancient Epistolary Theorists*. Atlanta: Scholars Press, 1988.

Manson, T. W. "St. Paul's Letter to the Romans—and Others." In *The Romans Debate*, edited by Karl P. Donfried, 3–15. Rev. and expanded ed. Peabody, MA: Hendrickson, 1991.

McKnight, Scot. *A Light among the Gentiles: Jewish Missionary Activity in the Second Temple Period*. Minneapolis: Fortress Press, 1991.

Metzger, Bruce M. *A Textual Commentary on the Greek New Testament*. New York: United Bible Societies, 1971.

Meyer, Heinrich August Wilhelm. *The Epistle to the Romans*. New York: Funk & Wagnalls, 1884.

Michel, Otto. *Der Brief an die Römer*. Göttingen: Vanderhoeck & Ruprecht, 1957.

Minear, Paul S. *The Obedience of Faith: The Purposes of Paul in the Epistle to the Romans*. SBT 2/19. London SCM, 1971.

Moo, Douglas J. *The Epistle to the Romans*. NICNT. Grand Rapids: Eerdmans, 1996.

Morris, Leon. *The Epistle of Paul to the Romans*. Grand Rapids: Eerdmans, 1988.

Moulton, W. F., and A. S. Geden. *A Concordance of the Greek Testament*. Edinburgh: T&T Clark, 1970.

Mounce, Robert H. *Romans*. NAC. Nashville: Broadman & Holman, 1995.

Mullins, Terence Y. "Formulas in New Testament Epistles." *JBL* 91 (1972): 380–90.

Murray, John. *The Epistle to the Romans*. 2 vols. NICNT. Grand Rapids: Eerdmans, 1965.

Munck, Johannes. *Paul and the Salvation of Mankind*. Richmond, VA: John Knox, 1959.

Nanos, Mark D. *The Mystery of Romans: The Jewish Context of Paul's Letter*. Philadelphia: Fortress Press, 1996.

Nygren, Anders. *Commentary on Romans*. Translated by Carl C. Rasmussen. Philadelphia: Fortress Press, 1949.

Penna, Romano. *Paul the Apostle: A Theological and Exegetical Study*. Vol. 1, *Jew and Greek Alike*. Translated by Thomas P. Wahl. Collegeville, MN: Liturgical Press, 1996.

Rapa, R. K. *The Meaning of "Works of the Law" in Galatians and Romans*. New York: Peter Lang, 2001.

Richards, E. Randolph. *The Secretary in the Letters of Paul*. WUNT 2/42. Tübingen: J. C. B. Mohr (Paul Siebeck), 1991.

Ridderbos, Herman. *Paul: An Outline of His Theology*. Translated by John R. DeWitt. Grand Rapids: Eerdmans, 1979.

Rutgers, Leonard Victor. "Roman Policy toward the Jews: Expulsions from the City of Rome during the First Century C.E." In *Judaism and Christianity in First-Century Rome*, edited by Karl P. Donfried and Peter Richardson, 93–116. Grand Rapids: Eerdmans, 1998.

Sanday, William, and Arthur C. Headlam. *The Epistle to the Romans*. New York: Charles Scribner's Sons, 1897.

Sanders, E. P. *Paul, the Law, and the Jewish People*. Philadelphia: Fortress, 1979.

Schlatter, Adolf. *Gottes Gerechtigkeit: Ein Kommentar zum Römerbrief.* Stuttgart: Calwer, 1959.

Schmithals, Walter. *Der R?merbrief als historisches Problem.* Gütersloh: Mohn, 1975.

Schürer, Emil. *The History of the Jewish People in the Age of Jesus Christ.* Revised and edited by Geza Vermes, Fergus Millar, and Martin Goodman. Vol. 3. Edinburgh: T&T Clark, 1986.

Smallwood, E. Mary. *The Jews under Roman Rule.* Leiden: Brill, 1976.

Stern, M. "The Jewish Diaspora." In *The Jewish People in the First Century: Historical Geography, Political History, Social, Cultural and Religious Life and Institutions,* edited by S. Safrai and M. Stern in cooperation with D. Flusser and W. C. van Unnik. Compendia Rerum Iudaicarum ad Novum Testamentum I-1. Philadelphia: Fortress Press, 1974.

_____. "The Jews in Greek and Latin Literature." In *The Jewish People in the First Century: Historical Geography, Political History, Social, Cultural and Religious Life and Institutions,* edited by S. Safrai and M. Stern in co-operation with D. Flusser and W. C. van Unnik. Compendia Rerum Iudaicarum ad Novum Testamentum I-2. Philadelphia: Fortress Press, 1976.

Stirewalt, Martin Luther, Jr. "The Form and Function of the Greek Letter-Essay." In *The Romans Debate,* edited by Karl P. Donfried, 147–71. Rev. and expanded ed. Peabody, MA: Hendrickson, 1991.

_____. *Studies in Ancient Greek Epistolography.* Atlanta: Scholars Press, 1993.

Stoessel, Horace E. "Notes on Romans 12:1-2." *Int* 17 (1963): 161–75.

Stott, John R. W. *The Message of Romans.* Downers Grove, IL: InterVarsity Press, 1994.

Stowers, Stanley K. *The Diatribe and Paul's Letter to the Romans.* SBLDS 57. Chico, CA: Scholars Press, 1981.

_____. *Letter Writing in Greco-Roman Antiquity.* Philadelphia: Westminster, 1986.

_____. "Paul's Dialogue with a Fellow Jew in Romans 3:1-9." *CBQ* 46 (1984): 707–22.

_____. *A Rereading of Romans: Justice, Jews, and Gentiles.* New Haven: Yale University Press, 1994.

Stuhlmacher, Peter. *Paul's Letter to the Romans.* Translated by Scott J. Hafemann. Louisville: Westminster: John Knox, 1994.

Tcherikover, Victor. *Hellenistic Civilization and the Jews*. Philadelphia: Jewish Publication Society of America: Philadelphia, 1959.

Thiele, Friedrich. "Guilt, Cause, Convict, Blame." In *The New International Dictionary of New Testament Theology*, edited by Colin Brown, 2:137–39. Grand Rapids: Zondervan, 1975.

Tobin, Thomas H., SJ. *Paul's Rhetoric in Its Contexts: The Argument of Romans*. Peabody, MA: Hendrickson, 2008.

Walters, James C. *Ethnic Issues in Paul's Letter to the Romans: Changing Self-Definitions in Earliest Roman Christianity*. Valley Forge, PA: Trinity Press International, 1993.

____. "Romans, Jews, and Christians: The Impact of the Romans on Jewish/Christian Relations in First-Century Rome." In *Judaism and Christianity in First-Century Rome*, edited by Karl P. Donfried and Peter Richardson, 175–95. Grand Rapids: Eerdmans, 1998.

Watson, Francis. "The Two Roman Congregations: Romans 14:1–15:13." In *The Romans Debate*, edited by Karl P. Donfried, 203–15. Rev. and expanded ed. Peabody, MA: Hendrickson, 1991.

Wedderburn, A. J. M. "Adam in Paul's Letter to the Romans." In *Studia Biblica 1978, III: Papers on Paul and Other New Testament Authors*, edited by Elizabeth A. Livingstone, 413–30. JSNTSup 3. Sheffield: JSOT Press, 1980.

____. *The Reasons for Romans*. Edinburgh: T&T Clark, 1988.

White, John Lee. *The Form and Function of the Body of the Greek Letter*. SBLDS 2. Missoula, MT: Scholars Press, 1972.

Witherington, Ben, III. *Paul's Letter to the Romans: A Socio-rhetorical Commentary*. Grand Rapids: Eerdmans, 2004.

Wiefel, Wolfgang. "Jewish Community in Ancient Rome and the Origins of Roman Christianity." In *The Romans Debate*, edited by Karl P. Donfried, 85–101. Rev. and expanded ed. Peabody, MA: Hendrickson, 1991.

Zahn, Theodor. *Introduction to the New Testament*. Edinburgh: T&T Clark, 1909.

Ziesler, John A. *Paul's Letter to the Romans*. London: SCM, 1989.

Index

Penna, Romano, 83, 85

Rapa, R. K., 37
Renan, E., 5
Richards, E. Randolph, 33, 167
Ridderbos, Herman, 156
Rutgers, Leonard Victor, 134, 135

Sanday, William, 5, 19, 44, 48, 73, 97,
 111, 175, 181
Sanders, E. P., 178
Schlatter, Adolf, 73, 85
Schmithals, Walter, 122
Schürer, Emil, 133–37
Smallwood, E. Mary, 128, 137
Stern, M., 134, 135
Stirewalt, Martin Luther, Jr., 34
Stoessel, Horace E., 87, 89
Stott, John, 111
Stowers, Stanley K., 10, 14, 58, 77,
 102–19, 124, 184

Stuhlmacher, Peter, 111, 120

Tcherikover, Victor, 133, 134, 138
Thiele, Friedrich, 178
Tobin, Thomas H., SJ, 23, 24, 25, 87

Walters, James C., 129–32, 154, 155
Watson, Francis, 140
Wedderburn, A. J. M., 2, 3, 100, 126
White, John Lee, 17
Witherington, Ben, III, 10, 26, 27,
 36, 91, 123, 124, 161, 167
Wiefel, Wolfgang, 128, 129, 132, 134,
 138

Zahn, Theodor, 9, 11, 89
Ziesler, John A., 72